Benjamin Moore

**History of Wesleyan Methodism in Burnley and East Lancashire**

Benjamin Moore

**History of Wesleyan Methodism in Burnley and East Lancashire**

ISBN/EAN: 9783337326494

Printed in Europe, USA, Canada, Australia, Japan

Cover: Foto ©ninafisch / pixelio.de

More available books at **www.hansebooks.com**

# METHODISM IN BURNLEY AND EAST LANCASHIRE.

JOHN WESLEY
AS HE WAS WHEN HE FIRST VISITED
EAST-LANCASHIRE.

# HISTORY OF
# WESLEYAN METHODISM IN BURNLEY
# AND EAST LANCASHIRE.

BURNLEY, COLNE, PADIHAM, NELSON, BARNOLDSWICK.

BY

B. MOORE, J.P.,
BURNLEY.

BURNLEY:
PRINTED AND PUBLISHED AT THE "GAZETTE" PRINTING WORKS,
BRIDGE STREET.
1899.

# Preface.

METHODISM in East Lancashire covers a period of history of almost one hundred and sixty years. The pioneers of Methodism were Darney and Grimshaw, but John Wesley himself appeared on the scene more than a century and a half ago. The frontispiece is a reproduction of a portrait of him as he was when he first visited East Lancashire. The portrait is the only one of the kind known to be in existence, and adorns one of the rooms of Didsbury College, by the governor of which institution, the Rev. R. Green, kind permission to reproduce it has been granted.

The important position which Methodism has taken in East Lancashire called, in the opinion of the author, for some permanent record of its origin and progress. Nearly twenty years ago he began to collect materials for such a book, never dreaming that he himself would have the responsibility of publishing it. The fathers of Methodism have, however, passed away so rapidly that it was felt that, if the the opportunity were not seized, not only would the advantage of living memories be lost, but many of the records would be dispersed beyond recovery, and the compilation of a satisfactory record become impossible. As the work proceeded, this was found to be already in some measure the case; and an amount of time and labour, never contemplated, has been spent in the collection of the historical data that are the basis of a work of the kind.

Even while the last sheets were passing through the press, additional particulars continued to come to hand. One gentleman writes in loving memory of Mary Overton and Elizabeth Titterington, of Benjamin Whittam and Henry Hargreaves, and of the great prayer-meetings under Wesley chapel when Mr. George Hopwood "used to pray with a voice of thunder." He describes too a sacramental service conducted by Dr. Lyth in the same chapel. At one point of the service the minister gave out the familiar hymn, "All ye that pass by." He read the verses one by one in the ancient fashion; and when he came to the sixth verse, "My pardon I claim, for a sinner I am," he paused for a moment and then said, "Bold language for a sinner that." As he went on to show that the claim was yet well within the sinner's right, the Spirit of God came down and filled the house. Another gentleman writes of Padiham and its early glories, when Mr. Ball was the schoolmaster, and Richard Cronshaw and others did yeomen's service. The Rev. Thomas Hitchon, though he actually entered the ministry from Nantwich, was a Padiham lad, whilst the Revds. S. Weaver and A. Edman found their wives there. From Colne the Rev. Alfred Barritt entered the ministry. And probably of every place that is mentioned in the following pages some further incident or detail might be added.

The book is designed to let the present and possibly future generations know the origin and wonderful development of Methodism in East Lancashire. No church within the same area and started within the same period can for a moment compare with it either in the value of its eccleciastical and educational buildings, in the accommodation provided, or in the number of its adherents. No serious attempt has heretofore been made to chronicle the events connected with its introduction and growth in this district. The early stages were marked by struggle and social persecution, the later by large enterprise and increasing influence. The prosperity of any church which seeks the higher welfare of the people should be a matter of deep interest to all. And without any disparagement of the valuable work of other churches historical accuracy warrants the statement, that no other religious movement has told more widely for good upon the various phases of the private and the public life of Burnley and East Lancashire than the Methodist revival of the eighteenth century. With a view to put on permanent record the local history of this great church, and to exhibit the progress it has made and the noble self-sacrifice of those who have contributed to its present position, the author undertook a task, which he probably would never have undertaken, had he known what labour was involved.

Valuable help, for which sincere thanks are tendered, has been received, particularly in the earlier stages of the book, from the Rev. J. Thackray, B.A., and from my elder daughter, upon whom much labour has devolved. Amongst other contributors special mention should be made of Mr. W. Lancaster, Mr. J. W. Laycock, of Keighley, Mr. Leonard Marsden, of Nelson, Mr. Craven, of Brierfield, Mr. John Blezard, of Padiham, His Honour Judge Ingham, of Birkdale, formerly County Court Judge, and a grandson of Benjamin Ingham, who founded the Inghamite chapels so well known in this district, and of Mr. John Stott, of Haslingden. Judge Ingham is the possessor of two manuscript books that were used by his grandfather. The one is a private account-book which throws much light upon the prices of food and articles of household use in the second half of the last century, and upon the style of living in the case of a family of some standing and substance. The other is a copy of the Minutes of a series of church meetings held by the so-called Inghamites at Wheatley Lane, Winewall, and elsewhere, chiefly in 1761. This was some years after Mr. Ingham had left the Moravians, and five or six years after his own followers had become so organised as to formally elect him their general overseer. The Minutes moreover relate almost exclusively to the admission or exclusion of members or to matters of internal controversy, and have no connection at all with the fortunes of Methodism. They or selections from them are however well worth printing for their bearing upon the early history of a church, that has never attained much magnitude, but has survived many vicissitudes.

Nov. 13th, 1899.             B. MOORE.

# Table of Contents.

|  |  | Page |
|---|---|---|
| Chapter I. | Darney and Grimshaw | 1 |
| Chapter II. | Haworth Circuit or Round, 1748-1776 | 12 |
| Chapter III. | Colne Circuit, 1776-1810 | 28 |
| Chapter IV. | Burnley Circuit, 1810-1899 | 74 |
| Chapter V. | Colne Circuit, 1810-1899 | 168 |
| Chapter VI. | Padiham, 1810-1899 | 176 |
| Chapter VII. | Nelson, 1810-1899 | 193 |
| Chapter VIII. | Barnoldswick Circuit | 217 |
| Chapter IX. | Biographical Notes and Sketches | 226 |

CHAPTER I.

# DARNEY AND GRIMSHAW.

THE first Methodist preacher to appear in the neighbourhood of Burnley was John Nelson, who for a short time assisted the Rev. Benjamin Ingham in preaching, and in forming religious Societies in the villages around Colne in 1742. Ingham, however, introduced Moravian helpers, and before the end of the year Nelson left him: and these Societies never became *Methodist* Societies. It is also probable, that John Bennet in travelling his extensive 'Round' may have preached thus early at Todmorden, but the evidence is not conclusive.

The first to form Societies, which ultimately became *Methodist* Societies, was William Darney, who seems to have carried on his work, chiefly in Rossendale and Pendle-forest, for three or four years, under the direction of or in friendly co-operation with the Rev. William Grimshaw, the vicar of Haworth.

William Grimshaw was born in 1708. After a course of study at Cambridge, he was ordained in 1731, and entered the ministry of the Established Church, not with any thought of saving souls, but, as he afterwards sorrowfully confessed, in the hope of getting a good living. After officiating a few months at Rochdale, he removed in September, 1731, to Todmorden. When he had been some time there, he began to be seriously concerned about his soul. It has been supposed that the loss of his wife, to whom he had been married four years, may have turned his thoughts to spiritual things; but we have it from his own pen that he made a solemn covenant with God in 1738. At or about that time he gave up the diversions in which he had delighted, retired for prayer four times a day, and began diligently to visit his people and to press upon them the importance of religion. He became an "earnest and exemplary minister," his wife remarking that "never was man more changed for the better." It is clearly established that his spiritual awakening took place while he was yet at Todmorden,

WILLIAM GRIMSHAW.

though by what means it was brought about cannot now be ascertained. After reading Owen on Justification, he spoke of its perusal as having given him "light and comfort," and "a taste of the pardoning love of God."

Soon after his removal to Haworth (May, 1742) he met with a pious family named Greenwood. Two tracts by the Rev. Robt. Seagrave, M.A., which had been greatly blessed to that family, he borrowed and eagerly read. His preaching at this time must have been 'evangelical,' for the Methodists of Keighley were in the habit of going to hear him. Writing to Dr. Gillies in 1754, he says of that year:—"The Lord was pleased to visit Haworth. A few souls were affected under the word, and brought to see their lost estate by nature, and to experience peace through faith in the blood of Jesus."

Still there seems to have been sometimes a lack of clearness in his teaching. Such at least is the testimony of John Wilkinson, the first Methodist, the first class-leader, and the first local preacher in Keighley. His grand-daughter reported that she had often heard her father say that his father knew Grimshaw before he had consciously passed from death unto life, and frequently heard him preach; that when he thought Grimshaw had not been sufficiently faithful, he would follow him into the vestry, and remind him of his failings; and that Grimshaw used to say that in those earlier times he sometimes felt as if he would as soon have seen the devil in the vestry as John Wilkinson.

Whatever the character of h's preaching in the early years of his rule at Haworth, it was not altogether in harmony with that of the Methodists, as understood by him: for, when it was announced that John Nelson was coming to preach in his parish, he warned the people not to go and hear him. Tradition adds that Nelson preached in the old Hall which stands near the present Railway Station, that his text was "These that have turned the world upside down are come hither also," and that many of the villagers went to hear him.

Soon after it was announced that William Darney was coming to preach. On this occasion, instead of exhorting the people to stop away, which possibly he had found was a sure way of inducing them to go, Grimshaw resolved to attend the preaching himself, that, having assured himself of what these preachers actually taught, he might refute their errors, and prevent his parishioners from being led away. Darney preached his first sermon in Haworth in a house in "the Ginnel" opposite the Church gates. His subject was "Salvation by faith," the very subject on which Grimshaw understood he was misleading the people. He appealed to the Scriptures, to the Liturgy and Articles of the Church of England, in support of what he advanced. The result was memorable. Grimshaw, who had intended to argue with him, began to think he was right, and sought a private interview. Not far from the Parsonage were some old quarries; in which and other out of the way places he and Darney quietly conversed on Christian doctrine and personal experience; and it was not long before Grimshaw took his stand by the side of the evangelist, at one meeting giving out the hymn before the sermon and at another concluding with prayer. Some of the villagers said that "mad Grimshaw," as they already called their vicar, had turned "Scotch Will's clerk"; and Grimshaw wrote to Dr. Gillies, "William Darney came to Haworth in 1745.[1] The Lord was with him indeed, and I have cause to bless God for it."

Whether Grimshaw found peace with God through reading Owen's book or Seagrave's tracts, or through Darney's preaching and conversation, cannot be accurately determined. The statements made on the subject are contradictory, and cannot now be harmonised. But whatever his experience up to September, 1744, he then enjoyed a sense of the pardoning love of God, which he never lost.

Some time before this he had begun a systematic visitation of his scattered parish. Selecting a dozen convenient places, he called together six, eight, or ten families, and gave them an exhortation. The round was completed in a year: "and wonderfully the Lord blessed it."

Early in 1746 we hear of further developments. Mr. Williams, a clothier, of Kidderminster, visited Haworth on business in the spring of this year, and was entertained presumably at the Parsonage. Some twelve months afterwards he

---

1. There is reason to believe that Grimshaw has made a mistake in this date: for he says in the same letter that Darney went from his parish to Rossendale. His visit to Rossendale took place in 1744; so that probably his visit to Haworth was in the early part of that year.

wrote a letter[1] to the Rev. Malachi Blake, of Blandford, in which he described the work that was being carried on in Grimshaw's parish. He writes that, as soon as Grimshaw "can discover good evidences of a thorough work" in the hearts of his converts, "he forms them into classes of ten or twelve in a class, and sets over each a man who has the gift of prayer to watch over them, and mark the increase or decay of grace in every one. The heads of these classes give an account to their pastor at meetings he holds with them."

It is difficult to decide whether in the establishment of these classes we are to trace the influence of Ingham or of Darney. The author of the "Life and Times of Selina, Countess of Huntingdon" says (i. 253) that Ingham became acquainted with Grimshaw about eight months after the latter began his ministry at Haworth, and that the two were soon afterwards closely united, Grimshaw labouring "unweariedly to diffuse the glad tidings of the Gospel among his [Ingham's] Societies." It is known that Ingham and Nelson were in the neighbourhood of Colne in 1742: but the tradition, that Grimshaw warned his people not to go and hear Nelson when he came to preach at Haworth, does not favour the idea of there having been such an association between him and Ingham as the writer just referred to believed to have existed. Grimshaw, moreover, writing to Dr. Gillies, says, "The parson and the mason laboured together with great success for some time, and formed Societies, whose exercise consisted in praying, singing, reading, and conferring together about the work of God in their souls. . . . In 1742 I am informed they separated." This language does not imply the existence of any great intimacy between himself and Ingham at this time, and prevents our believing that there was any close association in work. Still, Grimshaw knew of the formation of the Societies, and was acquainted by hear-say with the character of the meetings.

We have, however, reason to believe that Grimshaw was on more or less intimate terms with Darney. Williams in his "Letter" speaks of Grimshaw's being assisted by two laymen, of whom one held the doctrine of Particular Election and the other that of Universal Redemption. Mr. Williams may have been a little confused in his recollection of what Grimshaw said. It is probable that they had talked about several men, two of whom lived at Haworth, whilst a third, a Scotchman, frequently visited that place, and would on those occasions

---

1. The letter is printed at length in the *Methodist Recorder* of Jan. 12, 1899, from a copy made by Charles Wesley.

## ESTABLISHMENT OF CLASSES.

dispute about Election. This third man could be no other than William Darney.

We know that Darney's preaching and conversation had considerable influence on Grimshaw's preaching and personal experience; and it may be that he exercised still more influence in the formation of the classes in Grimshaw's parish than has been hitherto supposed. Against this supposition is the fact,

INTERIOR OF HAWORTH CHURCH IN GRIMSHAW'S DAYS.

that it is not certain that he was in the habit of forming classes before he came to Haworth; and in favour of it is the fact, that they were formed soon after his arrival, and the one at Haworth, at least in part, by him.

From Haworth Darney proceeded to Rossendale, and in May, 1744, preached and formed a Society at Gawksholme, near Todmorden. Towards the end of the year he did the same at Heap-barn, and Miller-barn; and at the latter place, a hamlet of but four or five houses, he took up his abode. He earned his living as a pedlar,[1] and as he tramped his rounds and sold his wares, he preached the Gospel and formed Societies at Padiham, and in many places in the district of Pendle, which will be mentioned as our story proceeds.

In January, 1747, Charles Wesley paid his second visit to Haworth. On that occasion he preached, but not in the Church, as Mr. Grimshaw was afraid to allow him, and afterwards he visited[2] "what were called William Darney's Societies."

On the 1st of May in the same year John Wesley visited Haworth, and preached in the Church. Thence he proceeded to Halifax, Armley, Birstal, and adds under the date of May 4th, "At his earnest request I began examining W. D.'s Societies." At this time he visited Roughlee, Hinden, Widdup, Stonesey-gate, Shore, Todmorden Edge, finishing his round in Rossendale on the Thursday, possibly at Miller-barn, where Darney at that time lived.

A few extracts from letters[3] which Grimshaw wrote to Wesley in the summer of 1747 follow. May 30th: "The Societies you formed in William Darney's Circuit, I hear are in a good state. I went amongst those about Todmorden the week after you were there, and, to my great comfort, found it so. . . . William Darney desires a particular letter from you respecting his going into Scotland. He would go soon after Whitsuntide, if you think proper. I shall see him, I hope, to-morrow, as also Mr. Bennet, who will both be at the chapel I am going to; and I intend that one of them shall preach at noon near the same place." He does not name the place at which, nor the clergyman for whom, he was going to preach. But he says it was fourteen or fifteen miles from Haworth, and not above two or three "from that place where you preached in Rossendale." The reference is probably to Chipping, of which the Rev. Mr. Milner was minister.

On the 20th of August he writes again to Wesley, and after referring to the offence he had given to the neighbouring clergy by going into their parishes, and saying that at one time he had almost resolved to keep himself in future to his own,

---

1. Jessop, *Methodism in Rossendale*, says he was a clogger.

2. Jackson, *Life of Charles Wesley*, i. 461. The first visit occurred in the previous October, when Grimshaw was ill, and Charles Wesley "read prayers and expounded Isaiah xxxv."—*ib.*, i. 452.

3. The letters are given in full in Everett, "*Methodism in Manchester*," 67 ff., and in Myles, *Grimshaw*, 156 ff.

he states that after much thought he has come to the conclusion "to preach the Gospel abroad." He continues: "The first thing suggested to me was to visit William Darney's Societies: I accordingly met one of them about a month ago. Last week I struck out into Lancashire and Cheshire, Mr. Bennet bearing me company." After mentioning the places they visited, and that he parted from Mr. Bennet in Manchester, he adds: "I called and spent a part of two days with William Darney's Societies, particularly those in Todmorden, Shore, Mellor-Barn, Rossendale, Bacup, Crostone, Stoneshawfate, Crimsworth-dean. . . . I am determined, therefore, to add, by the divine assistance, to the care of my own parish, that of so frequent a visitation of Mr. Bennet's, William Darney's, the Leeds and Birstal Societies, as my own convenience will permit, and their circumstances may respectively seem to require, all along eyeing the Lord's will and purposes for me. If I find the Lord's pleasure be that I must still launch out further, I will obey. . . . I desire to do nothing but in perfect harmony and concert with you, and therefore beg you will be entirely free, open, and communicative, to me. I bless God, I can discover no other at present, but every way a perfect agreement between your sentiments, principles, &c., of religion, and my own; and therefore desire you will (as I do to you) from time to time lay before me such rules, places, proposals, &c., as you conceive mostly conducive to the welfare of the church, the private benefit of her members, and, in the whole, to the glory of the Lord. My pulpit, I hope, shall be always at your's, and your brother's service; and my house, so long as I have one, your welcome home. The same I'll make it to all our fellow-labourers, through the grace of God."

There is a further letter, dated "Ewood, Nov. 27, 1747." Grimshaw writes: "You desire a particular account of the progress of the Lord's work here. Indeed, I have the pleasure of assuring you that I think it never went better, from its first appearance among us, than it has done within these two months. I may say, at Leeds, Birstal, Keighley, Todmorden, Rossendale, Heptonstall, Pendleforest, and in my own parish, the Societies are very hearty; souls are daily added to the church; and, I may say, multitudes, on all sides, (many of whom have been enemies to us and our Master's cause), are convinced of the truth, run eagerly to hear the Gospel, and (as I told you in my last) are continually crying out for more preachers. New and numerous classes have been lately joined. . . . I went to meet all the Heptonstall parish classes. Last week I met brother Colbeck, and all the Keighley parish classes; and about six weeks ago I visited those of Leeds and Birstal; about a month since, those of Todmorden, Shore, and some of Rossendale."

And now Grimshaw was an itinerant. Strongly built and in perfect health, he traversed the rough district in which he lived, and preached not only in his own parish, but in the parishes of his neighbours, from twelve to thirty sermons every week. The landlord at Colne said that a sermon he preached in that town "lasted two long hours," and "that every week and almost every day he preached in barns and private houses, and was a great encourager of conventicles." Wesley said that a few such as he would make a nation tremble, for he carried fire wherever he went.

To return to William Darney, Myles, in his "Chronological History of the Methodists," says that Darney was one of Wesley's lay-helpers in 1742; and on that authority the statement has been repeated by several later writers. But there are grounds for concluding that, as late as 1744, Darney was not in communion with any church; and that he began to work in connection with Wesley only shortly before, in May, 1747, he declared his readiness to go to Scotland if Wesley thought proper. At the Conference held June 3rd, 1748, he is named amongst the assistants whom "we now agree to receive into the work": and he appears to have been employed for two years in what soon came to be called the Haworth Round.

In those days the preachers had no regular allowances. They boarded and lodged with friends at the places where they preached, and were dependent on the Societies for their clothes. Darney, however, was married, and a somewhat small allowance seems to have been made irregularly for his wife. This will explain the following entries in the Circuit book:—

Oct. 10, 1748, Gave Wm. Darney - 1s. 7d.
Jan. 10, 1749, To Wm. Darney's wife - 1 10 0
         A pair of Boots for W. Darney   14 0
Ap. 8, 1749, To W. Darney's wife - 2 2 0
July 11,  ,,  To W. Darney's wife - 1 10 0

In the year 1750-1 he seems to have been in the neighbourhood of Rotherham, as his name is appended to an entry in the Circuit Book. During this year he published[1] "A Collection of Hymns." John Wesley condemned them as unfit for public worship: Charles Wesley called them 'nonsense,' and Thomas Jackson says they are "amongst the most rude and unpolished compositions ever put to the press." The publication of this volume is supposed to have led to the regulation that no preacher should publish anything without Wesley's approval.

---

1. *A Collection of Hymns*, by William Darney, in four parts. Leeds: Printed by James Lister, 1751. 12mo. pp. 296. The volume is now rather scarce.

In 1752 Darney was again associated with Grimshaw. In an old Society Book at Osmotherley, a village in the north of Yorkshire, is the entry: "for Wm. Grimshaw and Wm. Darney, 1s. 3d.": whether this was for the entertainment of themselves or their horses is not recorded. The Todmorden Steward's Book for the same year is another evidence that he was in the neighbourhood. One entry runs:—"1752. April 20. For William Darney, foreside of his waistcoat, 7s. For trimming for his coat, 9s. 11½d. To him, for his wife, 20s."

After serving in Wales in 1753 and in Scotland in 1755, with apparently several breaks in his connection with the Wesleys, three years later his case was formally considered. The Minutes of the Conference of 1758 contain the following question and answer:—

"Q. Can we receive William Darney?

A. Not till we are assured that he does not rail, print, or sell wares without a license."

Darney had incurred the displeasure of Wesley by publishing a second volume. Its title was "The Fundamental Doctrines which are contained in the Scriptures." The work was dedicated "To the Religious Societies in England called by the name of Methodist; and in a more particular manner to those who are joined in Christian fellowship in these parts of Lancashire and Yorkshire, where the Lord was blessed of His infinite mercy to send me, His unworthy servant, to call them in His name, out of darkness into His marvellous light, and from the power of Satan unto God; being an instrument in His alone hand, for that holy purpose."

Darney's explanation and promises must have been considered satisfactory by Grimshaw, for he was sent on October 18th, 1758, in charge of a pastoral letter to the Society at Newcastle, in which Grimshaw wrote, "Brother Darney's labours have been useful in these parts; may they be blessed among you." The following year he seems to have returned to Haworth; and there he remained until Grimshaw's death in 1763. The following entries in the Circuit Book show that he had in the latter part of the time the regular allowance of twelve pounds a year, the additional five shillings being probably paid him in the last three quarters because he had a wife.

| | | | | | |
|---|---|---|---|---|---|
| Jan. 17, 1760, | to W. Darney | - | 1 | 1 | 0 |
| Oct. 14, 1762, | „ „ | - | 3 | 0 | 0 |
| Jan. 16, 1763, | „ „ | - | 3 | 5 | 0 |
| „ „ | to W. Darney's horse | | 3 | 1 | 7 |
| Apr. 14, 1763, | „ W. Darney | - | 3 | 5 | 0 |
| „ „ | „ W. Darney's horse | | 12 | | 0 |
| July 7, „ | „ W. Darney | - | 3 | 5 | 0 |
| „ „ | „ W. Darney for his journey to London | | 1 | 15 | 4 |

His next appointments were successively Cornwall, London, Yarm, Newcastle, and Derbyshire; but from 1768 his name ceases to appear in the Minutes of Conference. Then, or shortly after, he returned to the scene of some of his earliest, and perhaps his most successful labours. He spent several years at Southfield, but finally took up his abode in the "Old Cottage," Upper Houses, Barley, a little nearer to Pendle than Roughlee, probably because the scenery of the neighbourhood reminded him of his native Scotland. The "Old Cottage" is not now occupied, but is still standing not far from Windy Harbour, to which place it is said that Darney walked every week for a pound of butter, which then could be had for threepence. He had now become a very feeble, white-haired old man. He died in 1779, and was probably buried at Newchurch (in Pendle).

Like most of his contemporaries he met with great and sometimes violent opposition, and once at least he was imprisoned. When he first attempted to preach at Padiham, the vicar and some boon companions attacked him and drove him away. He was frequently dragged through the river, and otherwise abused by the mobs that gathered in the neighbourhood of Colne. Near Accrington he was treated with the greatest indignity, being thrown into the Hyndburn, and his wig filled with indescribable filth. At Yeadon, a mob led by the curate of Guiseley threw eggs in his face as he was preaching, dragged him down and stamped upon him. At Almondbury he was knocked down, pulled by the hair, and almost killed by a mob who kicked him with their clogs.

Once, at least, his courageous temper saved him from violence. Near Alnwick, a number of strolling players were heard to say in a tone sufficiently loud for him to hear, "Here's Scotch Will: let's mob him." Darney hearing this, and being a man of "prodigious size, and when he chose, of a terrific countenance," rode up to them, made his horse rear, raised his whip, and cried out with a voice of thunder "Ye sons of Belial, come on." The poor players were sadly frightened, begged his pardon, and promised to behave better in the future: which, the narrator adds, "they were very careful to do."—*(Meth. Mag.,* 1826, p. 797). At another time he escaped by gentler means. Having preached at Roughlee, he was passing through Colne on his way to Wycollar. Meeting the mob, in order to appease them, he offered the leader all the money he had, which amounted to a shilling: and on this occasion they did not molest him, but led him through the town in peace.

Of Darney's character and preaching, the Rev. Jacob Stanley writes that he was "a man possessing few personal attractions, of a broad Scotch dialect, and, when dwelling on the terrors of the Lord, terrible to behold; but a man of deep piety, strong sense, and burning zeal, with a courage that fearlessly defied all opposition. There was a rich vein of evangelical truth in his preaching, often delivered with the quaintness of some of the old Puritan Preachers, which pleased and profited many."—*(Meth. Mag.,* 1826, p. 796). Whitefield seems to have met with Darney when he visited Haworth in 1749, and speaks of him as "seemingly unqualified," but candidly admits that many were awakened under his ministry. Wesley describes him as "rough." But he had a kindly heart; children loved him, and always looked forward to his visits with pleasure. He was odd and eccentric, somewhat wayward also, and not easily advised, showing himself a little restive under Wesley's guiding hand: but a pure-minded, zealous, hard-working, useful man.

## CHAPTER II.

# THE HAWORTH CIRCUIT OR ROUND, 1748-1776.

AT Wesley's third Conference, held at Bristol in May 1746, occurs the first reference to "Circuits." Of these at that time there were seven. The fifth was *Yorkshire*, which included six counties in addition to the one from which it was named :— Cheshire, Lancashire, Derbyshire, Nottingham, Rutland, and Lincoln. According to the "Bennet Minutes," at the Conference of 1748 the number of circuits was increased to nine, Lancashire being taken from the Yorkshire, and included in the Cheshire circuit. The following year (1749) twelve circuits were reported, one of which was called " Haworth," the name of the little moorland village being probably used because it was the residence of the Rev. W. Grimshaw, who whilst continuing to be vicar was now formally recognised as one of Mr. Wesley's "Assistants." He was really what would be called at present the "Superintendent" of the Haworth circuit. As such, he visited the classes, gave tickets of membership, presided at Quarterly Meetings, and regularly preached in the Methodist Chapels, of several of which he became a Trustee. He also attended the Conference, whenever it was held in Leeds. He entertained the itinerants at his house, and as he could not lawfully allow them to preach in his pulpit, he permitted them to preach in his kitchen, announced their services, and finally built a chapel in his parish for their use.

In considering the Rise and Progress of Methodism in this district, two places claim attention first, Roughlee and Padiham ; and first of these, because it received one of the earliest, if not the very earliest visit of the founder of Methodism to this neighbourhood, comes Roughlee.

## ROUGHLEE.

The work here was commenced by William Darney, possibly before his meeting with Grimshaw. When Grimshaw wrote to Wesley in August, 1747, that he had recently visited Darney's Society at Roughlee, and found it "very hearty," he was writing about a Society with which Wesley was personally acquainted. For before this visit of Grimshaw, Wesley himself had paid his first visit to Roughlee. Meeting with William Darney he had "at his earnest request" examined his Societies. He continues in his Journal under May 4th, 1747, "At three I preached at Great-Harding [? Harwood]; in the evening at Roughlee, where there was a large society. But since the men of smooth tongue broke in upon them, they are every man afraid of his brother; half of them ringing continually in the ears of the rest 'No works, no law, no bondage.' However, we gathered about forty of the scattered sheep, who are still minded to stand in the old paths."[1]

On the 5th of May he preached at Roughlee at five in the morning, at Hinden about eleven, and at Widdup about three.

The account of Mr. Wesley's second visit to Roughlee is full of interest. On the 25th of August, 1748, he writes:—" I rode with Mr. Grimshaw to Roughlee, where T. Colbeck, of Keighley, was to meet us. We were stopped again and again, and begged not to go on, for a large mob from Colne was gone before us. Coming a little farther, we understood that they had not yet reached Roughlee. So we hastened on that we might be there before them. All was quiet when we came. I was a little afraid for Mr. Grimshaw, [who up to this time does not seem to have met with any violent opposition,] but it needed not; he was ready to go to prison or to death for Christ's sake.

"At half-hour after twelve I began to preach. I had about half finished my discourse, when the mob came pouring down the hill like a torrent. After exchanging a few words with their captain, to prevent any contest, I went with him as he required. When we came to Barrowford, two miles off, the whole army drew up in battle-array before the house into which I was carried, with two or three of my friends. [This house is supposed to have been the White Bear, which is still standing, near the mills of Thomas Barrowclough, Esq.] After I had been detained above an hour, their captain went out and I followed him, and desired him to conduct me whence I came.

---

1. This falling away is referred to in Darney's Poem. The 'men of smooth tongue' were *probably* Moravians. See the Journal of John Nelson *passim*.

He said, he would; but the mob soon followed after; at which he was so enraged, that he must needs go back to fight them, and so left me alone. . . . .

"Between four and five we set out from Roughlee. But observing several parties of men upon the hills, and suspecting their design, we put on and passed the lane they were making for before they came. One of our brothers, not riding so fast, was intercepted by them. They immediately knocked him down, and how it was that he got from amongst them he knew not.

"Before seven we reached Widdop. The news of what had passed at Barrowford made us all friends."

At Widdop they spent the night, and there next day at noon Wesley preached on a stone on which the late Mr. Peter Phillips caused to be engraved in memory of the event the date, "August 26th, 1748." That morning, Mr. Wesley addressed the following letter, to the Rev. G. White, the Vicar of Colne:—

"Widdop, August 26th, 1748.

"Sir,—Yesterday, between twelve and one o'clock, while I was speaking to some quiet people, without any noise or tumult, a drunken rabble came, with clubs and staves, in a tumultuous and riotous manner, the captain of whom, Richard B[annister], by name, said he was a deputy-constable, and that he was come to bring me to you. I went with him, but I had scarce gone ten yards, when a man of his company struck me with his fist in the face with all his might; quickly after, another threw his stick at my head: I then made a little stand; but another of your champions, cursing and swearing in the most shocking manner and flourishing his club over his head, cried out 'Bring him away!'

"With such a convoy I walked to Barrowford, where they informed me you was; their drummer going before, to draw all the rabble together from all quarters.

"When your deputy had brought me into the house, he permitted Mr. Grimshaw, the minister of Haworth, Mr. Colbeck, of Keighley, and one more, to be with me, promising that none should hurt them. Soon after you and your friends came in, and required me to promise, I would come to Roughlee no more. I told you, I would sooner cut off my hand, than make any such promise; neither would I promise that none of my friends should come. After abundance of rambling discourse (for I could keep none of you long to any one point), from about one o'clock till between three and four, (in which one of you frankly said 'No; we will not be like Gamaliel, we will proceed like the Jews,') you seemed a little satisfied with my saying 'I will not preach at Roughlee at this time.' You then undertook to quiet the mob, to whom you went and spoke a few words, and their noise immediately ceased. I then walked out with you at the back door.

"I should have mentioned that I had several times before desired you to let me go, but in vain; and that when I attempted to go with Richard B[annister], the mob immediately followed, with oaths, curses, and stones; that one of them beat me down to the ground; and when I rose again, the whole body came about me like lions, and forced me back into the house.

"While you and I went out at one door, Mr. Grimshaw and Mr. Colbeck went out at the other. The mob immediately closed them in, tossed them to and fro with the utmost violence, threw Mr. Grimshaw down, and loaded them both with dirt and mire of every kind; not one of your friends offering to call off your blood-hounds from the pursuit.

"The other quiet, harmless people, who followed me at a distance, to see what the end would be, they treated still worse, not only by the connivance, but by the express order of your deputy. They made them run for their lives, amidst showers of dirt and stones, without any regard to age or sex. Some of them they trampled in the mire, and dragged by the hair, particularly Mr. Mackford, who came with me from Newcastle. Many they beat with their clubs without mercy. One they forced to leap down (or they would have thrown him headlong) from a rock, ten or twelve feet high, into the river. And when he crawled out, wet and bruised, they swore they would throw him in again, which they were hardly persuaded not to do. All this time you sat well-pleased close to the place, not attempting in the least to hinder them.

"And all this time you was talking of justice and law! Alas, sir, suppose we were Dissenters, (which I deny), suppose we were Jews or Turks, are we not to have the benefit of the laws of our country? Proceed against us by the law, if you can or dare; but not by lawless violence; not by making a drunken, cursing, swearing, riotous mob, both judge, jury and executioner. This is flat rebellion against God and the King, as you may possibly find to your cost."

In October, 1748, when the first quarterly meeting of 'Leaders' on record was held at Todmorden Edge, there were six leaders at Roughlee, namely:—Alice Dyson, Bernard Dyson, James Varley, Edward Holt, Thomas Laycock, and James Hunter. The Society must, therefore, at that time, have been numerically strong.

Mr. Wesley paid a *third* visit to Roughlee on June 8th, 1752. He writes in his Journal:—"We rode to Roughlee; and found a large, serious, and quiet congregation. There have been no tumults since Mr. White was removed. He was for some years a Popish Priest. Then he called himself a Protestant, and had the living of Colne. It was his manner first to hire, and then head the mob, when they and he were tolerably drunk. But he drank himself first into a gaol, and then into his grave."

The *fourth* and last visit of Wesley to Roughlee was on the 20th of May, 1757. Under that date he writes, "I preached near Padiham at eight, to a large, wild congregation : about noon, at Roughlee; where those who stood firm in the storm had melted away in the calm. At Keighley I had neither voice nor strength left; but while I was preaching my strength returned."

How it was that the large Society which Wesley found at Roughlee, and which Grimshaw had pronounced to be very hearty, had in ten years melted away, can only be surmised. Possibly the evil which Wesley noticed on his earliest visit had again made itself felt.

The two houses in which Mr. Wesley is said to have preached in Roughlee are still standing : one in a row of cottages parallel with the present chapel, and the other near to a farm lately occupied by Mr. Holgate. It is said to have been near the stone bridge in the village, that Mr. Wesley was attacked by the mob from Colne.

It will doubtless be interesting to the reader to have some further account of the principal person concerned in the riot at Roughlee, as given in Myles' *Grimshaw*, p. 68 ff.

The Rev. George White was educated at Douay College in France for the Romish priesthood. After his recantation he was received into the Church of England, and was, seemingly by the Vicar of Whalley, on the recommendation of Archbishop Potter, appointed Vicar of Colne and Marsden. He was a careless, worthless man, shamefully inattentive to his duty, frequently leaving his parish for weeks together. On one occasion he is said to have read the Burial Service more than twenty times in a single night over the dead that had been interred without any ceremony in his absence from home. He was also a notorious drunkard; and further sought to distinguish himself by riotous opposition to the Methodists. In fact but for this his name would have long since passed into oblivion. Whenever he heard of the arrival of any Methodists in the neighbourhood, it was his practice to call the people together by beating a drum. He would then issue a proclamation at the Colne Market Cross, and enlist a mob for the defence of the Church! The following is a copy of this curious proclamation :—

"Notice is hereby given, that if any men be mindful to enlist into His Majesty's service under the command of the Rev. Mr. George White, Commander-in-chief, and John Bannister, lieutenant-general of His Majesty's forces, for the defence of the Church of England, and the support of the manufactory in and about Colne, both which are now in danger, &c., let them now repair to the drum-head at the Cross, where each man shall have a pint of ale for advance, and other proper encouragements"—see also Myles' *Life of Grimshaw*, p. 110.

It is more than probable that Mr. White knew in 1748 of the approaching visit of Mr. Wesley, for he preached a sermon against the Methodists, as if in preparation for it, at Colne on the 24th of July and at Marsden on the 7th of August. It was based on 1 Cor. xiv. 33, "For God is not the author of confusion, &c.," and was published with a dedicatory epistle to the Archbishop of Canterbury.[1] On each occasion of its delivery the foregoing proclamation was read. White writes that he has taken pains to "inquire into the characters of these new sectaries," and "has found their teachers shamefully ignorant," and criminally arrogant, while many of them have been prevented arriving at the order of priesthood by early immoralities. He charged Wesley, Grimshaw, and their fellow-labourers with being "authors of confusion; open destroyers of the public peace, flying in the face of the very Church they may craftily pretend to follow; occasioning many bold insurrections which threaten our spiritual government; schismatical rebels against the best of Churches; authors of a farther breach in our unhappy divisions; contemners of the great demand, 'Six days shalt thou labour' &c.; defiers of all laws, civil and ecclesiastical; professed disrespecters of learning and education; causing a visible ruin of your trade and manufacture; and, in short, promoters of a shameful progress of enthusiasm and confusion not to be paralleled in any other Christian dominion."[2] He speaks of the Methodists as "a weak, illiterate crowd," and of their system as "a labyrinth of wild enthusiasm." Their preachers are "bold, visionary rustics," setting up to be guides in matters of the highest importance, "without any other plea but uncontrollable ignorance." He declares that "these officious

---

1. The title is - "A Sermon against the Methodists," Preach'd at Colne and Marsden, to a very numerous audience, by George White, M.A., Minister of Colne and Marsden: and Author of 'Mercurius Latinus.' Publish'd at the request of the audience. Preston: printed for the author by James Stanley and John Moon; and sold by W. Owen near Temple Bar, London, and the Booksellers of Yorkshire, Lancashire, Northumberland, and the Bishoprick of Durham. The Dedicatory Epistle is dated, Colne, Nov. 7, 1748, and signed George White. 8vo. 24 pages.

2. As summarised by Grimshaw in his "Answer," p. 114.

haranguers . . . cozen a handsome subsistence out of these irregular expeditions: . . . that Mr. Wesley has in reality a better income than most of our bishops: . . . that the under lay praters, by means of a certain allowance from their schismatic general, a contribution from their very wise hearers, and the constant maintenance of themselves and horses, may be supposed in a better way of living than the generality of vicars and curates; and doubtless find it much more agreeable to their constitution, to travel abroad at the expense of a sanctified face and a good assurance, than to sweat ignominiously at the loom, anvil, and various other mechanic employments, which nature had so manifestly designed them for."

To this nonsense, Grimshaw next year wrote a reply. The "Answer" was a closely printed duodecimo of eighty-six pages, "an able and well-written defence of the poor persecuted Methodists." Grimshaw says that White's sermon is "so full of palpable contradictions, absurdities, falsities, groundless suggestions, and malicious surmises, that it in some sort vindicates the people it was intended to asperse." He tells the reverend author of the Roughlee riots that "the very tinkers and colliers of your parish have of late acted the parson as well as you have done, and with as much regard to truth and the honour of God. . . . I believe, if we will but speak the truth, as we hope to answer for it at the day of judgment, we must own that they (the Methodists) have, through the divine assistance, who sends by whom He will send, wrought a far greater reformation in our parishes than we have done. . . . Sir, I make the following appeal to your own conscience, whether you do not believe that trade receives more obstruction and real detriment in one week from numbers that run a hunting, from numbers more that allow themselves in various idle diversions an hour, two, sometimes three, daily, for what is vulgarly called a noon-sit, and from many yet more, who loiter away their precious time on a market-day in your town in drunkenness, janglings, and divers frivolous matters, than from all that give the constantest attendance to this new model of worship in the space of two or three months."[1]

There is very little more to say about this rowdy Vicar of Colne. Dr. Whitaker in his History of the Parish of Whalley writing of him says:—"After one of these maudlin outbreaks," referring doubtless to the periods of absence from his parish, "he brought home Madame Helen Maria Piazza, an Italian,

---

1. Grimshaw's Answer is printed in full in Myles' *Life and Writings of the late Reverend Wm. Grimshaw*. This work, White's "Sermon," and Grimshaw's "Answer," in its separate form, are now very scarce, and are highly prized by collectors.

whom he married at Marsden. But soon after he was torn away from his bride by being imprisoned for debt." Within three years of the riot he died at Langroyd, and was buried in the Church at Colne. In the burial Register is the simple entry under April 29th (1751)—"George White, who came to be minister here, October 5th, 1741." It was reported, and believed in Colne, that before he died, he sent for Grimshaw, expressed his regret for his conduct at Roughlee and elsewhere, and begged the assistance of his prayers. Mr. Mackford, of Newcastle, who was with Wesley and Grimshaw, on the same occasion received such injuries at the hands of the mob that he soon after died.

Mr. John Bannister, "lieutenant-general of His Majesty's forces" at Roughlee, purchased some cottage property at Barrowford, and resided in the village. There his two sons afterwards gladly received the word of God, and became good Christians.

Thomas Colbeck, of Keighley, was at that time about twenty-five years of age. He was one of Grimshaw's travelling companions, a faithful and laborious local preacher, and by him Methodism was introduced into not a few of the villages in the neighbourhood of which he lived. His house was Wesley's home, and the resting-place of his itinerants. He was one of six preachers who signed the book in which the accounts of the Haworth Round were kept in 1758. He died in 1779.

## PADIHAM.

It is doubtful whether Roughlee or Padiham was first visited by Darney. He is said to have preached at Padiham as early as 1742, but there is some reason to doubt the accuracy of this statement. It is more likely that his first appearance was two years later. Padiham was then a place of some thousand or twelve hundred inhabitants. He took his stand on the riding steps, which were then at the corner of the churchyard wall, opposite to the Old Black Bull Inn. The first time he came, he was driven away by a mob led on by the clergyman of the parish, who just before had been drinking in a neighbouring inn. But he came again, and again, preaching 'repentance, faith and the witness of the Spirit.' On one occasion when a mob was attempting to pull him down from his stand, with the evident intention of doing him serious personal injury, a tall, well-built man who had been listening to what he said, and was greatly affected, stepped up to his side and declared he would knock down the first that touched him. His name was John Wood, the uncle of the late Thomas Wood.

This John Wood was one of the first Methodists at Padiham, and one of Mr. William Sagar's firmest friends. He and Mr. Sagar were frequent co-workers in schemes of Christian service, and Mr. Sagar one day observed to him at Southfield, "You and I, John, have built many a chapel in this parlour." He went to the Sessions at Preston to obtain a licence to preach, and the Magistrate who was a clergyman, having granted it, and seeing a number of disorderly people outside the Sessions House, sarcastically said, "There, go and reform that crowd." John bowed, thanked His Worship for the licence, availed himself of the opportunity, and preached what was perhaps the first Methodist sermon those men of Preston had ever heard.[1]

The first Society at Padiham was formed in 1748, and was locally known as "Darney's Society." The members were John Wood and wife, Ighten Hill Park; Thomas Pollard, Simonstone; James Hargreaves, Fir Trees; James Hunter, Margaret Wilkinson, George Wood, John Wilkinson, and Henry Robinson, all of Padiham.

The leader of this class was James Hunter, who was the first to embrace the "new faith" at Padiham. It met in his house, a thatched cottage, that stood where the old Unitarian Chapel now stands.

In 1757, Mr. Wesley paid the first of his six recorded visits to Padiham. He writes May 20th, "I preached near Padiham, at eight, to a large, wild congregation." Grimshaw also visited the town about the same time.

The first preaching-house was built in 1758, and was used for about fifteen years, the services being transferred in 1773 to the house of Abraham Sharp. It was opened in November, Grimshaw and Darney being the preachers. The interior was twenty-nine feet long and twenty-four feet broad. The total cost was £186. It afforded sitting accommodation for two hundred and thirty people. It stood at the top of the town, and was known as the "Old Chapel." There were two doors, and the pulpit was fixed against the wall between them; the women entered by one door and the men by the other, the sexes sitting apart during worship, as was the general rule at that time. The builder was a person named Whitehead, who was a member of the Society. He began as if he intended, as possibly he did, to build some cottages, but the other members arranged with him to throw two cottages into one, and so make the building into a preaching-house. Accordingly he built the outside walls or shell of the house first; and when anyone, noticing that there were no *interior* walls, asked him what he was doing, he

---

1. Jessop's *Methodism in Rossendale*, p. 116.

said he wanted to get the outside walls up and the slates on while the fine weather lasted, as he could build the inside in the winter. When finished, it was licensed as a place of worship before it was known in the neighbourhood for what purpose it was intended.

The first trustees of this chapel were John Wesley, Clerk, Bristol; Charles Wesley, Clerk, Bristol; William Grimshaw, Clerk, Haworth; Thos. Colbeck, Grocer, Keighley; John Nelson, Birstal, Gent.; Paul Greenwood, Stanbury, Gent.; and Jonathan Maskew. A few years afterwards, seven others were appointed:—William Charles, Jonathan Wood, James Pollard, Robert Hartley, John Dewhirst, William Clayton and Thomas Pollard.

In front of this chapel was a grave-yard in which several interments were made. It is now used as a garden, the chapel being occupied as a dwelling-house, in which for many years resided the late Mr. Thomas Holland. Some years ago, when repairs were being made to the drains in the house, the workmen came in contact with a grave which is supposed to have been dug near the pulpit.

Sometime after the erection of the preaching-house, a dwelling-house was built. At the back part of the house was the stable in which the horses of Mr. Wesley and his itinerants fed, and took their rest. The way to the stable was by a passage between the chapel and the house. The hook on which the bridles were hung, was, till quite recently, in its original position, and is possibly still to be seen. Over the stable was the preacher's sleeping-room. In connection with this chapel was one of the dispensaries which Wesley established in various parts of the country.

The somewhat stealthy way in which the first preaching-house was built and licensed shows, that the little Society feared there might be some opposition to their undertaking. This was no groundless fear. Darney had been mobbed by the incumbent on his first appearance in the town, and for some years after the erection of the chapel a service could not be peacefully conducted in the open air. Thomas Taylor writes of a period almost twenty years later[1]:—"A little before the Conference (1776), having to preach one Sunday evening at Padiham, the house was far too small for the congregation. It being a fine evening we chose a convenient place to preach on out of doors. While I was preaching to a large congregation, the minister came at the head of a mob, in his gown and cassock, and dragged me down. As soon as I could, I mounted again, and again was jostled down. I attempted standing up a third

---

1. *Lives of Early Methodist Preachers*, 4th ed., v. 46.

time, but to no purpose; so we adjourned to the preaching-house."

Wesley's first visit to Padiham has been already noticed. On three other occasions during this period he preached in the town. He writes under July 13th, 1761, "About five I preached at Padiham, another place eminent for all manner of wickedness. The multitude of people obliged me to stand in the yard of the preaching-house. Over against me, at a little distance, sat some of the most impudent women I ever saw; yet I am not sure that God did not reach their hearts, for

> They roar'd, and would have blushed, if capable of shame."

The entry under July 29th, 1766, is, "In the evening I preached near the preaching-house at Padiham, and strongly insisted on communion with God, as the only religion that would avail us. At the close of the sermon came Mr. M. His long white beard showed that his present disorder was of some continuance. In all other respects he was quite sensible; but he told me, with much concern, 'You can have no place in heaven without—a beard! Therefore, I beg, let yours grow immediately.'" Again, April 29th, 1776, "I preached at Padiham, in a broad street, to a huge congregation. I think the only inattentive persons were, the minister and a kind of gentleman."

The Todmorden Society's Book contains the following entries :—

"Oct. 18th, 1748. At a meeting, then held at Major Marshall's, of the Leaders of Classes of several Religious Societies, the following persons were chosen *Stewards:* James Greenwood, John Parker, John Maden, and James Dyson." It is the first notice, and possibly the first formal election of Stewards in Methodism. Of course Mr. Grimshaw, like a good superintendent, copied the particulars into the Circuit Book at Haworth, with, however, some important additions. He states that the place of meeting was Todmorden Edge; the Societies for which Stewards were appointed were those at "Rossendale, Roughlee, Hepponstall, and Todmorden," and the object of their election was that they might "transact the temporal affairs" of the Societies.

"It was then agreed," so the entry proceeds, "that if there be any just cause to exchange any of the above Stewards, it shall be done at the next Quarterly Meeting held for the said Societies by the approbation of the leaders then present. If any dispute arise touching the choosing of Steward or Stewards, the greater number of voices shall have the choice to elect a fresh Steward. This shall be mentioned to our minister, Mr. John Wesley, or his successor, who shall end any dispute of this kind."

This last entry is important, as showing that Grimshaw at this time considered himself acting as Wesley's 'Assistant'; and the Societies, by whomsoever they had been formed, were regarded as Wesleyan Methodist Societies.

The amount contributed from Roughlee was £1 4s. 7d. The sum of 15s. 2½d. had been disbursed at Roughlee, but for what purpose we are not told; probably for turnpikes, keep of horses, &c.; the only entry is "Charges as per bill." The balance was given to William Darney.

James Hunter, the leader of the recently formed Society at Padiham, was also present at this meeting, and paid in the first contribution from that place, the amount being 3s. 6d. For several years he attended the quarterly meetings of the " Round," which seem generally to have been held at Keighley.

The book in which these accounts are preserved is in the hand-writing of Grimshaw. Four other meetings are reported, in which the contributions from Padiham are given :—

|  |  |  | s. | d. |
|---|---|---|---|---|
| January 10th, 1749, | James Hunter | ...... | 3 | 10 |
| April 18th, | ,, ,, ,, | ...... | 6 | 2 |
| July 11th, | ,, Thomas Asden | ... | 4 | 2 |
| October 31st, | ,, James Hunter | ... | 9 | 4 |

There are no more entries in this book until July 25th, 1754, under which date the following occurs:—"Whereas it appears no accounts are herein inserted from October 31st, 1749, to this present day, July 25th, 1754; Be it known that the reason of it is the discontinuance of Quarter Meetings from that to this day."

From 1754 the meetings were regularly held, and payments from Padiham, with the names of the Stewards, duly entered, until 1776. The amounts contributed vary from 2s. 6d. to £1 12s. 10d.

It is impossible to give the precise limits of the Haworth Round. Circuit boundaries in those days were not very clearly defined. Some idea of its size may be gathered from the fact that in the year of Grimshaw's death it included 66 Societies with 1803 members. These Societies were scattered over East Lancashire and the districts of Craven and Bolland. In Haworth there were only 15 members, but in Keighley 163, whose practice was to attend Haworth Church regularly on Communion Sundays and frequently on other occasions.

Grimshaw died on the 7th of April, 1763, after having worked in more or less close connection with Wesley for some fifteen years. There was every reason to fear that, when the man, who had superintended a circuit so extended and at the same time so feeble in its different parts, passed away, the work would receive a serious check. But no such ill result followed. John Pawson who was sent to the Haworth circuit in 1763, writes[1]:—" Upon coming into the circuit we found all the people mourning the loss of that eminently faithful servant of God, the Rev. William Grimshaw. . . . Many, very many had, I am inclined to think, put that excellent man in God's place, and seriously thought that the prosperity of the work entirely depended upon him. Hence they thought, 'Now he is gone, all is over with us; we shall surely come to nothing.' God, we know, is a jealous God, and will not have us to ascribe that to any creature, which we ought to ascribe to Him alone. As the people, I am satisfied, did this, the Lord called His faithful servant away; and, it was very remarkable, the work prospered wonderfully; and I believe there was much more good done in that circuit in that one year, than had been done in seven years before that time. In Keighley, also, and the neighbourhood, there was a glorious revival of the work of God, such as no one then living could remember to have seen. It seemed as if the word of God could carry all before it, and men, women, and children were converted on all sides."

Such indeed appears to have been the growth of the circuit in the next few years, Methodism being established in more and more places within its area, that at last it became altogether unwieldy. Consequently its outskirts were first of all separated from it, and at last in 1776, on the advice of Thomas Taylor, who was then its superintendent, its complete partition was effected. Haworth disappeared from the list of circuits, and Keighley and Colne took its place. Mr. Taylor, who was appointed Superintendent of the former (still occasionally for a time known as the Haworth circuit) at the Conference of 1775, writes[2]:—" My next remove was to Keighley. This circuit was a mere scarecrow on various accounts; so that I entered into it with little less than horror. There was a family in the preacher's house, which I was obliged to remove. The house was to furnish, and put into repair; and I had to beg the money up and down, which is not pleasing work.

"The Circuit was a large rambling range. I was to be but three or four days at Keighley in six weeks; and many of the congregations were very small; all of which were completely disagreeable circumstances. However, I entered upon my work in the best manner I could. I soon got the house put into good repair and well furnished; so that my family were comfortably situated. God likewise revived His work in

---

1. *Lives of Early Methodist Preachers*, 4th ed., iv. 28.
2. *ib.*, v. 45-47.

many places, so that between four and five hundred were added to us during the year ; and the greater part were able to give a reason of the hope that was in them. . . .

"In July, 1776, I went to the Conference at London . . . Returning to Keighley, I divided the circuit into two very compact rounds, making Colne and the societies which surrounded it into a circuit by itself; by which means both the circuits are become very agreeable. But an unhappy affair happening at Colne, put a great damp on the work there." This "unhappy affair" will be referred to when we come to speak of Methodism at Colne.

It is also impossible to give any complete list of the preachers appointed to travel in this large circuit during the earlier years of its existence. The "Stations of the Preachers" do not appear in the printed Minutes of the Conference till 1765 ; and moreover, the men appointed at Conference did not at first always remain in their 'Round' for twelve months, but only for one or two, changes being made by Wesley during the year as the necessities of the work in various parts required. The earlier appointments can only be gathered from the manuscript memoranda and published Journals of the preachers, etc.: and it seems as if these sometimes included the names of preachers, who were not at that time, though some of them afterwards became, Wesley's Itinerants. Darney's connections with the circuit have already been described.

In 1753, there were in the "Yorkshire and Haworth" circuit the following ministers—Jonathan Maskew, John Whitford, Enoch Williams, Joseph Jones, William Shent, John Edwards.

In 1755, there were William Grimshaw, John Nelson, James Schofield.

In 1758, there were again six preachers : at least six signed the book of accounts. These were Alexander Coates, James Oddie, Thomas Colbeck, William Greenwood, Parson Greenwood, Samuel Fielden.

John Nelson was a stone-mason at Birstal ; William Shent was a barber and one of the first Methodists in Leeds ; Jonathan Maskew was a native of Bingley, and for some time seems to have had charge of Grimshaw's glebe. Nelson died in the work in 1774 : Shent seems to have returned to his business in Leeds; and Maskew married and settled at Dean-Head, acting as a 'local' preacher till his death. These three were at one time stationed in the York circuit, and are referred to in the following lines from a Satirical Poem on the Methodists :—

"A stone-cutter leads, a barber succeeds,
    The third is a clergyman's servant."

The following is a list of the preachers appointed to the Haworth Circuit from 1765 to 1775. In the case of those who remained in connection with Mr. Wesley till their death, the date of entering the ministry and the date of death are given. Where no date is given, it is to be understood that for some reason the preacher ceased from travelling.

1765. Isaac Brown (1760-1815), John Atlay, Nicholas Manners, James Stephens, Robert Costerdine (1764-1812).
1766. Isaac Brown, J. Shaw (1762-1793), Robert Costerdine, John Atlay.
1767. Robert Costerdine, Joseph Guilford (1761-1777), John Wittam (1767-1818), Thomas Cherry (1767-1772).
1768. T. Mitchell (1748-1784), Joseph Guilford, William Ellis, Thomas Newall.
1769. T. Mitchell, George Hudson, Thomas Wride (1768-1807), David Evans.
1770. Richard Seed (1768-1805), George Hudson, David Evans.
1771. Jeremiah Robertshaw (1762-1788), Stephen Proctor, John Poole.
1772. Thomas Johnson (1752-1797), John Poole, Thomas Tatton.
1773. Thomas Johnson, Edward Slater, Robert Costerdine (second time).
1774. Robert Costerdine, Richard Seed (second time), Robert Swan (1770-1810).
1775. Thomas Taylor (1761-1816), Robert Swan, Samuel Bardsley (1768-1818).

It will also be noted that in those days there were frequently very young superintendents, and that a man having occupied that position was sometimes sent afterwards as second or third preacher to the same neighbourhood.

In this list there are the names of twenty-five men. Of these only fourteen died in the work; and eleven, or forty-four per cent. of the whole 'retired.' This retirement was not so much occasioned by misconduct or divergence from the accepted standards of doctrine, as by 'family reasons.' The allowances were too small for the decent support of a family, hence many of the preachers ceased to travel, though they did not cease to work; some obtaining ordination in the Established Church, some settling as pastors of Dissenting Churches, and still more returning to their former calling. Of two hundred and eighteen, whom Myles considers as the "first race of Methodist preachers," one hundred and thirteen, or more than half retired from the itinerancy.

The support of the preachers was considered at the Conference of 1752. Up to this time they had boarded with

the members of the society as they travelled through their
'Rounds'; their travelling expenses were supposed to be paid
by the circuit stewards: for clothes and books they were
dependent on the gifts of the people. It was now resolved
that each preacher should be granted "eight pounds at least,
perhaps ten pounds per year," for clothing. Even this regulation may not have been general, as it was adopted at a
Conference held at Limerick. In 1769 it was further resolved
that each preacher's wife should receive ten pounds a year: a
little later the amount was raised to twelve, with four pounds a
year for each of the children. Forty-three of the itinerants
(about a third of the entire number) were married.

These resolutions were not fully carried out in England,
as appears from the following extract from the Bradford Circuit
Book for the year 1770.[1] The circuit may have been poor,
but there is reason for believing that the allowances in neighbouring circuits did not differ largely from those of Bradford.

|   | £ | s. | d. |
|---|---|----|----|
| The preacher's board, thirteen weeks, at 3s. 6d. | 2 | 5 | 6 |
| The preacher's quarterage ... ... ... | 3 | 0 | 0 |
| ditto ditto ... ... ... | 1 | 17 | 6 |
| Allowed for servant ... ... ... ... |  | 12 | 6 |
| Allowed for turnpikes ... ... ... ... |  | 6 | 0 |
|   | 8 | 1 | 6 |

---

1. Stamp's *Methodism in Bradford*, p. 55.

## CHAPTER III.

# COLNE CIRCUIT, 1776-1810.

COLNE—BARLEY—SOUTHFIELD—PADIHAM—BARROWFORD—
HIGHAM—BURNLEY—MERECLOUGH—HURSTWOOD.

IN this period, from the formation of the Colne to that of the Burnley circuit, a period of thirty-four years, the interest centres chiefly around three places—Padiham, Burnley, Colne. And first, as the place from which the circuit took its name, the work in Colne may be briefly noticed.

### COLNE.

The 'unhappy event,' to which reference was made near the close of the last chapter, was an accident which happened at the opening of the first chapel in this town. Methodism had already been established in several small places in its neighbourhood. The first to provide a home for the Methodist preachers in the town itself was Richard Lancaster, who came originally from Gisburn (Everett, *Methodism in Manchester*). Richard Lancaster, in all probability the same man, is recorded to have paid in a contribution from the society at Roughlee on the 19th of October, 1758.

The first Methodist preacher to visit Colne was John Jane. Wesley writes (Journal, April 30, 1776) that as Jane was innocently riding through the town the mob pulled him off his horse and put him in the stocks, and that he seized the opportunity to exhort them to "flee from the wrath to come." Wesley does not say when it was that Jane thus preached, but it must have been before 1750, for this young man only travelled three years, dying at Epworth, August 25th, 1750. In the report of his death to Wesley it was stated that "all his clothes, linen and woollen, stockings, hat, and wig, are not thought sufficient to answer his funeral expenses, which amount to £1 17s. 3d.; all the money he had was 1s. 4d." Whereupon, Wesley commented (*ib.*, Sep. 6, 1750), " Enough for any unmarried preacher of the Gospel to leave to his executors."

Wesley himself paid several visits to Colne. The first was on Friday, July 20th, 1759. He writes in his Journal: "We went on to Colne, (formerly I suppose a Roman colony,) situate on the top of a high round hill, at the edge of Pendle Forest. I preached at eleven in an open space, not far from the main street; and I have seldom seen a more attentive or decently behaved congregation. How is the scene changed, since the drunken mob of this town used to be a terror to all the country!"

A second visit was made on Monday, July 13th, 1761. Wesley writes, "At noon I preached in Colne, once inaccessible to the Gospel; but now the yard I was in would not contain the people. I believe I might have preached at the Cross without the least interruption."

On the occasion of his third visit on Tuesday, July 29th, 1766, the record is simply, "I preached at Colne."

His fourth visit was on Sunday, April 28th, 1776. At this period the churches were generally open to him, and on this occasion he preached in the pulpit from which George White had several years before delivered his fulmination "Against the Methodists." In his Journal Wesley writes:—"The church at Colne is, I think, at least twice as large as that at Haworth. But it would not in anywise contain the congregation. I preached on 'I saw a great white throne coming down from heaven.' Deep attention sat on every face; and, I trust, God gave us His blessing."

Thomas Taylor, who was then the superintendent of the Haworth circuit, in his unpublished diary[1] describes this visit more fully. On Saturday the 27th, Wesley had preached at Bradford at five in the morning, and in Bingley church at half-past ten. Taylor had never seen him weep while preaching till then. "He spoke awfully, and the congregation heard attentively." His text was Acts xxiv. 25. Mr. Taylor continues :—
"The next day (Sunday) I heard him at Keighley in the morning, and then at Haworth church. Afterwards the sacrament was administered, but in too great a hurry. Several hundreds communicated in less than an hour. We then dined, in haste and confusion, and drove off to Colne. I rode fast, and got thither before Mr. Wesley. The street was filled with people waiting to welcome him; but, when about two miles from Colne, his chaise broke down, which somewhat delayed his coming. He mounted a horse, however, and so arrived in safety. The crowd was so great that it was with difficulty we got into the church. The

---

1. Quoted in Tyerman, *Life and Times of John Wesley*, iii. 225, 226.

sexton led us to the reading desk, and thereby I got a seat. Mr. Wesley's text was Rev. xx. 12. At the beginning he was rather flat, but at the end he spake many awful things." That was not a bad day's work for an old man of seventy-three.

On the following Tuesday, Wesley writes again :—" In the evening I preached in a kind of Square, at Colne, to a multitude of people, all drinking in the word. I scarce ever saw a congregation wherein men, women, and children stood in such a posture ; and this in a town wherein thirty years ago no Methodist could show his head !"

Shortly after John Jane preached from the stocks, John Nelson came and held a service in a house situated in a part of the town called Niniveh. Services were afterwards held in other houses, and finally in a room extending over several cottages in Dent Back.

In July, 1774, the society, which had been in existence some sixteen years, contained thirty-five members. The year afterwards the number had risen to sixty-three, and the need of a preaching-house was felt. To erect one was a great undertaking for a society which, though rapidly increasing, was still both small and very poor ; but Mr. Sagar, of whom more will be heard, entered with two others into a solemn engagement to stand true to one another, and not desert the work until it was completed. This determination was adhered to until the walls were about half-way up, when difficulties from the scarcity of money began to be felt. Mr. Sagar, on his way home from one of his Scotch journeys, stopped at Colne, no doubt to enquire about the progress of the chapel. He was soon informed that all was at a stand-still, and that his two friends had broken their promise and abandoned the enterprise. The workpeople began asking for their wages, which he was unable to pay. His father was not at this time at all friendly to Methodism, and he had not the means to meet the claims of the builders. He left the town and the unfinished walls, much distressed and not knowing what to do. Having reached the top of the Lenches[1] on his journey homewards, he turned round his horse, and looked at the half-built chapel, visible on the other side of the valley. Then he alighted, and kneeling on the ground with his face toward the unfinished house of God earnestly cried for help. On the next market-day at Colne, a man tapped him on the shoulder in the old Piece Hall, and said, " Mr Sagar, don't you want some money for that chapel." He replied, "Yes, I do." "I have a certain sum," said the man, "which I will lend you." " But," said Mr. Sagar, "I cannot give you any security for it, and no one will join me in a bond." "No matter for

---

1. Then called the Lanshaws.

that," said the man, "Your word is as good as your bond, and you shall have it." Soon after, a second man accosted him in the same way, making a similar offer and returning the same reply to his objections. The generous offers were accepted, and with this seasonable supply the work was carried on without further interruption till the building was ready for the roof, when an equinoctial gale blew down the western gable-end into the area and shook the whole fabric. This disaster rendered it necessary, after repairing the damages, to erect a house against the chapel, and so strengthen the whole edifice. With laudable zeal and perseverance, the pious few engaged in the arduous task struggled on through the winter, and in the month of June, 1777, the chapel, though not then quite finished, was formally opened by Wesley.

CHAPEL OF 1777, WITH HOUSE BUILT TO SUPPORT IT.

This William Sagar, who took such a prominent part in the building of the first Colne chapel, was born at Southfield in 1751. His father was a cloth-merchant, who by industry and prudence was very successful in business, and amassed a considerable fortune. In his youth, William was steady and respectable, but careless about religion. His father was very fond of hunting, and, as William grew up, his father's great desire was to see him first in the field. For a time the son was as ardent a sportsman as the father, and the two hunted together all day, and then, to make up for lost time, worked hard all night. Accustomed to travel in Scotland on business, he was converted at Edinburgh. As he did not conceal his religious principles, his father at first contented himself with expressing his disapprobation; but when he avowed himself a Methodist, he frequently found the door of his home locked against him, and had to seek a lodging elsewhere. At length the father became so far reconciled to his son's connection with the Methodists as to receive Mr. Taylor, the superintendent of the Haworth (Keighley) circuit, into his house at Southfield. In December, 1781, the son married a kindred spirit, Miss Elizabeth Halstead, of Cockdane; and their influence and generosity contributed largely to the establishment of Methodism in this neighbourhood upon a firm basis.

Mr. Sagar was a decidedly religious man. His diary abounds in evidence that he enjoyed close communion with God. One example must suffice. On June 1st, 1808, he writes:—"While I was at private prayer this morning, I found the power of the Lord present to heal. What an unspeakable mercy, from so gracious a Redeemer, [that] He has looked upon me with a compassionate eye, remembered me in much mercy, restored unto me the joy of His favour." The following are the rules[1] according to which he endeavoured to spend each week day of his life when at home. "Rise at five, if health permit. Spend two hours in meditation and prayer. Call the family together at seven in winter. After prayer, spend until eight in going through tenter-crofts and workshops. Breakfast at eight. From that time till noon in some useful employment, but observe to live in the spirit of prayer and watchfulness; and beware of getting my mind damped with earthly things. Spend three quarters of an hour at noon in reading and prayer. From one till five in some useful employment. Then, if business permit, spend till seven in visiting the sick, following the backsliders, speaking a word of comfort to the mourners. From seven to nine retire. Then bed."

One of the latest entries in his diary is dated June 23rd, 1808. He writes:—"The Quarterly Meeting for this circuit was this day held at Southfield. The local preachers, stewards, and leaders who dined here were upwards of thirty. Was much gratified in being honoured with so respectable a company. The greatest unity subsisted among us while transacting our temporal concerns."

Amongst the papers of Mr. Sagar, who was expecting a visit from Wesley at Southfield, was found the copy of an itinerary,[2] which the latter had prepared for the spring of 1790

---

1. See James Carr, *Annals of Colne*, p. 44.

2. This itinerary is dated "London, March 1, 1790." The arrangements for a week in April were—"Saturday 10th, Bolton : Monday 12th, Blackburn : Tuesday 13th, **Colne** : Saturday 17th, Keighley." On March 22nd, however, Mr. Roger **Crane wrote** to Mr. Sagar, " I this day received

and distributed amongst his friends. It began with the business-like statement, "As many persons desire to know where I am from this time till the Conference, I here set down my route, which, if God permit, I shall keep till that time:" and it closed characteristically, "Many persons are continually teasing me to visit more places. Now let them judge whether I have work enough."

Mr. Sagar died as only a Christian can. Shortly before his death, his wife said to him, "William, I hope we shall be enabled to follow you, as you have followed Christ." "Yes," he replied, "but do it more faithfully; religion is worth living for, a never-failing source of comfort." He then asked to see an old local preacher, who was charitably supported by the family; and on his coming into the room, he said, "James, the Lord will not forsake us in our old age." James replied, "You find religion good now?" "Yes," returned he, "and I want more of it." As the end drew near, he began to sing, "I'll praise my Maker while I've breath." Whilst singing, his countenance brightened into an expression more than human, especially while endeavouring to raise his faltering voice higher to repeat the final line, "Or immortality endures." His last words were, "Take me, take me"; and then he quietly fell asleep in Jesus in the fifty-ninth year of his age.[1]

---

a letter from Mr. Wesley, and he has altered his plan as follows, viz., April 10th, Bolton : Monday 12th, Rochdale : Tuesday 13th, Padiham : Wed. 14th, Preston : Thursday 15th, Blackburn : Friday 16th, Colne. I have acquainted Mr. Collins of the said alteration. I have also wrote to Blackburn to the same purpose. Mr. Wesley desires me to meet him at Rochdale, and I think I shall go, if you be there. Please to give me a line immediately." Roger Crane was one of the most active Methodists in Preston and the Fylde. His sister was the wife of the Rev. Charles Atmore, and his daughter afterwards married George Fishwick, of Scorton. The rest of the letter refers to some dispute with Mr. Collins, the superintendent of the Colne circuit, but the particulars are not given. A sister of George Fishwick married into the Hopwood family, by whom the following unpublished letter from Wesley to Roger Crane has been preserved :—

"Dear Roger,                        Conway, April 9, 1785.

What you observe is true. The new places ought not to be neglected. Therefore it is not expedient to remove William Bramwell yet. So I have sent to Derbyshire, and hope Nathaniel Ward will speedily remove to Chester to assist Mr. Wright. Meantime take care that *you* be not weary of welldoing. In due time you shall reap if you faint not.

                 I am, dear Roger,
                       Your affectionate Brother,
                                   J. WESLEY."

1. This account of Mr. William Sagar and that of the building of the Colne chapel, are taken from a Memoir drawn up for the use of the family by one of his daughters. Interesting extracts are cited in Carr, *Annals of Colne*, pp. 41-43.

To return to the opening of the chapel. In June, 1777, it was still far from finished, building materials were strewn about the premises, the gallery had no protection in front and was without pews; but as Wesley was proceeding through the district on one of his regular visitations, it was arranged that he should open it. A sad accident marred the service. Wesley thus tells the story (*Journal*, iv. 101), "I had appointed to preach in the new preaching-house at Colne. Supposing it would be sufficiently crowded, I went a little before the time; so that the galleries were but half full when I came into the pulpit. Two minutes after the whole left-hand gallery fell at once, with a hundred and fifty or two hundred persons. Considering the height, and the weight of people, one would have supposed that many lives would have been lost. But I did not hear of one. Does not God give His angels charge over them that fear Him? When the hurry was a little over, I went into an adjoining meadow, and quietly declared the whole counsel of God."

Thomas Taylor, the superintendent of the Keighley circuit, in his account of the accident writes (*Early Methodist Preachers*, v. 47)—" We had with much difficulty raised a fine large chapel; and being completed, Mr. Wesley came to open it. Being much crowded, both above and below, and the timber of the galleries not being sufficiently strong, just when Mr. Wesley and I had got into the pulpit, before he began, all of a sudden one of the galleries sunk down, and abundance of people had legs, arms, or thighs broken. The confusion, as may easily be imagined, was very great; and the cries of such as were maimed, and such as were frightened, were truly piercing. Many false reports were spread concerning this awful adventure. Some said the whole chapel was in danger, and therefore durst not come into it. By one means or other, the work got a dreadful stun, which I fear it will not recover very soon." One of the false reports spread abroad, to which Mr. Taylor refers, was that the accident was occasioned by the contractor for the wood work having purposely cut the gallery timbers too short. The real cause seems to have been that the people crowded too much together, sitting on the floor of the gallery with their feet hanging over the front. The weight concentrated thus too much on a single spot forced the beams out of the newly erected walls. Many of the people who were injured by this accident were poor, and a great distance from home. They were obliged to remain for some time in Colne, and their maintenance and medical attendance increased the burden of the trustees, already serious enough through the cost of the repairs.

At the Conference of 1777, Alexander Mather was

appointed to the circuit with instructions to make a private collection in the neighbouring circuits for the sufferers. He writes (*Early Meth. Preachers*, ii. 185, 186)—"In the year 1777 I was appointed for the Colne circuit. It was not long before, that the gallery in the preaching-house, being full of people, had fallen flat to the ground. And though no one was killed, yet some limbs were broken, and many poor people bruised. This obliged me to travel through many societies, in order to defray those large expenses, of taking care of those that were hurt, and rebuilding the gallery, as well as building and furnishing a house for the preacher. But whatever fatigue I had was made up by the kindness and liberality of our brethren."

It was a long time before there was a general feeling that the chapel was safe. Nearly two years afterwards Mr. Wesley came again to Colne (April 13th, 1779). Having recorded that he preached at one o'clock in Padiham, he proceeds, "In the evening I preached at Colne; but the people were still in such a panic, that few durst go into the left-hand gallery."

Wesley paid several visits to Colne after this. He wrote to Mr. Sagar from Bristol, March 12th, 1780—

"My Dear Brother,—
   To-morrow morning I am to set [*sic*] from hence. I expect to be at Manchester on Good Friday, at Bolton on Easter Eve, at Warrington on Easter-day, at Liverpool on Easter Monday. If I go to Ireland (concerning which I am not fully determined) I shall then set sail as soon as possible. If I do not, I shall have time to visit our friends at Colne, which would give me a particular satisfaction. If we are zealous and active, our Societies will increase; otherwise, they will moulder away.

I am,
   Your affectionate Brother,
      J. WESLEY."

He managed to visit Colne, for he writes in his Journal under Sunday, April 30th,—"We had a lovely congregation at Colne; but a much larger at one and at five. Many of them came ten or twelve miles; but I believe not in vain: God gave them a good reward for their labour."

Another visit is recorded without particulars on Wednesday, July 14th, 1784:—"I preached at Colne."

On February 25th, 1786, Wesley writes to Mr. Sagar—"I expect to be at Manchester, on Wed. April 5; at Chester, Monday 30th; at Liverpool, Wed. 12th [May]; at Warrington, Sat. 15; at Preston Mond. 17th; at Blackburn, Tuesday 18; Wedn. 19 at Padiham; Burnley 12 [o'clock], Colne 6 [o'clock]: so as to lodge with you on Thursday 20th. I am to be in the evening at Keighley. I am obliged to make haste. Concerning Building and other matters, I hope we shall have time to talk when we meet.

I am,
Your affectionate Brother,
J. WESLEY.

If you know how to mend my plan, send me word to Manchester."

The plan was carried out in substance, as the Journal shows.

In connection with this visit there is an interesting letter to Mr. Sagar from Richardson, the vicar of Haworth, which deserves to be recorded.

"Haworth,
April 18th, 1786.

Dear Sir,
Mr. Cross, the vicar of Bradford, was at my house yesterday, and informed me that Mr. Wesley was expected to be at Southfield to-day; therefore I write to you to beg the favour that you will present my Christian and humble respects to him, and acquaint him that I shall be very glad to have my pulpit honoured with him the next Sabbath day. I learned from Mr. Cross that Mr. Wesley had offered him his services then; and as for some particular reasons Mr. Cross chooses to decline the acceptance of his kindness, (of which Mr. Wesley will be informed by letter from Mr. Cross to-morrow), I flatter myself Mr. Wesley will be disengaged for that day. I highly esteem and venerate that great and good old man; and I assure you that the disagreeable interruption of our friendly intercourse was not in the least measure owing to me. I would cordially cultivate love and peace with all men, especially those who fear God. My kind respects to Mrs. Sagar. I shall be glad to see you both at the time mentioned to dine with me along with Mr. Wesley, if I be so happy as to be successful in my application.

I am, dear Sir,
With much esteem,
Your Friend & Servant,
JOHN RICHARDSON."

Wesley appears to have accepted the invitation, for he preached in Haworth church on Sunday, April 23rd.

There are only scattered notices of Methodism in Colne for the next few years.

Christopher Hopper was appointed to the circuit in 1779. He writes (*Early Methodist Preachers*, i. 217)—"I met with many agreeable, and some disagreeable things. The great enemy had wounded many, who I hope are now healed again. We had a severe winter, many crosses and trials, and many blessings. The Lord owned our weak labours, and gave us a little success. The last time I visited the classes in this circuit, we added thirty-eight to our number, and twenty-three to the church of the living God, who had found remission of sins through the blood of our adorable Saviour. Nine died in peace, and are now with the spirits of just men made perfect in the paradise of God."

A little after this there seems to have been a fear of Calvinistic teaching spreading in the neighbourhood; and Mr. Sagar must have written to Wesley on the subject, for Wesley replies :—

"August 11th, 1782.

Certainly nothing can more effectually stop the work of God than the breaking in of Calvinism upon you. I hope your three preachers will calmly and diligently oppose it, although not so much by preaching as by visiting the people from house to house, dispersing the little tracts as it were with both hands.

Your affectionate brother,

J. WESLEY."

Charles Atmore was appointed to the circuit in 1784. He writes[1] in his diary that Colne had been "proverbially dead" for many years, but now "people flocked to the house of prayer in such numbers that we were constrained to leave the chapel and preach in the fields." The good work beginning at Colne spread to every part of the circuit except in the district north of Pendle. Mr. Atmore described the two years he spent in the Colne circuit as the most useful in his life. Nearly eight hundred members were added to the society. About the same time Mrs. Sagar wrote to her husband, "We had a wonderful good love-feast at Colne. We had more than the chapel would hold by hundreds, so that Mr. Atmore was obliged to preach on the garden wall, and, as Mr. Atmore observed, to the most attentive congregation he ever spoke to. His text was 'Let the wicked man forsake his way, &c.' Likewise at night the chapel was quite full." Again she writes, evidently near the Conference of 1786 when Mr. Atmore left the circuit, "I found it a very great cross to part with Mr. Atmore. The chapel was quite full on the Tuesday night . . . I could scarcely believe Mr. Atmore could have been so affected . . . It was thought there were more than a thousand people at Lower Bradley." Mr. Ridall was one of the preachers the next year, and threw himself with such ardour into the work that even Mr. Wesley considered he needed a little gentle restraint, and recommended in a letter that someone should "advise brother Ridall not to please the devil by preaching himself to death."

---

1. Quoted in *Wesleyan Meth. Magazine*, 1845, p. 16.

In 1788 Mr. Atmore was appointed to the circuit for a second time, with Mr. Ridall, also re-appointed, as his colleague. One of their immediate predecessors had adopted sceptical notions on the subject of revelation, and in other ways greatly disturbed the church. His place unfortunately was supplied by a man, who quickly turned Calvinist, and joined another communion. The effect upon the circuit was disastrous and not easily corrected. "We began to rebuild," writes Mr. Atmore, "the temple of the Lord which in many places was thrown down, and to repair the waste places. Our labour was not wholly in vain. We saw the breaches in some degree repaired; but the building was far from being so fair and noble a structure ... as it once was." As the ministers appointed in 1789 were both mighty men of God, William Collins and William Bramwell, the recovery of the circuit was soon complete, and its growth was so marked that the following year the services of a third minister were needed.

John Wesley died on March 2nd, 1791, and his death filled the circuits with a natural apprehension as to the perpetuation of his work and the possible changes that would be introduced into his methods. The following month Mr. Atmore wrote Mr. Sagar a letter, which has been preserved. The only local particulars it records are that Mr. Sagar was increasing in riches, and had recently become a lay preacher. Incidentally there is a criticism of the newly-published Life of Wesley, by John Hampson, that "it deserves burning by the hands of the common hangman." But the main interest lies in the allusions to the critical event, of which the minds of all Methodists were at that time full. "Many," writes Mr. Atmore, "are waiting for our halting; our friends fear it, our enemies hope for it, but I trust the Lord will appear for His own cause, and still shew that He is on our side." He considers himself "that things bear an agreeable aspect, and there is the greatest probability that peace and brotherly love will continue and abound." The preservation of "itinerancy and a pure uncorrupt ministry" appears to him the sole condition of continued progress. And, he adds, "the steps that have been taken by the preachers in Yorkshire and Lancashire for our future union perfectly meet with my approbation, and in my judgment they bid fair to lay a sure foundation for permanent peace among us." The figures are a little mixed, but the allusion is to the meetings that were held, not only in the counties that are named, but in various parts of the kingdom, for the purpose of agreement upon the course to be followed and the arrangements to be made at the approaching Conference. In these meetings is to be seen the origin of the District Committees, which were afterwards according to the laws of legitimate ecclesiastical development more appropriately styled District Synods. The Conference determined "to follow strictly the plan which Mr. Wesley left us at his death;" and whatever agitation there was, except in relation to a question of polity, though not always free from bitterness, was generally reasonable in its expedients and patient of opposition.

Joseph Entwistle was appointed at the age of twenty-eight to Colne by the Conference of 1794. Arrived at Keighley, he heard that smallpox was very prevalent, and that his predecessor had left a child dangerously ill in the preacher's house. He therefore left his youngest child, then seventeen months old, at the house of a friend in Keighley, and proceeded to Colne. His son and biographer writes that "the congregations at Colne and some other places were small, and religion was but at a low ebb." In the evening of the day on which he arrived, Mr. Entwistle preached to a congregation of about thirty persons only. He began to fancy that he had been sent to "a wilderness circuit," where he was "deprived of many outward comforts," for the good of his soul. However, the following week he had double the number, and at the end of September he writes of peace at the quarterly meeting, "a blessed time" at the love-feast in the afternoon, and a refreshing season at the watch-night (which was then in some places held quarterly, at an earlier period even more frequently), and sees "the prospect of a glorious revival" in the neighbourhood of Colne.

In December 1795 he wrote to a friend at Huddersfield:— "Many have lately been brought to Christ. We hear almost daily of the conversion of sinners. In the neighbourhood of Colne seventeen at least have experienced 'the knowledge of salvation by the remission of their sins' since Conference. Some months ago my dear wife began to meet a number of girls, which has been made very useful already, and promises much more. We have a meeting for the lads also." Other indications of Mr. Entwistle's good work at Colne survive. He was amongst the youngest of superintendents, but his colleague, the Rev. C. Gloyne, wrote of him, "His management of the circuit was admirable. He was strict in enforcing discipline, and governed with ministerial authority, yet did not seem to govern. I do not remember having a single jar in the circuit during the year; we had peace and prosperity in almost every society." For another colleague he took a house "on his own responsibility, and begged as much money as enabled him to furnish it in the homely style of those olden times" (*Memoir*, p. 160). Whatever Mr. Sagar and the other lay officials thought of their supersession in this matter, they shared Mr. Entwistle's views on the subject of the administration of the Lord's Supper in Methodist chapels. He prepared a reply to the various circulars with which the circuit was being inundated, many of them of the most factious and wilful character. The reply was characterised by the utmost moderation and catholicity, closed with the statement "that our whole circuit has been preserved in peace," and was "signed in behalf of the Quarterly Meeting of Colne circuit, held at Padiham, July 9, 1795" (*ib.*, pp. 155-157).

Other matters besides the due equipment of their church with sacramental privileges occupied at this time the thoughts of the Methodists. Wesley was an autocrat, and at his death means had to be devised for the proper distribution of the authority which he naturally wielded alone. Suggestions were made without number; and out of the conflict of opinion gradually issued a polity that has proved at once effective and capable of adaptation to changed times. For years a vigorous war of pamphlets was waged. On the 26th of May, 1795, Mr. M. Longridge[1] sent Mr. Sagar a bundle, with a covering letter in which he wrote, "Mr. Atmore requests me to send you a few of these. Please to accept twelve Essays and Letters. The value of them lay out in some work of mercy, if you think right, as I mean to receive nothing for them. Till the Methodists agree to let each member and society act for themselves, we may not expect any plan will succeed. I have aimed at two things: 1. To promote an avowed and regular intercourse between Conference or districts and circuits; 2. That the majority of members in a society should determine all prudential things for themselves."

About eleven months later, on April 11, 1796, Mr. Sagar drafted a letter to John Pawson, the President of the Conference in 1793 and again in 1801. Whether the letter was actually sent is doubtful, as both signature and closing sentences are wanting: but the handwriting is unmistakeable, and the contents throw some light upon the condition and the state of opinion in the Colne circuit. "I make no doubt," writes Mr. Sagar, "but Mr. Entwistle will inform you that, notwithstanding the calumnious pamphlet from the North has made its appearance in these parts, nothing but concord and unanimity prevails throughout this circuit; and we have every reason to believe that there is a mutual love subsisting betwixt preachers and people, without which it is not likely the work of God should prosper. But I am sorry to find this is not the case in some of our neighbouring circuits, particularly the West Riding of Yorkshire. The principal topic of conversation last year among some of our friends was 'Nothing but the old plan.' Now

---

1. Mr. Longridge was an influential Methodist in the North of England, by trade an ironfounder, from whose employment George Stephenson refused to be tempted away.

there is another kind of hubbub, which is beginning to make a great stir in some of our societies, namely, about who is to have the management of the temporal concerns of the church, or in other words who is to be entrusted with the purse. . . If the collections for our Preachers' Fund were either totally suspended, or else the moneys arising from such collections disposed at the District meeting according to the exigencies of each, this would cut off all occasion of jealousy and surmise, particularly if a layman was elected annually to assist the president of each District in the distribution of the same, and a printed account were rendered, and the receipts and disbursements sent annually to the steward of every society through the District. I think there is far too much of the preachers' time taken up at Conference in settling the temporal concerns of the church. There is a great deal of time spent at Conference in transacting money matters, which might be equally well managed at the District." It is curious to find from what a remote period the last familiar complaint dates.

For the next few years the information as to the state of things at Colne is but scanty. A few details are however available. Habits in those days, when small beer was the customary beverage at boys' schools, and tea and coffee were luxuries of the wealthy, differed from present ones, and should not be judged by comparison. A small bill has been preserved, which was made by S. Milne against Mr. Sagar more than a century ago for "1 doz. port" supplied to one of the ministers. The price was £1 10s., to which was added 1s. 6d. for "Bots. and Tub." The wine was probably a gift from Mr. Sagar, according to a custom that flourished in many circuits in those days.

At a later date, in August, 1798, one of the ministers wrote Mr. Sagar a letter which is pathetic enough, but also of some historical value. It is a revelation of the woeful penury of which the preachers for their work's sake made the best, as well as of circuit economy and finance. The preacher in question had served in Blackburn before, and writes thus, "The difference of quarterage between Blackburn is as follows:—

| Blackburn. | | | | Colne, &c. | | | |
|---|---|---|---|---|---|---|---|
| | £ | s. | d. | | £ | s. | d. |
| 1. Quarterage | 4 | 4 | 0 | 1. Quarterage | 3 | 0 | 0 |
| 2. Toll Bars | | 10 | 6 | 2. Toll Bars | | 5 | 0 |
| 3. Washing | | 10 | 6 | 3. Washing | | 6 | 0 |
| 4. Board | 3 | 10 | 6 | 4. Board | 2 | 8 | 6 |
| | 8 | 15 | 6 | | 5 | 19 | 6 |

Difference, £2 15s. [sic], for one quarter. Exclusive of a gallon of rum they sent me here, and a gallon of wine they sent my wife: and the doctor's bill brought forward at quarter-day or any time." The memory of past joys leads him to add, "And afterwards sent to Colne in a post-chaise." His only further allowances appear to have been £6 a year, paid by the Conference towards the support of his wife, and £6 a year, divided between himself and another minister under the head of servants' wages. He had in consequence to keep himself and wife, and to dress decently, on rather less than thirteen shillings a week; and he had reason to write, "After I had got my house repaired, I made free to bring in my little bill, at which time I told my necessities to Mrs. Sagar. She therefore kindly gave me a guinea, as I could not have got bread for my family. . . In the depth of winter the Burnley people saw my threadbare coat, and kindly united without my knowledge, and purchased me a new one. . . And some other little tokens of love they and others have manifested, or I could not have subsisted without contracting debts there appeared no probability of discharging." In another sentence he states that two of his predecessors had each spent twenty-four pounds per annum besides their allowances; and there is every indication that in the early years of the Colne circuit, as of others, the Gospel was made as nearly as possible without charge.

In the autumn of 1798 Mr. Sagar received the following letter from Richard Hardacre, one of the preachers in the Huddersfield circuit. In the course of the dispute that issued in the separation of Alexander Kilham from the Conference, several chapels had been appropriated by his supporters. Nottingham and Huddersfield were amongst the greatest sufferers, and at the Conference the ministers both subscribed amongst themselves a considerable sum in relief, and ordered a public collection to be made through the Connexion. Mr. Hardacre writes, "Mr. Highfield [his colleague] having returned to town for a few hours, I took the opportunity of conversing with him respecting the best way of making the collection in Colne circuit; and at the last it was agreed upon that I should come to be at your house on Thursday, the 8th of November, and take Colne on the Sunday, or proceed according to your direction. I suppose Mr. Highfield will write to the preachers, and consequently you will agree among yourselves. Mr. Highfield sends his respects to you, and hopes you will consider the situation that we are in, and will assist us all that is in your power." Altogether a considerable but barely adequate sum was raised; and there is little doubt that the Colne circuit assisted according to its ability.

Next to William Sagar, John Wood of Padiham appears to have been the man of most influence in the circuit. A small correspondence between the two has been preserved. On

May 2nd, 1800, the latter describes the steps he was taking to circumvent any attempt on the part of a Dr. Collings to stop preaching in places not licensed. He had already sent to York and Chester to secure licenses for the Clitheroe and Bradford chapels, and had advised the people there to refer any curious enquirer to Mr. Sagar, as the likeliest man to apply to on business of that kind. A second letter, dated eleven days later, shows the two officials discussing finance. "Since our last quarterly meeting," writes John Wood, "I have had an opportunity of conversing with most of the stewards and leaders in our societies at Bradford, Clitheroe, Burnley, etc., and find many of them are in a tried state, their expenses being much larger than last year, and many of the poor members giving very little. Also at Padiham we find a wide difference, and I begin to fear that we shall not be able to manage so well as we expected. Having seriously thought upon the present state of this circuit, I am thoroughly persuaded in my own mind, that it will not be well for us to have three preachers next year. I intend to make a plan for two preachers and one horse, and will send it you. I know of no place where they want more preaching, if it will be more expense. I think our friends at Bradford and Waddington could like to have one night in the fortnight less, and have heard that Sawley friends want the preachers to go only once a month, and am inclined to believe Downham and Gasquil[1] have had them more (of late) than we can expect they will continue to wish for. Also I believe the Conference will complain of this circuit, and perhaps will neither be able nor willing to do much for us another year. I shall not say much about this excepting to a very few, till I see or hear from you."

The proposal thus to reduce the staff seems to have been under discussion at the next quarterly meeting, as was also a proposal to cut off some of the places on the other side of Pendle; but no decision was reached on either matter. Just before Conference the chairman of the district wrote that, as no resolution had been passed, he considered himself at liberty to recommend what he thought best. And from the Stationing Committee itself came an urgent communication to Mr. Sagar for information as to the number of ministers to be appointed. The ultimate result was the formation of the Skipton circuit, and the reduction of the ministers in the diminished area left from three to two.

At first the change was not entirely an advantage, and

---

1. This place is identified by Mr. T. Wilkinson with the homestead now called Gasten, which stands some half mile to the right of the road from Downham to Chatburn.

the funds continued low. One of the ministers was removed the next year from Colne to Todmorden, and John Wood was not disposed to pay the expenses. He writes to Mr. Sagar, "I told him I would pay the doctor's bill which is 6s., and his expenses to the District Meeting which is [sic] 7s. 3d., but that I would pay nothing towards his remove without your orders. I think it will be well for you to tell him either that nothing will be paid, or that he must send a bill of his expenses as Mr. Day [a previous minister] did, and that you will mention it the next quarterly meeting, and if anything is allowed, he shall have it." In a subsequent sentence John Wood suggests that Mr. Sagar's decision should be communicated directly to the minister in question; and it is possible to suspect that there was a little friction as well as an inadequate revenue in the circuit in those days. For two or three years the membership of the circuit continued to decline, until in 1806 it suddenly sprung from 566 to 700. An increase of fifty more was reported at the next Conference, which appointed again a third preacher. By 1810 the membership had risen to 800; and Burnley with the adjacent places was separated, and constituted the head of a new circuit.

## BARLEY.

It has been related that William Darney spent the latter part of his life near Barley, and there may have been a society there at that time, but no means of arriving at certainty on the matter are now known to exist. All that can be ascertained is that about the year 1803 a number of zealous young Methodists from Downham, among whom was Richard Broxup, began to hold services in the village, in the house of William Robinson. At this time the travelling preachers from Skipton visited Barley, and were entertained by William Hartley, a local preacher, who lived at Barley Green, and to whose house, built in 1796, the preaching was soon removed. When the house was too small for the congregation that assembled, the service was held on the Green.

One Sunday, when Mr. Hartley was preaching on the Green, a youth named John Foster passed by. He had been spending the fine day in the Ogden Valley, and as he returned he heard the singing, and wondered how he would be able to get past without being seen. Attempting to pass by the brookside he heard one sentence that the preacher uttered, "Be sure your sin will find you out." This led to his conversion, and he soon after joined the society. He became choir-master at Barley, and the office has remained in his family from that day to this. This John Foster also began a Sunday School at Barley. At that time Mr. Metcalfe, who kept a public-house in the village, rented two farms of Mr. Bollard of Whitehough. As one of the houses was empty, he offered it rent free to John Foster, if he would conduct a Sunday School in it. The offer was gladly accepted; reading was taught on the ground-floor, and writing in the room above. The superintendents were John Foster and Richard Brown, a farmer of Higher Black Moss.

Some time after, the school was removed to a room in Barley Green Mill, and there were soon above 200 scholars on the books. The tenant of the mill, however, failed, and the manager of the new tenant persuaded him not to allow the Methodists the use of the room they had had. Again the school had to be removed; first to a room in Narrow-gate Mill, and then to a cottage just above the present Barley Chapel. For the use of this cottage the school paid ten pounds a year.

## SOUTHFIELD.

Southfield, which at the time could hardly be regarded as a village, was, as we have seen, the place at which William Darney made his home for some years after he had retired from the active work of the ministry. There his son too, who travelled about the surrounding villages as a pedlar, lived and died. But in local Methodism the place is noted as the residence of the Sagar family. Mr. William Sagar as we have seen was converted in Edinburgh in 1751, other members of the family were led to hear and receive the word of God, and ultimately a home of more than ordinary comfort was always open to Mr. Wesley when he came into the locality. After his death, the bedstead on which he had slept was treasured for many years as a relic.

There can be no doubt that a society was formed at a very early period at Southfield; and that half of Mr. Sagar's barn was converted into a chapel, which was deemed amply sufficient for the population of the neighbourhood. In this chapel a Sunday School was commenced as early as 1797. Several members connected with the society at Southfield are worthy of mention: Miss Sagar, who had the advantage of godly training and the holy example of Christian parents, and early became a member of the Wesleyan Society, was eminent for her piety and exemplary in her life beyond many; William Whittaker, a humble, consistent Christian, most attentive to everything connected with the house of God, even to the ringing of the bell which always sounded forth its invitation in good time; Richard Kershaw, a local preacher of some originality, whose sermons abounded in quotations from Scripture and from Wesley's hymns. As a testimony of respect, the Colne circuit presented him with a large and beautiful

Bible, which he valued highly to the end of his life.

A curious story is told of Grace Hartley, who kept a small grocer's shop. She had occasion to go to Colne to buy some potatoes. Hearing that a Missionary Meeting was being held that afternoon in the chapel, she went to it, and was so moved with what she heard that she put all her money into the collection box, and had to go home without the potatoes. Next morning having arisen early to begin her weekly washing, she heard a knock at the door.. On opening it, a man enquired if Grace Hartley lived there, she replied that she was Grace Hartley. "Then," said he, "I have brought you a load of potatoes." Grace told him he must have brought them to the wrong house. "But," the man said, "my master told me to leave them at Grace Hartley's, and as that is your name I shall leave them here."

Jonas Lee more than once changed his residence, but was always regarded as a Southfield man. Jonas, though not a mason, built a chapel at Thurstone, and made the pulpit one step lower than the floor. His own house was three storeys high, and the topmost room was turned into a chapel. The pulpit was made apparently of the body of an old gig, a bookboard being fixed to the splash board, and the seat behind remaining. Jonas was a tall, large-boned man, and used to wear a long blue coat with flat brass buttons, knee breeches, brown stockings, and low shoes with very large buckles. He was acknowledged to be the best mower in the district, and went from farm to farm, cutting grass by contract. He was a local preacher, and took journeys to various parts. On one occasion, not being able to procure a horse, he rode a bull. Tradition adds that, thus mounted, he set out for Derby, but was made to dismount in Manchester, as such a mode of travelling did not accord with local ideas of propriety. He preferred to preach in the open air, his subject being previously announced. His peculiarities drew large congregations. One of his favourite subjects was "A cart wheel" (Isaiah xxviii. 27). He interpreted the nave as representing Christ; the spokes, the apostles; the felloes, the disciples in general; and the hoop, the grand uniting principle of Divine Love, which binds and holds the whole church together.

## PADIHAM.

The younger of the two preachers appointed to the Colne circuit in 1777 was Richard Condy, who was very popular; and when he preached at Padiham, the little chapel was so crowded, that the service had to be held in the open air. The society also quickly increased; and the need of a new and larger chapel was felt. This second chapel was built on what was called the Tithe-barn Croft purchased from Miles Aspden, of Brookfoot, whose grandfather of the same name purchased it in 1659 from a John Dodgson. In the course of its erection the anti-Methodist feeling in the town seems to have been considerably stirred; and a dispute also arose between the trustees and a person named J. Willion, who owned the adjoining property, with respect to the boundary lines. The following account is given by Alexander Mather, the superintendent of the Colne circuit, and also the architect of the chapel (*Lives of Early Meth. Preachers*, ii. 186-188). "Having prepared the materials for the preaching-house at Padiham, the next year, on the 1st of October, we laid the foundation. But a person pretending a claim to the ground, when the wall was about a yard high, threw a part of it down. We bore this outrage, and proceeded in the work. This emboldened him to engage three masons, who came in the night, when the roof was on, wrested out the sides of both doors with the lintels, with a yard of the wall above. They broke the sides of the two large windows, near three feet on each side; they then made a large hole in the pillar between the two windows, intending to throw down the house. But suddenly such a panic seized them, that first one and then the other stopped short and ran away. These returned no more. But their employer, with the third man, resolved to finish their work. Presently he was himself struck with a fear of being killed, and ran away, dragging his fellow with him.

"Being averse to law, we bore this also; but we set a watch on the house every night, till it was covered in and licensed, in hopes we should then be quiet. But on December the 21st he brought two men at eleven in the forenoon, with a pickaxe and a crow, and directed them to begin at one of the doors, which was not quite repaired. The workmen stood amazed: but several of the townsmen quickly came to the place, two of whom were remarkably weak men, and one of them lame besides. One laid hold of the pickaxe, and one on the crow. They that held them were stout men, the terror of the country. Many took part on each side. I was in my room, and at first thought not to stir out. But fearing mischief might be done, I sent for a constable, and myself walked to the chapel. The young man was struggling with him that held the pickaxe, to whom I spoke, and he promised to be quiet. Meantime some took the crow from the other man, which their employer observing struck a lad that helped them. He returned the blow. A battle ensued, wherein the gentleman was worsted, and rolled in the dirt.

"Finding there was no other way, I procured a warrant from Serjeant Aspinwall, for the chief rioters. This was served immediately. The next morning we waited upon him, at his house, and he bound them all over to the assizes. But I, recollecting that Mr. W——n had said before the serjeant, he was willing to refer the whole affair to him, I sent him word, I was willing too ; and desired him to name the time and place. But he would do neither. After preaching at Millend in the evening, I went to bed ; but my sleep departed from me. However, I rose as usual ; but before I went out of my room, I heard a knocking at the door. It was one from Padiham, who mournfully cried out, 'O sir, we are all ruined ! Mr. W——n has got a warrant for seven-and-twenty of us, and you are the first in it. We must all be at the serjeant's by noon.' I told him, I would be there. As soon as I came, I saw Mr. W——n just going into the yard. I followed him close, to the great joy of my friends. We were near forty in number. The serjeant coming to the door, I asked why I was summoned. He answered, ' For a riot.' I said, ' Sir, you cannot but know that Mr. W. has done this out of mere litigiousness. But why should we trouble the whole country with our affairs ? Cannot we settle it between ourselves ? ' To this Mr. W. agreed. So, as we had no bonds of arbitration ready, we both signed a memorandum to the same effect. The poor people then went home in peace. After some difficulties the bonds were signed ; and after hearing all parties, the serjeant's sentence was, (1) That the ground (part of which we had purchased) should be equally divided between us and Mr. W. ; and, (2) That he should pay us five pounds for the damage which he had done. Thus we were at length delivered out of our trouble, and peace re-established at Padiham."

The first sermon in the chapel was preached by Wesley on the 13th of April, 1779. He writes in his Journal, I preached "at one in the shell of the new House at Padiham." This was before the roof had been put on, so that a considerable time elapsed before the chapel was opened for regular worship. There is a stone now to be seen on the wall of the chapel, placed there at the request of Mr. Mather, which bears the following inscription, " They have thrust sore at me that I might fall, but the Lord hath taken my part with them that helped me." In this chapel there was a gallery on three sides of the building, with sitting accommodation for 246 people ; whilst the floor, provided with forms without backs, seated 334, thus giving a total sitting capacity for 580. The cost of the building was £419 12s., towards which the Conference made a grant of £20. In 1798 two cottages were built on the site of the old chapel, as shown in the illustration, at a cost of £171.

Wesley's visit to Padiham at the opening of the Hall Hill chapel was his fifth. His sixth was made on Tuesday, the 18th of April, 1786, when he simply says, " I preached at

COTTAGES ON THE SITE OF THE FIRST CHAPEL.

Padiham, Burnley, Southfield, and Colne." The last visit occurred on Tuesday, April 22nd, 1788, and concerning it the entry is, "I preached at eleven to as quiet a congregation, though not so lively, as at Bolton."

THE CHAPEL OF 1779.

The Sunday School was commenced with thirty scholars in the body of the chapel in 1792 by John Hudson and James Whalley. In 1800 additional premises were taken in Helm's Ground, amongst the leading spirits being John Stott, William Horne, Charles Tunnycliffe, and George Ainsworth. When these premises were needed for business purposes, an upper room in a house on Hall Hill was substituted for them. But these were only makeshifts, and increased accommodation being urgently required, a site was purchased in Club Street in 1805, and a two-storied building erected at a cost of £300 8s. 8½d. The principal subscribers were John Wood, William Taylor, John Tickle, John Dewhurst, John Lord, John Hudson, Richard Smith, and Henry Thompson, each of whom contributed five guineas, while the sum of £200 was borrowed at five per cent. from James Walmsley. The first anniversary sermons were preached by the celebrated Samuel Bradburn, when the collections amounted to £25 9s. 11d., and, still greater cause for gratitude, many persons were converted to God. There were 57 scholars when these schools were opened. In nine years the number had increased to 148. This school has been turned into cottages, which are now the third and fourth houses from the top of St. Giles' Street on the right hand, going up the street.

## BARROWFORD.

It is impossible to say when Methodism was commenced in Barrowford. All that can be ascertained is that there was a society there in 1779, which was connected with the society at Colne. The leader was James Ridehalgh.

There is a tradition that Wesley sometimes preached at Clough, near Barrowford. It is said that he stood at the bottom of the fold, with his back against a tree; that his hearers sat or stood on the steep brow facing him; and that immediately after the service, having carefully examined his horse, and satisfied himself that the saddle was secure, he mounted, and rode off to some other place. That Wesley did preach at Clough, we know from his Journal. Under the date, April 22nd, 1774, he writes, "I rode and walked to Bradshaw House, standing alone in a dreary waste. But although it was a cold and stormy day, the people flocked from all quarters. So they did at noon the next day, to Clough (two or three miles from Colne), where, though it was cold enough, I was obliged to preach abroad."

Wesley's next and last recorded visit to Clough was on April 29th, 1776. He writes: "I preached at Padiham. ... I saw none inattentive at Clough in the evening. What has God wrought, since Mr. Grimshaw and I were seized near this place by a furious mob, and kept prisoners for some hours! The sons of him who headed that mob now gladly receive our saying."

It cannot be ascertained whether there was any regular preaching or indeed any preaching at all at Barrowford during the time it was part of the 'Haworth Round.' At the Conference succeeding Wesley's last recorded visit, this large Round was divided, and Barrowford was included in the area that was to be worked from Colne, but it was some time before it found a place on the circuit plan.

At the beginning of the nineteenth century Barrowford contained about 130 houses, 30 standing above the present Wesleyan Chapel, and 100 below it. There is reason to believe that Methodist preaching services were held in the houses of Mrs. Dolly Isherwood, grocer, of Higherford, and of Mr. James Ridehalgh, farmer, of Park Hill, and that a prayer meeting was held at the Old Row, Lowerford, for some time before Barrowford was put on the plan. Tradition gives the names of two other leaders in these early days, John Tattersall, and John Wilkinson. In the last year of the eighteenth century the friends set to work in earnest to build a small chapel. Mr. James Walton gave the land, Mr. Abraham Hargreaves, of Heirs House, £100, and many others helped according to their ability; and the sanctuary was opened on Whit-Monday, 1801, by the Rev. C. Atmore, who had previously travelled in the circuit. The trustees were Christr. Lister, Rd. Sagar, Thomas Wilkinson, J. Tattersall, Wm. Preston, Abm. Beanland, John Kaye, Geo. Battison, Jas. Ayrton, Nathan Pickles, Henry Myers, John Watson. The trustees thought it desirable to have a bell on the chapel, large enough to be heard through the village, and for more than half-a-century this bell was rung twice for public service, once half-an-hour before, and again at the appointed time. It was ultimately sold to Mr. Wm. Tunstill, and is still in his possession.

This little chapel was at the time the only place of worship in the neighbourhood. Through the instrumentality of the Rev. A. Haigh, a considerable number of people from Blacko and the surrounding district began to attend it regularly. Two or three society classes were formed there, and Blacko-Hill became one of the regular preaching-places of the Colne circuit. In the Circuit Book, Blacko stands third, though it never had that position on the plan. This Blacko society was finally merged into the one at Barrowford.

Among the members at Barrowford at this time should be mentioned Hagar Towler, who, having a large heart and a fairly large house, was ever ready to find a home for the Methodists. Several of her sons, and a daughter became members. William was a leader at Roughlee, Blacko, and Barrowford, till increasing deafness compelled him to resign. Thomas, another son, was a local preacher for many years.

For some time there were four constables connected with the chapel. In their official capacity they regularly attended the morning service, occupying a pew near the door. During the singing of the second hymn they went out, and scoured the village, and if they met any one loitering about, they compelled him at once either to go to chapel or to go home. Each constable was furnished with a staff bearing his initials. The staff was six feet long, and painted black, with a large knob at one end. On this knob was a crown, and the letters G.R. (i.e. Georgius Rex). These staves were for some time in the custody of Mrs. England. They afterwards passed into the care of the late James Clegg, who preserved them until his death.

## HIGHAM.

By whom, and at what time, Methodism was introduced into this village is not certainly known. There is no reason to suppose that Wesley ever preached in the village, though he probably often passed through it on his way from Padiham to Roughlee and Colne. Probability points to the fact that it was introduced by William Darney, or by some members of the society at Padiham, which had been formed by him. The time of its introduction can be, at least, approximately fixed. Darney appeared in the district in 1744; in 1749, a contribution was sent from Higham to the quarterly meeting of the Haworth Round; and in 1751, Darney in his poem refers to there being Methodists in Higham:—

"And in Higham there's a few."

The fewness of the members may be inferred further from the fact that the contribution just referred to, taken by Thomas Lowcock on the 18th of April, 1749, amounted to three shillings. During the quarter three shillings and ninepence more had been raised and spent, probably for stabling the preacher's horse.

For some five years no quarterly meetings were held, and there are no means of ascertaining the society's condition. The members were still but few in number, when Grimshaw wrote out the list of members in the 'Round' in November, 1763. There were then only five residing at Higham,—Jane Croskey, Ellen Dewhirst, Thomas Lowcock, Betty Laycock, Mary Marross. While it is noted that they lived at "Hickham," they are significantly included among the members at Padiham. To Padiham they doubtless went to meet in class, having at that time no leader of their own.

When the Haworth Round was divided in 1776, Higham was included in the area visited by the preachers of the Colne circuit, but it does not appear on the plan of that circuit for 1786; and what Methodists there were, probably continued to attend preaching and to meet in class at Padiham.

From March, 1794, there are a few materials for a history of the society in an Autobiography of Mr. Henry Houghton Wilkinson, who was born April 10th, 1771, and died January 12th, 1848. Mr. Wilkinson was appointed a leader in 1820, and continued to meet his class for twenty-six years. He attended the prayer meeting that was held at Padiham at six o'clock on the morning of Christmas day for fifty-four years, for the same length of time he entertained the travelling preachers at his home, and during his connection with the Higham society he officiated at more than a thousand funerals. He seems to have completed the record of his life on the 18th of May, 1847, only a few months before his death. "In old time," says he, "God blessed the house of Obed-edom for the ark's sake, and God hath condescended to bless both me and my family."

From Mr. Wilkinson's book we can see something of the struggles of the early Methodists, and note the progress of the work. There was a society of six members in 1794, but no regular preaching. Mr. Wilkinson and a friend, named John Robinson, used to go to the Methodist services at Padiham or Colne on Sundays, and ultimately induced some of the local preachers to visit Higham. Mr. Wilkinson records a somewhat singular fact, that none of the members of the little society could sing: so he and his wife learned a few tunes, and taught them, and soon afterwards some of the young people, who had begun to meet in class, also met to learn to sing. These Higham Methodists were full of zeal, a zeal that took them on Sundays to conduct prayer meetings at Barley, Rimington, Chatburn and Clitheroe, thus making a circuit of Pendle Hill. The classes soon increased, the leaders being John Crawshaw and John Robinson. The travelling preachers, who had called once a quarter to renew the tickets on their way to Padiham, promised, if a bed could be found them, to stop and preach on the Tuesday night at Higham. Mr. Wilkinson at once provided a bed, and service for the next seventeen years was held in his house.

## BURNLEY.

Very little is known of Methodism in Burnley, while it formed part of the Haworth Round. As early as 1749 Goodshaw is mentioned in the Circuit Book as in conjunction with Padiham "making a charge" of 6s. 4d. Ten years later

Dunnockshaw appears in the same book as paying in 4s. on January 12th, through Dion. Haworth, a local preacher and probably also a leader; the next quarter the payment was sixpence less. In 1763 the names of seventeen members are recorded. Bentley Wood Green is also entered for the first time in 1759, when Jonathan Wood paid in 17s. on January 18th; and four years later a list of sixteen members is given. In none of these places is Methodism now in any way represented. No doubt Burnley itself was occasionally visited by the preachers of the Round, but what preachers actually did visit it cannot be ascertained, beyond the fact that Grimshaw possibly more than once preached in the parish church. Mr. John Stott in his "Methodism in Haslingden" (p. 16) says that the Methodist evangelists, called by some "New Lights" and by others "Damnation Preachers," were then (1775) attracting considerable interest and attention, and that a man named Ralph Rishton, accompanied by a friend, walked over from Haslingden to hear one of them preach in the open air at Burnley Wood. Whether this preacher was one of the two itinerants then on the round, or one of the local preachers, is not known. Except Mr. Grimshaw, the first Methodist preacher who is certainly known to have preached in Burnley is John Wesley himself in 1784. We have seen that he frequently passed round the town, at some short distance, but it was not until he was an old man that he entered it. There is a tradition that he once preached at the Cross Roads, near the Bull and Butcher Inn. If he ever preached there, it would probably be when he was passing from Bacup on his way to Padiham. There is also a tradition of a visit to Burnley, the details of which were given by the son of a man who took a very prominent part on the occasion, John Riding, who lived on what was then called Burnley Green, but is now Cannon Street. In front of this house was a riding stone. Wesley, finding an open space of sufficient dimensions for his purpose, and a pulpit so conveniently at hand, at once mounted the stone, and after the usual preliminaries began to preach to a large crowd of people. His text is said to have been "The eye that mocketh at his father, and despiseth to obey his mother, the ravens of the valley shall pick it out, and the young eagles shall eat it" (Prov. xxx. 17). Either the text or the sermon was too much for the audience, and a shower of clods of earth, and whatever other missiles were within reach, soon began to fall upon the preacher. At last Wesley was obliged to desist from his efforts to appease the crowd, and taking refuge in retreat, he managed quietly to get out of the sight of the mob in Bridge Street. John Riding led him round to the back door of his own house, and hid him in the meal chest until counsel was taken of the authorities of the town. Their wish was only to get rid of Wesley as soon as possible; and when the uproar had ceased, the old man was smuggled to the Old Bull Hotel, where he had put up his carriage, and despatched from the town without delay.

No date is assigned to this supposed visit, and its incidents cannot be identified with any of those to which reference is made in the Journal. It will at once strike most readers that the text from which Wesley is said to have preached is not like one of his texts, and his taking refuge in retreat is altogether unlike his conduct in the presence of a mob. In addition to this there is his entry on the occasion of his last visit, in which he uses the expression, "both times before when I preached at Burnley," so that on his own statement he preached three times in Burnley. It cannot, of course, be expected that he should record all the occasions on which he preached, but these three are all recorded in his Journal; and the incidents above related cannot have taken place on any of them, for Wesley remarks that he had "acceptable seasons" whenever he preached at Burnley. If the visit took place at all, it must have been after his last recorded visit in 1788. This is not altogether impossible, as he was in the neighbourhood of Blackburn two years later: but as Methodism had then obtained a good footing in the town, we are compelled to regard the story as improbable. It is a tradition for which no foundation can be found. Some Methodist preacher may have attempted to preach from that text, and have been hidden from the fury of the people in a meal chest, but it is almost certain that it was not John Wesley.

His first recorded visit was on Tuesday, July 13th, 1784. Wesley writes, "I went to Burnley, a place which had been tried for many years, but without effect. It seems the time was now come. High and low, rich and poor, now flocked together from all quarters; and all were eager to hear, except one man who was the town-crier. He began to bawl amain, till his wife ran to him, and literally stopped his noise: she seized him with one hand, and clapped the other upon his mouth, so that he could not get out one word. God then began a work which, I am persuaded, will not soon come to an end."

Several considerations lead to the conclusion that the statement, that Burnley had been tried for many years but without effect, must not be taken too literally. There is reason to believe that a society was formed at Burnley as early as 1763. In those remote days, the 'assistant' had to leave a complete list of the members in his circuit, arranged according to their 'classes,' for the use of his successor. A few of these books have been preserved. One of them is at Haworth, and from this has been copied the following list of members at Burnley, in the year in which Grimshaw died:—James Varley, Alice Varley, Lawrence Roberts, Margaret and Mary Fort, Roger Foulds, Richard Taylor, Isabella Taylor, Mary Blakey, Jon. Heap, Ann Heap. It is probable, however, that this society soon melted away. We have seen how the one at Roughlee decreased. In 1748 it had six leaders, and in one quarter contributed £1 4s. 7d.; whilst in 1758 the contribution was only 3s., and in 1763 the number of members was only twelve! The society at Brimicroft, a small hamlet near Hoghton, numbered thirty-six members in 1774; soon after there was no society at all. A class was commenced again in 1787 by William Livsey; it was attended by Martha Thompson, the first Methodist in Preston, who walked twelve miles every Sunday for the purpose; but this class also soon ceased to exist. Mr. Wesley's remark in his Journal seems to point to something of the same kind at Burnley: the small society had for some time practically ceased to exist, and another was formed, possibly in connection with his own visit.

This view of the case receives some confirmation from the statement of Thomas Dixon, who was at that time one of the preachers in the Colne circuit. Thomas Dixon, like a wise man, kept a diary, but again like a wise man, did not publish it. It has, however, been preserved in manuscript, and there is the following entry relating to Burnley at this period,—"The work of God at Burnley was very young, but" he adds, "many during this year (1784) were converted. The great men of the place were angry, and agreed to banish the Methodist preachers from the town. The proprietor of the preaching-house sent us notice to quit the premises, and the rest of the gentlemen pledged themselves not to let us have another; but about a month before the expiration of the notice, the Lord converted a man who had a house of his own which he gave to the preachers, and now we had a better preaching-house than before. Soon after, a chapel was erected." Unfortunately it is not stated in what locality the original preaching-house was situated, and, beyond a tradition that it was in the neighbourhood of Lane Bridge, all memory of it and of the proprietor appears to be lost. The man who was converted shortly before the expiration of the notice to quit was Peter Hargreaves, a joiner by trade; and it was his workshop, in what is now called Muschamp Yard, that was used by the Methodists from the close of 1784 to the time of the erection of Keighley Green chapel.

A second visit was paid by Wesley on Tuesday, April 18th, 1786. On the previous day he had preached at Blackburn to a large crowd of people, who had been attracted to the fair. His work on the Tuesday is thus briefly summarised, "I preached at Padiham, Burnley, Southfield, and Colne." On this occasion Mr. Wesley chose the front of the Thorn Inn, as the most convenient place at which to preach. There was at that date, and very many years later, a thorn tree growing before the Inn. Round the tree was a railing of some rude kind, and hard by it was the riding stone, which Wesley adopted as his rostrum. When he was in the midst of his sermon there came by a young couple, who had been married that morning at the parish church. Something about the appearance of the white-haired preacher, who was then 83 years of age, or else some remark of his that they overheard, attracted their attention, and the mutual engrossment of their novel experience of that day proved less strong than the influences that drew both of them to Wesley. Conviction awoke within them, and they stopped to listen. When the sermon was over, and the couple reached their new home, the fiddler who had been engaged for the customary festivities of the afternoon was dismissed, and the day became memorable in their lives as that of their consecration to God and first connection with Methodism, as well as that of their marriage. A long career was granted to each of them, for they lived to see their children and their children's children in high repute, alike amongst their fellow townsmen and in the church of their choice; and it was not until June 8th, 1838, that Mr. William Hopwood, who had listened on his wedding day when Wesley preached in front of the Thorn Inn, and had yielded himself to God, died, full of honour and of years.

Mr. Wesley's third visit was when he was 85 years of age, but in the habit of travelling almost as rapidly as ever. Leaving Bristol in March, he preached daily as he journeyed northwards to Liverpool, and thence through Bolton, Bradford, etc., to Scotland. Under the date of Thursday, April 24th, 1788, he writes: "About ten we began the service in the church at Todmorden, crowded sufficiently. I found uncommon liberty among these poor mountaineers. We had a pleasant road from hence to Burnley, where a multitude of people were waiting; but we had no house that could contain them. Just then the rain ceased: so we went into the inn-yard, which contained them well; and it was an acceptable season, as indeed it was both the times before when I preached at Burnley." The inn-yard was probably that of the Thorn, or it may be that of the Bull, at which Wesley seems to have generally put up his carriage. According to the testimony of the wife of Mr. Abel Bridge, of Lane Bridge, who was one of Wesley's audience either on this occasion, or on the previous one in 1786, the sermon lasted only about twenty minutes, and at its close the large concourse of people quietly dispersed.

There is some reason for believing that Wesley visited Burnley once more. In the Society Stewards' Book is the following entry:—"7 Sep., to Jno. Wood for expenses wen Mr. Wesley was at Burn. 8s. 0d." This seems to refer to the year 1791; and if so, the amount was paid six months after Wesley had been laid in his grave. We can hardly suppose that Mr. Wood had delayed bringing in his account for above three years, or that the stewards had forgotten to enter it for so long a time: so that it can hardly refer to the visit of April, 1788. Moreover when Wesley came to Burnley in 1788, he came from Todmorden; and Jno. Wood, who was evidently with him on the later visit, lived at Padiham; and therefore through Padiham almost certainly Wesley came on the occasion to which this entry[1] refers. According to Wesley's plan[2] he was to be at Blackburn on Monday, April 12th, 1790; on Tuesday at Colne; on Saturday at Keighley; on Sunday at Haworth. On the 15th he was the guest of Miss Emmett of Walton (from whose house he wrote a letter to Ann Cutler), and preached at Preston. As he went out of his way to visit Preston, it is possible to suppose that he managed on his journey from Rochdale to Padiham, or on that from Blackburn to Colne, to come also to Burnley, to see, and preach in, the New House, of which the site had been purchased, and the building probably commenced when he was there nearly two years before.

At Burnley, we are told, the rich people did what they could to hinder the work, and drive the Methodists from the place; but they preached in the most public parts of the town, and "a large and commodious chapel was speedily built." The writer (C. Atmore, as quoted in *Wes. Meth. Mag.*, 1845, p. 17) is speaking of the revivals, with which Lancashire was favoured in the years 1783-84; and the hopeful spirit in which Wesley wrote of Burnley in 1784 will be borne in mind. Samuel Bardsley, writing[3] on the 27th of October, 1787, to Mr. W. Sagar, of

---

1. The steward did not always enter the amounts he paid at the time he paid them. For instance, after November 14th, 1814, he enters the contribution paid to the quarterly meeting in September, 1813, and the Rev. L. Hargreave's funeral expenses are entered after September, 1814, though he died in 1812: so that there is nothing unusual in the entering of a payment that had been made some time before.

2. See note on pages 32, 33.

3. This letter is still preserved by Mr. Sagar's descendants. The date as it stands is "1897"; but its contents afford conclusive evidence that it was written in 1787, shortly after Mr. Bardsley moved from Colne to Plymouth. It is a letter of kind messages to Mr. Sagar and his family, to John Wood, to "Brother Hall, and Brother Edwards, and all the leaders."

# FIRST CHAPEL IN BURNLEY.

KEIGHLEY GREEN CHAPEL OF 1788, NOW THE COURT-HOUSE.

Southfield, says, "I hope you are preparing to build at Burnley." Steps, no doubt, were at that time being taken to secure a site, for the deed conveying the land was signed on the 16th of July, 1788. When Wesley visited Burnley in April of that year, he does not refer to any chapel being in course of erection, though probably the work had been commenced during the summer. At a Trustees' meeting held December 23rd, 1788, the Rev. Charles Atmore in the chair, Richard Birtwistle and Jeremiah Spencer were appointed "joint stewards for the galleries and pews" for the following year. There were 44 pews in the chapel, containing 271 sittings; and the quarterly rent of a sitting ranged from 4d. to 1s., which seems to have been the maximum charge. The income of the trust for 1789 (omitting all collections, for there is no record of any) was as follows :—

|  | £ | s. | d. |
|---|---|---|---|
| First quarter's pew rents | 6 | 6 | 2½ |
| Second   ,,  ,,  ,, | 6 | 6 | 5 |
| Third   ,,  ,,  ,, | 5 | 14 | 2 |
| Fourth   ,,  ,,  ,, | 5 | 12 | 6 |
|  | £23 | 19 | 3½ |

The singers' pew was No. 41, and contained 20 sittings, but only half of them were occupied, for the last entry on the page is "William Pollard for singers, 5s." Up to the year 1810, this chapel at Keighley Green was the only place of worship in the town, set apart solely for worship, that was open twice every Sunday. There were one or two rooms in various houses occupied by little congregations belonging to as many non-conformist denominations, of which as much might be said. But Keighley Green and St. Peter's were the only places solely set apart for public worship, and the practice at that time was for St. Peter's to be opened only once on the Lord's Day.

A short extract from the Journal of the Rev. Joseph Entwisle may fitly close our present notice of Keighley Green chapel. On August 24th, 1794, he writes, "Set out early this morning from Colne to Burnley. Preached three times at Burnley with considerable freedom and warmth; and I hope with profit to the people. It is a populous little market town. The chapel is large and elegant; but few of the town's people will attend preaching. My congregations, being a stranger, were nearly double the usual number. But still the chapel was not one-third filled." It is interesting to note that the "populous little market town" six years later contained only 2,224 inhabitants.

Charles Atmore, after an absence of two years, was appointed superintendent of the circuit in 1788. On the 22nd of December in that year he wrote in a small quarto, bound in rough calf, "An Account Book for the Stewards of the Methodist Society in Burnley"; and on the following day on the next page, "I appoint Thos. Driver and Christopher Hartley joint Stewards of the Society in Burnley." To each of these entries he appended his peculiar signature, a fac-simile of which may be seen in "Wesley and his Successors."

There is no further reference to the appointment or re-appointment of stewards for twenty-seven years; and during this period, with the exception of the first page, which looks uncommonly like the work of Atmore himself, and a few entries which the recipients of various amounts themselves made in the book, the writing is all by one hand till 1815. The writing is uniform, but the orthography is peculiar, and not uniform.

From this book we gather that the society at Mereclough, which was then in existence, and the societies at Pendle, New Laund, Worsthorne, and "Abergham Eaves," as they came into existence, paid their contributions to the stewards at Burnley. The first entries are simply "Received from the classes"; and the earliest recorded list of leaders in Burnley is for the year 1790:—Jeremiah Spencer, Robt. Riding, Joseph Marshall, Richard Birtwistle, Thomas Driver.

The accounts for the year 1789 are as follows:—

|  | £ | s. | d. |  | £ | s. | d. |
|---|---|---|---|---|---|---|---|
| Received from the classes | 3 | 5 | 0 | Preachers' board and horse | 1 | 8 | 9 |
| ,, ,, | 3 | 9 | 9 | ,, ,, |  | 15 | 11 |
| ,, ,, | 3 | 12 | 8 | ,, ,, | 1 | 5 | 3 |
| ,, ,, | 3 | 5 | 6 | ,, ,, | 1 | 13 | 0 |
| Extra Collection | 1 | 11 | 6 | Quarterly Meeting | 7 | 17 | 6 |
|  |  |  |  | Candles |  | 12 | 9 |
|  | 15 | 4 | 5 | ,, |  | 15 | 9 |
|  |  |  |  | Books |  | 15 | 0 |
|  |  |  |  |  | 15 | 3 | 10 |

The quarterly contribution to the circuit funds was at that time £1 11s. 6d.; but in July, £3 3s. was paid, the usual contribution being increased by the amount of the extra collection which was probably made in the classes. When collections are recorded in the book during the earlier years, they were not called 'quarterly', for they were not made four times a year, but "publick" collections. The average amount of the first four separately entered was 14s. 7d.: not till the chapel had been in use eight years did the public collection exceed one pound.

It may be interesting to know the amounts contributed by the country societies in the early years of Methodism, while Burnley and the places in its vicinity were in the Colne circuit. As far as they are separately recorded in the Burnley Society-Stewards' book, (frequently they would be included in the comprehensive entry, "received from the classes,") they are as follows:—

MERECLOUGH (First leader, James Owsen [sic]) 1792: Jan. 1, 2s. 6d.; Dec. 25, 2s. 6d. 1806: Jan. 9, 17s. 3d.; Mar. 28, £1 2s. 6d.; June 27, £1 0s. 9d.; Sep. 20, £1 1s. 3d. 1807: Jan. 24, £1 3s. 3d.; April 4, £1 3s. 6d.; Sep. 19, £1 0s. 0d.; Dec. 26, 15s. 0d. 1808: Mar. 19, 16s. 6d.; June, 16s. 6d.; Sep. 17, 18s. 6d. 1809: Jan. 7, £1 3s. 0d.; April 1, 14s. 0d.; [June] 15, 13s. 6d.; Sep. 30, 11s. 6d.; Dec. 23, 17s. 0d. 1810: Mar. 17, 17s. 6d.; June 22, 17s. 6d.

WORSTORN (First leader, probably Abel Bridge). 1807: Sep. 19, 3s. 6d. 1809: April 15, 10s. 0d.; July 29, 8s. 6d. 1810: Jan. 6, 9s. 0d.; Mar. 17, 9s. 6d.; July 20, 10s. 0d.

NEW LAUND ("New Lon"). 1807: Sep. 19, 9s. 0d. 1808: Mar. 19, 8s. 6d; June, 8s. 6d.; Sep. 17, 8s. 6d. 1809: Jan. 7, 9s. 0d.; April 1, 9s. 0d.; [June] 15, 11s. 6d.; Sep. 30, 12s. 0d.; Dec. 23, 11s. 6d. 1810: Mar. 17, 10s. 6d.; June 22, 10s. 0d.

PENDLE or PENDLE-BOTTOM. 1796: June 16, 4s. 0d. 1798: June 28, 2s. 5d. 1801: Mar. 16, 2s. 6d. 1802: June 21, 8s. 0d. 1804: Dec. 8s. 0d. 1806: April 5, 9s. 0d.; June 27, 9s. 0d.; Sep. 20, 9s. 0d.; Dec. 27, 9s. 6d. 1807: May 2, 9s. 0d.

Many of these entries clearly refer to "ticket money," which was then paid at the time the tickets were renewed, and would be taken by the preacher to the society stewards. Habergham-Eaves, so far as we have observed, is only specially mentioned once, its contribution being 4s.

There is a separate account of the sums paid in by the leaders at their fortnightly meeting. To this regular leaders' meeting great importance was then attached, as may be seen from an entry which has been copied *literatim* from the stewards' book preserved at Colne. "June 29, 1785. Agreed upon between the preachers, stewards and leaders of Colne Society, that each leader for neglecting meeting the preachers once in a fortnight, except John Boint, John Bracewell, and Michael Pickles, who is to meet once a month, forfeit sixpence for each offence, without showing a sufficient cause for staying away, and the case to be determined by a majority present." This was signed by C. Atmore, John Easton, Thos. Dixon, Thomas Wilkinson, Thos. Whitaker, John Bracewell, Towneley Harrison X his mark, John Barritt, James Foulds, Richard Shaw. The first three are the preachers, John Barritt became an itinerant the following year.

The society stewards paid for the preachers' board, and for the care of his horse when he came to Burnley; most of the bills for these purposes are in the name of Robt. Riding. The preachers at first received the actual sums they had spent (1s. 10d. : 2s. 4d. : &c.); afterwards they each received a fixed amount for board, when once a fortnight they came to Burnley, which amount was gradually increased as the income of the society increased.

Twice at least during this period a special contribution was made to the Quarterly Meeting : "toward debt that was on the serchet [sic] £2 9s. 3d.," and again "to pay of the old debt on the Serkit [sic] £5 10s." A guinea was paid towards the removal expenses of Mr. Booth, nine shillings for a box for books for Mr. Entwisle, and half-a-guinea toward the purchase of a horse for the circuit.

The quarterly meeting of the circuit seems to have been held twice at Burnley in this period, and the cost of the dinner is duly recorded : April 11th, 1802, £1 13s. 7d. ; April 18th, 1806, £1 0s. 5d.

Sometime during this period one of the three preachers appears to have come to reside at Burnley. The Colne books have mostly disappeared, so that the date cannot be fixed. But there is some indication of a preacher's house in 1805, when 18s. 6d. was paid for window-tax; and the entries of the following year put its existence beyond a doubt, for the stewards paid poor rate ("poor ley") and house-tax. Zechariah Taft, moreover, was the second minister in the circuit for two years from the Conference of 1805, and Mrs. Taft appears as a leader in the Burnley society on October 19th of that year. In the autumn of 1806 and the earlier part of 1807, she had three classes under her charge, after which her name disappears from the list. And the conclusion is probable, that Burnley first had a resident minister in 1805. Mrs. Taft herself writes, in her autobiographical Memoirs (pt. ii. p. 140), under the date of August of that year, "We arrived in safety at Burnley, in the Colne circuit, to which we were appointed, and to which my husband had been invited. I felt greatly favoured in being stationed among my old friends and in my native county ; and though the glory was in part departed, especially at Burnley, where I had witnessed a mighty outpouring of the Spirit of God and a wonderful ingathering of souls, nevertheless we found many, and thank God some of my children in the Lord, truly alive to their best interest and to the prosperity of God's cause." She lost no time in getting to work : for the entry under September 1st is, "I spoke at Burnley, to a vast crowd of people : I felt great freedom. This week I began a new class with my mother, who is come to reside with us, myself, and two more. May the Lord send prosperity !"

The society stewards also took upon themselves charges which are now borne by the trustees. The chapel was cleaned at their cost, though at first that involved no large drain on their resources. The first who was employed in this work was James Lun, the next John Ashworth, and the third "Saley Balmford." Each of the first two was paid at the rate of fourpence per week; but during "Saley's" term of office the amount was raised to a shilling a week. In addition to the cleaning the society stewards paid for the lighting. For this purpose candles were used, which were then 8½d. per lb.; and they were candles that needed snuffing, for three pairs of snuffers had to be bought at a cost of nine-pence. Once and once only, do we read of mould candles; two dozen were bought for seventeen shillings. Once and once only, do we read of "oyl"; if mould candles and 'oyl' were ever used again, their cost is included in the &c., which frequently follows the entry of the cost of candles.

The stewards also paid for various requisites and repairs usually charged upon the trustees. Thus we read of bookbinding, printing, mending of windows and slates; also of the purchase of shovels, brushes, sash-cord, Bible, candlestick and "adision of window," which last item cost half-a-crown! In September, 1794, they paid to John Wood, "for intrist," £7; and this must have been for money borrowed by the trustees. The money, or at least part of it, was a loan from Mr. Sagar, and the payment of interest was very irregular. On September 9th, 1793, John Wood wrote to Mr. Sagar, "I was at Burnley on Monday, and the stewards for the chapel promised to send you what money they could get by Jno. Ashall to-night. When I come to Colne, I intend to stay till Monday morning, and settle the whole, if anything is left unpaid." But the money was not forthcoming; and on September 23rd John Wood wrote again, "Next Monday week the seats in Burnley chapel will be let for the Michaelmas quarter. Then I hope we shall be able to pay up the interest for your money. I have often been ashamed to think it should be unpaid so long, but could not help it. I trust another time we shall be able to pay sooner." The following year the society stewards came to the help of the trustees. And four years later they paid William Hindle for deeds, &c., £1 12s. 8d., the reference being probably to the conveyance of the house adjoining the Keighley Green Chapel.

On July 20, 1797, occurs the entry, "rent for a house taken, 9s. 9d."; and again in the following year, 6s. So far there is nothing to show where the house was situated, or for what purpose it was taken. The succeeding entries give the desired information:—"Aug. 12, 1799, rent for a house at Worstorn, 18s. . . . Aug. 4, 1800, to William Halstead for rent of house to preach in at Worstorn, £1 1s. . . . Aug. 28, 1801, received from Southfield toward Worstorn rent, 15s. . . . To William Halstead, for rent at Worstorne, £1 18s." There is no further reference to this house in the stewards' book, and it was probably given up and the preaching discontinued. There seems to have been no society at Worstorn for the next six years.

The amounts contributed at this time by Burnley to the Yearly Collection, then apparently the only Connexional Fund, cannot now be clearly ascertained. The only contribution of which any record remains is that for the year 1806, the amount being, for nine classes, £6 8s. 3d.

The Conference of 1800 was constrained to appeal to the people in a formal address for relief. It had been burdened with increasing debts ever since the death of Wesley. The multiplication of the preachers and their families, and the deficits in their support by the circuits, had rendered it necessary for them to draw largely on the Book Room at London, and on the Preachers' Fund, for the relief of effective but harassed men; a debt of more than a thousand pounds was thus imposed upon their publishing house. Their appeal to the societies proposed an average addition to the yearly collection of a shilling from each member. It was so far responded to that at the Conference of 1802, every debt was swept away, and the Connexion was enabled to pursue its course unembarrassed.[1] The Burnley society responded in part to this appeal, and contributed sixpence per member "towards Debt on Conference." The names of the leaders are duly entered, but only in some cases is the number of members given, the total number being 197.

|  |  |  |  |  |  |  |  |
|---|---|---|---|---|---|---|---|
| Received of | James Smith | - | - | - | - | 17 | 6 |
| ,, | Benj. Fielding | 27 | members |  |  | 14 | 0 |
| ,, | Richard Birtwistle | 19 | ,, |  |  | 9 | 6 |
| ,, | Edwd. Pollard | 23 | ,, |  |  | 11 | 6 |
| ,, | Thos. Kay | 24 | ,, |  |  | 12 | 0 |
| ,, | Wm. Hopwood | 14 | ,, |  |  | 7 | 0 |
| ,, | James Brown | - | - | - | - | 12 | 0 |
| 26 Ap. | R. Birtwistle | - | - | - | - | 1 | 0 |
| 1 May | rec. | - | - | - | - | 14 | 0 |
|  |  |  |  |  | £4 | 18 | 6 |

It would be unfair to the memory of a godly woman, who in humble circumstances did her best to serve God, and advance His kingdom in the world, to omit from the account of this period, the name of Miss Catherine or "Kitty" Scott, as she was generally called. She lived in a house facing the

---

1. Stevens, *History of Methodism*, ii. 96.

Calder, at the back of the old mill, in St. James' Street, and maintained herself by keeping a dame's school, at which a few not uninfluential men received the beginnings of their education. A society class met in her house; but it is impossible to say in what year it was formed. But that little cottage of hers beside the Calder was undoubtedly one of the places in which Methodism first rooted itself in Burnley. It was pulled down about twenty years ago. William Moor, a local preacher, should also be mentioned, and John Eagin, a shoemaker, who died in great peace in 1836. Of this John Eagin several stories are told, of which one may be given here, though all belong to a later date. It was customary to hold a prayer meeting in various houses after the Sunday evening service. One evening John was present at such a meeting, held in the house of a Mr. Foulds, who kept a shop in Sandygate. When John engaged in prayer, he was in the habit of giving emphasis to his petitions by vigorous thumps on whatever happened to be in front of him as he knelt. On this occasion he chanced to kneel against a sack of flour, without perceiving what it was. And as he prayed, he thumped and thumped, till at the conclusion, when he and the little assembly rose from their knees, they found themselves, to their no small dismay, powdered over with flour which John had thumped out of the sack.

## MERECLOUGH.

In April, 1786, Methodism was introduced into Mereclough by William Banning, a local preacher, who carried on the business of grocer and baker at Blackburn. He entertained Wesley on his visits to Blackburn. His son relates, in a brief Memoir which he wrote, that on one of these occasions his father took Wesley to see a new chapel, which was being erected in a neighbouring village. The building met with Wesley's approval; but he added,[1] "I have a favour to beg, that you have no pews in the bottom of this chapel, except one for the leading-singers; and be sure to accommodate the poor as well as your circumstances will admit; they are God's building materials in the erecting of His church. The rich make good scaffolding, but bad building materials: they require so much polishing."

In the following year (1787), William Halstead opened his house, which stood hard by the present chapel, but a little beneath it, for a class-meeting. The leader of the class was Mr. Sutcliffe. In this cottage services were held, week by week, without intermission for thirty-seven years.

---

1. Ward, *Methodism in Blackburn*, p. 27, where a fuller account of Mr. Banning may be found.

About the same time the Methodists found their way to HURSTWOOD, and for a while there was regular preaching in Hurstwood Hall, then occupied by Mr. Eltoft. But this did not lead to any permanent results.

The Colne Circuit was in 1776 very large. At one time it extended from twenty miles north of Colne nearly to Rochdale, and from near Halifax to beyond Preston. The following circuits have since been formed on the ground, over which the first Colne preachers travelled:—In 1787 Blackburn, divided in 1878 into Clayton Street, Darwen, and Harwood Street. In 1792 Lancaster, from which Morecambe was separated five years ago. In 1799 Preston, from which Chorley was separated for a year in 1819 and permanently in 1858, and which in 1866 was divided into Lune Street and Wesley. In 1799 Todmorden, from which in 1862 Hebden Bridge was separated. In 1801 Skipton, from which Grassington was taken in 1809, Clitheroe in 1812, and in part Settle in 1830. In 1807 Ulverston, which in 1871 parted with Barrow-in-Furness. In 1810 Burnley, which lost Padiham in 1861, and in 1898 was divided into Wesley and Fulledge. Other circuits once included are Bacup and Rawtenstall; Garstang, Blackpool, Lytham; Otley, Bingley, and Pateley Bridge; Haslingden and Accrington; Clitheroe, Nelson, and Barnoldswick. In 1776 when the Keighley circuit was divided the membership was 1640; the following year the membership in the Colne circuit was 754.

The preachers appointed to the Colne circuit from its formation to that of the Burnley circuit in 1810, were as follows:—

1776. Samuel Bardsley (1768-1818), William Brammah (1762-1780).
1777. Alexander Mather (1757-1800), Richard Condy (1776-1800).
1778. Alexander Mather, Thomas Vasey (1775-1826).
1779. Cristopher Hopper (1747-1802), William Percival (1773-1803).
1780. Christopher Hopper, Thomas Longley (1780-1809).
1781. Thomas Hanson (1760-1804), Thomas Readshaw, Parson Greenwood (1762-1811).
1782. Thomas Hanson, Thomas Johnson (1752-1797), David Evans.
1783. John Easton (1762-1813), Robert Costerdine (1764-1812), Thomas Warwick (1778-1809).
1784. John Easton, Thomas Dixon (1769-1820), Charles Atmore (1781-1826).
1785. Charles Atmore, Edward Jackson (1777-1806), Robert Hayward.
1786. Edward Jackson, Samuel Bardsley, James Ridall (1785-1822).

1787. James Hall, Samuel Edwards.
1788. Charles Atmore, James Ridall.
1789. William Collins (1767-1797), William Bramwell (1786-1818).
1790. Thomas Longley (1780-1809), William Bramwell, William Hainsworth (1790-1823).
1791. Thomas Longley, Charles Tunnycliffe (1788-1828), William Saunderson (1788-1810).
1792. Lancelot Harrison (1766-1806), John Beanland (1775-1798), James Evans, (1786-1820).
1793. Lancelot Harrison, Charles Gloyne (1793-1845), John Ward (1792-1838).
1794. Joseph Entwisle (1787-1841), Richard Seed (1768-1805), John Atkins (1786-1805).
1795. Joseph Entwisle, Jonathan Edmondson (1786-1842), Charles Gloyne.
1796. Jonathan Edmondson, John Atkins, Charles Gloyne.
1797. Timothy Crowther (1784-1829), John Denton (1789-1851), Richard Hardacre (1792-1828).
1798. Timothy Crowther, John Denton, Thomas Shaw (1796-1801).
1799. 1800. Simon Day (1766-1832), John Barritt (1786-1841), Thomas Gill (1786-1828).
1801. John Booth (1779-1820), John Chettle (1797-1850).
1802. John Booth, Thomas Hutton (1789-1839).
1803. Thomas Hutton, James Ridall.
1804. John Kershaw (1788-1855), James Ridall.
1805. John Kershaw, Zechariah Taft (1801-1848).
1806. George Snowden (1769-1812), Zechariah Taft.
1807. George Snowden, Zechariah Yewdall (1779-1830), Abraham Haigh (1803-1810).
1808. John Crosby (1783-1816), Isaac Muff (1792-1830), Abraham Haigh.
1809. John Crosby, Isaac Muff, Richard Arter (1809-1810).

The figures in brackets give the years in which the preachers commenced their ministry, and in which they died. In cases of re-appointment the figures are not repeated. Where no figures are given, the preacher for some reason "retired from the work." In this period there are only five who thus retired.

Of these preachers, Joseph Entwisle was twice President of the Conference; Alexander Mather, Charles Atmore, and Jonathan Edmondson, once. Thomas Vasey is stated in Hill's Arrangement to have been a Clergyman of the Established Church. At a later date another Thomas Vasey was stationed at Colne. He died in the circuit, and was interred in the burial ground attached to the chapel at Trawden. Charles Tunnycliffe resided in the circuit as a supernumerary in 1804-05, and again from 1806 to 1809.

Samuel Bardsley was "a man of great simplicity of character and ardent zeal for God." His one aim was so to preach as to save the souls of those who heard him. He had a slight impediment in his speech and his acquaintance with English grammar was but small; but he was mighty in the Scriptures, and "full of the Holy Ghost and of power." His evenness and sweetness of temper were proverbial. At one of his quarterly meetings the steward intimated, that the circuit would not require his services another year because he was such a poor preacher. "Brethren," said Bardsley, with inimitable good temper, "it is not that I am so poor a preacher, but that you are poor hearers: and I intend to stop and see you mend." He remained, and had the joy of witnessing a great revival.

Two more of these preachers require brief notice, because of their connection by birth with the neighbourhood.

William Bramwell was born near Elswick in 1759. He was brought up in the Church of England, and felt the gracious influence of the Holy Spirit 'from a child.' Meeting with some Roman Catholics in Preston, he tried for a time to satisfy his heart with austerities. He cut his flesh, knelt to pray with his bare knees on a sanded floor, and almost starved himself to death by frequent and long fasts. Failing to find what he sought, he returned to the Church of England, and was first assured of God's forgiving love while receiving the sacrament. This joy however he soon lost, and fell again into spiritual darkness. But in 1777 he heard Christopher Hopper preach at Preston, and at once said, "This is the kind of preaching I have long wanted to hear: these are the people with whom I am resolved to live and die." Soon afterwards he found peace, and gave himself to evangelistic work in the Fylde, devoting to it all his evenings and the whole of his Sundays for the next five or six years. Among his converts was Ann Cutler, who "became one of the holiest women of her times." Being urged to give up his employment and devote himself entirely to the ministry of the Gospel, but not seeing his way plain, it is said that he went into a quarry near Preston and remained, without food or drink, for thirty-six hours in continuous prayer. The conviction of his call being there confirmed, he sold all that he had, bought a horse and saddle-bags, and for the next thirty-two years travelled among the Methodist societies as a flame of fire, witnessing a gracious revival wherever he went.[1]

John Barritt was the son of a man in a good social position, who lived near Colne. He was opposed to all

---

1. Taylor, *Apostles of Fylde Methodism*, pp. 30-37.

religion, especially to the teaching of Wesley, and warned his children never to listen to the Methodists. When John joined them, and was urged to become a travelling preacher, his father tempted him to refuse by offering him one of his farms. John accepted the offer, took the farm, and married. Within a year his wife died, leaving him with a little girl, eight days old. Then said John Barritt, 'This is the voice of God,' left his farm, and took his place among Wesley's itinerants. The little girl grew to womanhood, and became the mother of the late Dr. J. B. Melson, of Birmingham.

No history of Methodism in this circuit would be complete without some notice of his sister Mary. She was of a serious disposition, and sought peace in a strict and self-denying life. When about twenty-two years of age she went to hear John Wesley, found the peace she had sought in vain, and joined the Methodists. Her father was greatly annoyed, and tried in every possible way, both by promises and threats, to draw her from their society. Finding these useless, he told her she must either leave the Methodists or leave his house. Declining to leave the people of her choice she accepted the latter alternative, and was without a home till years after she became the wife of Zechariah Taft. After conducting religious services of various kinds, she ultimately began to preach, and preached "with masculine eloquence and womanly tenderness." To say that hundreds, if not thousands, were converted under her preaching might be an exaggeration, but she was undoubtedly made very useful.

The question of female preaching exercised at the time the minds of some Methodists considerably, and Mary Barritt's name was often mentioned in the controversy which arose.[1] While it was still a matter of dispute whether she should be allowed to preach in the pulpits of Methodism, she was requested to preach before the Conference. At the close of the sermon, Dr. Adam Clarke said to her, "Well done, Mary,

---

1. *Life of Bunting*, ed. 1887, p. 106. In a note it is added that William Atherton, when preaching on the death of the second Joseph Taylor, said with all possible solemnity, "God often works by strange instruments. Balaam was converted by the braying of an ass, and Peter by the crowing of a cock; and our lamented brother by the preaching of a woman one Good Friday morning." This woman was Mary Barritt. Her husband afterwards became a very ardent advocate of female preaching. In 1803 he published "Thoughts" on the subject, and six years later defended his views against an attack made in the *Wes. Meth. Mag.* of that date. In 1820 he returned to the subject, and issued a statement of what he called the Scriptural doctrine. Five years later he printed a volume of "Biographical Sketches of the Lives and Ministry of various holy Women." A second volume appeared in 1828, with a portrait of the author as a frontispiece. His wife is not included in either volume.

go on with your preaching, and the Lord will own and bless your efforts." Early in the year 1801, John Gaulter wrote to his friend, Jabez Bunting, a letter in which among other things he says, "We have had the Reverend Miss Barritt here; and, as usual, a *mighty stir!* and, consequently, a number of professions of conversion: and, as you may believe, we are neither worse nor better for it." In 1797, she preached to a large congregation on Clifton Green, York. It began to rain heavily, whereupon she prayed that God "would stay the bottles of Heaven for a few minutes." The rain ceased, and in the prayer-meeting which followed the service several persons found peace with God. Mr. William Lancaster heard her preach in Keighley Green Chapel in 1828. Her text was "The righteous also shall hold on his way, and he that hath clean hands shall be stronger and stronger" (Job xvii. 9). In Memoirs, written by herself, but unfortunately not carried further than a few months after her husband's appointment to Burnley, she describes two or three visits to the town. On March 15th, 1801, and again about a fortnight later, she took part in the services of a great revival, in which she says that above fifty members were added to the society in two days. The following August she preached at Burnley "noon and night," and asked the prayers of the congregation for her father, who was lying on his death-bed. She was once preaching in the chapel at Colne, when a slight crash was heard caused by the breaking of a form. Not knowing what it was, and possibly remembering the sad accident which occurred at the opening of the chapel, the congregation, which was very large, became seriously alarmed. Some in their eagerness to get out leaped from the upper windows: but happily no lives were lost, though many lost part of their clothing, "and a promiscuous heap of hats, caps, bonnets, shoes, aprons, handkerchiefs, &c., were put into a large cask in front of the chapel, that those who had lost such articles might select and reclaim them."[1]

The plans in those days were *written* and simply stated the work that was to be done by each of the preachers. A copy of one of these plans for the Colne circuit is here given, from Jessop's *Methodism in Rossendale*. It will be seen that this circuit was what was called a six weeks' round. Except that the preacher visited a few places twice in the time, it took him six weeks to pass through his round, and during that time he preached sixty-one sermons and travelled 231 miles. With reason were the men called "travelling" preachers. There were then three preachers in the circuit, and two horses were

---

1. *Annals of Colne*, p. 41, note.

# A Plan for Preaching in the Colne Circuit in the Year 1786.

| DAYS. | PLACE. | TIMES. | SERVICES. | MILES. | DAYS. | PLACE. | TIMES. | SERVICES. | MILES. |
|---|---|---|---|---|---|---|---|---|---|
| *1st Sunday* | Colne | Morning, noon & night | 3 | 0 | *4th Sunday* | Bolton Hall | Morning, noon, night | 3 | 5 |
| " | Do. | | " | | " | Blackburn | | " | 6 |
| " | Do. | | " | | " | Do. | | " | 6 |
| Monday | Stocks | | " | 6 | Monday | Ribchester | | " | 6 |
| Tuesday | Caxton | Noon, night | 2 | 10 | Tuesday | Blackburn | | " | 8 |
| Wednesday | Mawen | Noon, night | | | Wednesday | Grave | Noon, night | 2 | 5 |
| | Long Preston | Noon, night | | 13 | | Flaxmoss | Noon, night | " | 2 |
| Thursday | Settle | Noon, night | 2 | | Thursday | Bank-Top | Noon, night | " | 1 |
| | Wigglesworth-row | Noon, night | | 8 | | Mill-end | Noon, night | | |
| Friday | Newhurst | Noon, night | 2 | 7 | Friday | Syke Side | | 2 | 7 |
| Saturday | Gisburn | Noon, night | 2 | 10 | Saturday | Haslingden | | " | |
| | Rimmington | | | | *5th Sunday* | Mill-end | Morning, noon, night | 3 | |
| | Padiham all day and rest | | | | " | Do. | | " | |
| *2nd Sunday* | Padiham | Morning, noon, night | 3 | 0 | " | Bacup | | " | 3 |
| " | Do. | | " | 0 | Monday | Wardlefold | | " | 8 |
| " | Do. | | " | 3 | Tuesday | Longclough Top | Noon, night | 2 | 8 |
| Monday | Burnley | | " | 6 | Wednesday | Todmorden | Noon, night | " | 4 |
| Tuesday | Rough Lee | | " | 4 | Thursday | Rothwell-end | | " | 6 |
| Wednesday | Colne | | " | 3 | Friday | Loddington | | " | 2 |
| Thursday | Haggat | | " | 3 | Saturday | Stocks | | " | |
| Friday | Rothwell End | Morning, noon, night | 3 | 14 | | Do. | | | |
| Saturday | Todmorden | Morning, noon, night | | | *6th Sunday* | Heptonstall | Morning, noon, night | 3 | |
| *3rd Sunday* | Do. | | " | | " | Do. | | " | |
| " | Do. | | " | 2 | " | Do. | | " | |
| Monday | Top o' th' Close | Noon, night | 2 | 14 | Monday | Widdup | Noon, night | 2 | 0 |
| Tuesday | Harwood | Noon, night | | 9 | Tuesday | Southfield | | " | 10 |
| Wednesday | Blackburn | | " | 12 | Wednesday | Fowlrigg | | " | 4 |
| Thursday | Preston | | " | 0 | Thursday | Colne | | " | 2 |
| Friday | Do. | | " | 10 | Friday | Barrowford | | " | 2 |
| Saturday | Chorley | | " | 10 | Saturday | Colne | | " | 2 |
| | Bolton Hall | | | | | | | | |

kept for their use. No Methodist services were held in what were called "Church hours." At noon or in the evening no service was held in any church, and "morning" would mean at such an hour that the preaching could be over in time for the congregation to go to the service of the Establishment. A week-day service at noon seems strange to us: but the people were largely hand-loom weavers, and could leave their work whenever they liked. It will be noticed that when there were two services appointed for any week day, one was at noon and the other at night; where only one is appointed the time is left unfixed. Bolton Hall is now Hoghton.

CHAPTER IV.

# BURNLEY CIRCUIT, 1810-1899.

THE Colne circuit reported to the Conference of 1810 a membership of exactly 800. This was not too large for one circuit, if all the members had lived in reasonable proximity; but they were distributed amongst societies over a wide area, and therefore to reduce physical labour and to secure more efficient oversight the circuit was divided. The good effect appeared at once; and at the next Conference the new circuit, to which Accrington had been transferred after a union for six years with Bury, was able to report a membership of 560, whilst that of the old fell only to 500.

An extract from the Stewards' book will show the income of the circuit for the first quarter of its existence, and the contributions of the various societies of which it was composed. It is the financial record[1] of its first September quarterly meeting:—

|  | £ | s. | d. |
|---|---|---|---|
| Burnley Quarterage | 12 | 0 | 0 |
| Padiham    ,, | 6 | 0 | 4 |
| Accrington  ,, | 6 | 0 | 0 |
| Warren Lane ,, | 1 | 10 | 0 |
| Oakenshaw   ,, |  | 10 | 0 |
| Whalley     ,, |  | 10 | 6 |
| Higham      ,, | 1 | 16 | 0 |
| Lowerhouse  ,, | 1 | 0 | 0 |
| Total | 29 | 6 | 10 |

The problem confronting the stewards was consequently how to work a circuit, in which the services of two ministers were required, upon an income of about £120 a year.

---

1. Quoted from T. Hargreaves, *Rise and Progress of Methodism in Accrington*, p. 38.

## CIRCUIT FINANCE.

Methodist finance, though not a branch of the higher mathematics, has an appearance of some complexity. It is the product of a long process of adaptation to varying conditions amidst the increasing claims of an organisation that was slowly completing itself. At first the preachers had no homes, and were strictly charged to receive no money. The societies they visited provided them with food and lodging, with boots and clothes, and sometimes even with a then fashionable wig, and paid the cost of stabling the preacher's horse, when he had one. But the preachers were not required or expected to give up entirely their secular calling. William Shent continued at intervals to carry on his barber's business in Leeds; and John Nelson sometimes worked as a stone mason for a week or two even while travelling with Wesley; and when James Rowell was sent to form a circuit in the Dales, his first care was to provide a basis of supplies by opening a shop. There is reason to believe that William Darney used sometimes at least to sell his wares as he tramped his rounds. When society stewards were appointed, their first duty was to provide for the necessities of the preacher, and as far as possible to pay his expenses from the contributions of the members.

This method was soon found to be very inconvenient, and it was recommended that each preacher should receive, in addition to his board and travelling expenses, £12 a year for books and clothes. But it was some years before this modest suggestion was generally adopted. A deputation from York attended the Conference at Manchester in 1765 to protest against so large a sum being allowed.

Still no provision was made for the preachers' wives and families, of whom some were left in charge of friends, whilst others supported themselves in various ways. It can cause little wonder that many of the earlier preachers returned to their businesses, or settled as pastors of other churches. When Alexander Mather entered the ranks of the itinerancy in 1757, the London stewards allowed his wife 4s. a week; and this is generally said to be the first case in which a regular allowance was made to a preacher's wife. But the records show that William Darney sometimes received an allowance for his wife in the Haworth Round as early as the year 1748, though it never amounted to 2s. 6d. a week. From the time when the London stewards made the allowance for Mather's wife, the custom gradually spread, and the amount was generally 50s. a quarter.

These allowances may seem very small, but it must be borne in mind, that money had a much greater purchasing power then than it has now, so that in reality the people gave more and the preachers received more than has been commonly supposed. Dr. Lyth, in his *Glimpses of Early Methodism in York*, (p. 111), quotes from Arthur Young to the effect that at Stillingfleet, a village about seven miles from York, in the year 1770, bread was 1d., butter 5¼d., cheese 2d., meat 3½d. per pound, whilst eggs were advertised in the York *Courant* at 12 for a penny. From the account book of the Rev. Benjamin Ingham, it appears that the prices of provisions, etc., at Aberford, a village about fourteen miles from York, were in the year 1768 as follows :—beef 3d. to 4d., mutton 3½d. to 4d., pork 3d., bacon and ham 4d. per pound; a goose cost from 1s. 6d. to 2s., a hare 1s., a rabbit 6d., a calf's head 1s. 2d.; pigeons were twopence and chickens sixpence each; Cheshire cheese was 4½d., soap 6d., and candles 7d. per pound. A careful comparison between these prices and those of the present day will show that the power of money in the purchasing of provisions was then about four times as much as it is now. Luxuries were more expensive; coffee was 6s. 6d., tea 12s., and sugar according to quality from 5d. to 7d. a lb. Clothing too was more costly than now, but is generally considered to have been more durable. Mr. Ingham paid 5s. 4d. for two pairs of stockings, and 6s. 6d. for a pair which are expressly said to have been cotton; but he obtained a coat and waistcoat of some material for 18s., and for 10s. sufficient cloth to make a pair of breeches. For four yards of black cloth he paid £2 10s. 0d., and for the same quantity of blue cloth £2; for making clothes and trimming 19s. 9½d. A pair of shoes cost him 5s.; William Darney's boots twenty years before, it may be remembered, cost 14s.; for the soling of his boots Mr. Ingham paid 2s. 6d.; a new wig cost £1 12s. 0d. The same book shows that for weeding a girl received 6d. a day; a man for ordinary labour 1s., and the gardener 1s. 6d. a day; for killing and dressing a cow the charge was 2s., for cleaning a clock 2s. 8d., sweeping four chimneys 2s. 4d.

To return to circuit finance, the system of payment not by salary but by allowances estimated to cover the different items of expenditure continued into very recent times, and has not yet been entirely given up. The early preacher received a fixed sum quarterly for books, clothes, etc., for his wife, for his servant, for candles, etc., and payment at irregular intervals for his board. That method of payment prevailed without change until March, 1860, when a formal resolution was passed by the quarterly meeting to the effect that the preacher's quarterly stipend should be £35. But even then the old system survived, and the resolution proceeded to state that "the following items compose the amount," and enumerated board, servants' wages and board, coal and gas, medicine, house-bill and stationery, washing, travelling expenses, ten guineas for the clothing of the whole household, closing with 16s. "extra to make an even sum." Though all these particulars are no longer entered in the circuit books, the system is still substantially the same, and a sum is paid quarterly that is estimated to meet the legitimate wants of the preacher and his family, but neither to cover extraordinary expenses nor to admit of provision for the future. The preacher is not now permitted to carry on any business, but all his energies are to be given to the work of the ministry: on his retirement through sickness or age, a scant and inadequate allowance is made to him from an Auxiliary Fund, whose claims upon the ungrudging and generous support of the societies are in fairness irresistible.

The small income of the circuit appears to have been ample for a time. The cost of the preachers' board was possibly met by payments made to him at the different leaders' meeting and not included in the schedule of income given above. From the authority there cited it appears that the items of expenditure were both curious and varied. "Washing, £1; coals and candles, 18s. 6d.; shoes cleaning, 3s.," are amongst the entries, followed by one over which at later times there has occasionally been much discussion, "Quarter-day dinner, £1 5s. 0d." That nearly five per cent of the income should be expended upon a single dinner, is perhaps warranted by old British customs, and at least an increase of good feeling and kindliness would be effected.

This quarter-day dinner was regularly attended for some years by John Eagin, who was one of the leaders in the Burnley society. On this occasion, it is said, a good supply of roast beef and plum pudding was provided; to such viands as these John Eagin was not accustomed at home, and after faring sumptuously and plenteously at the quarter-day dinner, he could hardly bring himself to relish his porridge next morning. When this was the case, he would put the porridge in the oven, and say to himself, "Oh, tha'l come to it." If at dinner time he was still disinclined for such plain fare, he would replace it again in the oven, and make the same prediction, "Tha'l come to it." How often the basin had to be put away, the story does not tell; but sometimes it was not until the morning of the second day that John would take the spoon, and set to work with appetite saying, "I knew tha'd come to it."

This innocent festivity seems to have been repeated without interruption till the end of 1837. At the Christmas quarterly meeting of that year however it was resolved, that the dinner should be discontinued, but that a tea should be provided for those who thought proper to remain after the business of the meeting had been concluded. The stewards were to meet at one o'clock, and business to commence at two precisely. In the September of the following year a special effort was ordered to be made to clear off the circuit debt, and at the same time it was resolved that the dinner should be resumed "as soon as the income of the circuit would justify such an expenditure of its funds." Mr. Hopwood kindly offered to provide the dinner at Christmas; he did the same in March, 1839; Mr. Howorth provided it in July; "a kind friend" in September; and Messrs. James Smallpage and Joshua Lord at Christmas. In June, 1840, the meeting resolved that dinner should be provided at their next meeting, each leader and officer pledging himself "to use his influence to increase the ordinary income at least to the amount required to cover it." But the practice, if renewed, was soon discontinued again; and instead of dinner a tea was provided at a charge varying from a few shillings to fifty. The cost is by no means entered regularly, and was probably met sometimes from private resources.

Several of the early plans of the circuit are still in existence, in the possession of Mr. John Howorth, of Park View. On another page is reproduced the second, which is headed "The Lord's Day Appointments of the Methodist Itinerant and Local Preachers in Burnley Circuit, 1811."

The Plan announced that the quarterly meetings were to be held at Burnley on Thursday, June 27th, and at Padiham on Thursday, October 31st. The list of itinerant and lay preachers is added:—1. T. Rogerson; 2. T. Davis; 3. J. Wood; 4. F. Watson; 5. J. Ackroyd; 6. J. Kenyon; 7. W. Lang; 8. J. Barlow; 9. W. Moon; 10. T. Farrar; 11. H. Seed; 12. G. Hargreaves (On trial); 13. J. Dean; 14. C. Lister; 15. D. Nunick; 16. — Downham; 17. W. Williams; 18. R. Holden; 19. T. Wilkinson; 20. J. Smith; 21. J. Crew; 22. J. Holden; 23. J. Walsh; 24. J. Illingworth; 25. R. Jackson; 26. J. Entwistle; 27. J. Coulthurst.

It appears from the plan that the Methodists in this circuit still avoided having their services during church hours. The morning services at Burnley and Padiham, where there was a church, began at 9 o'clock, and only at Accrington, where there was then no church, at 10-30. The itinerants preached each three times every Sunday, on which day their services were confined to the three principal chapels.

From a plan for the second half of the year 1830 it appears that the preaching places in the circuit were at that time Burnley, Padiham, Lowerhouse, Higham, Mereclough, Wheatley Lane, Back Lane, Bentley Wood Green, Castle Clough, Burnley Lane Head, Worsthorne, Pendle Bottom, Cheapside, Read, Sabden Hall, Haggate and Huncoat. The

# PLAN OF BURNLEY CIRCUIT, 1811.

| PLACES. | TIME. | MAY. | | | | JUNE. | | | | JULY. | | | | AUGUST. | | | | SEPT. | | | | OCT. | | | N. |
|---|---|---|---|---|---|---|---|---|---|---|---|---|---|---|---|---|---|---|---|---|---|---|---|---|---|
| | | 5 | 12 | 19 | 26 | 2 | 9 | 16 | 23 | 30 | 7 | 14 | 21 | 28 | 4 | 11 | 18 | 25 | 1 | 8 | 15 | 22 | 29 | 6 | 13 | 20 | 27 | 3 |
| Burnley { Morning | 9 | 2 | 1 | 1 | 1 | 1 | 1 | 1 | 1 | 1 | 1 | 1 | 1 | 1 | 1 | 1 | 1 | 1 | 1 | 1 | 1 | 1 | 1 | 1 | 1 | 1 | 1 | 1 |
| Afternoon | 1½ | 2 | 11 | 2 | 7 | 2 | 11 | 2 | 3 | 2 | 1L | 2 | 18 | 2 | 2L | 2 | 23 | 2 | 2 | 2 | 2 | 13 | 2 | 2 | 14 | 2 | 1L | |
| Evening | 6 | 2 | 1 | 2 | 7 | 2 | 1 | 2 | 3 | 2 | 1 | 2 | 2 | 2 | 7 | 2 | 1 | 2 | 2 | 13 | 2 | 1 | 2 | 2 | 2 | 2 | 1 | |
| Padiham { Morning | 9 | 1 | 5 | 1 | 2 | 2 | 2 | 1 | 2 | 1 | 7 | 5 | 1 | 2 | 4 | 7 | 1 | 2 | 7 | 1 | 2 | 2L | 1 | 2 | 2 | 2 | 5 | 1L |
| Afternoon | 1 | 1 | 5 | 1 | 1 | 2 | 11 | 1 | 2 | 7 | 1L | 2 | 15 | 2 | 1 | 2 | 23 | 1 | 7 | 2 | 1 | 16 | 1 | 2 | 2 | 1 | 5 | |
| Evening | | | | | | | | | | | | | | | | | | | | | | | | | | | | | |
| Accrington { Morning 10½ | | 24 | 1 | 21 | 1 | 26 | 2 | 7 | 1 | 20 | 2 | 5 | 1 | 22 | 2 | 7 | 1 | 23 | 2 | 6 | 1 | 20 | 2 | 2L | 16 | 18 | 1L | 5 | 2 |
| Afternoon | 1 | 24 | 2 | 21 | 2 | 26 | 2 | 7 | 1 | 20 | 2 | 5 | 1 | 22 | 2 | 7 | 1 | 23 | 2 | 6 | 1 | 20 | 2 | 2 | 3 | 18 | 1L | 5 | 2 |
| Evening | 7 | 1 | 5 | 1 | 2 | 1 | 1 | 2 | 1 | 1 | 7 | 5 | 1 | 2 | 1 | 7 | 1 | 2 | 1 | 1 | 2 | 13 | 1 | 2 | 15 | 2 | 5 | 1 | |
| Oakenshaw | 6 | 11 | p | 6 | p | 7 | p | 8 | p | 11 | p | 6 | p | 7 | p | |
| Warren Lane | 6 | 23 | 11 | 18 | 6 | 25 | 7 | 18 | 8 | 27 | 22 | 11 | 27 | |
| Whalley | 1 | 6 | 18 | 3 | 17 | 6 | 9 | 19 | 10 | 21 | 7 | 19 | 6 | 11 | |
| Higham | 4 | 3 | 9 | 10 | 12 | 4 | 3 | 5 | 11 | 3 | 12 | 9 | 10 | 4 | |
| Mereclough | 1 | 5 | 13 | 4 | 9 | 12 | 10 | 11 | 10 | 9 | 12 | 10 | 4 | 5 | |
| Lowerhouse | 3 | 12 | 10 | 3 | 9 | 11 | 4 | 3 | 5 | 11 | 3 | 9 | 11 | 3 | 10 | |
| New Laund | 6 | 9 | | 4 | | 3 | | 12 | | 9 | | 10 | | 4 | |

lay preachers were Messrs. Scarr, Crossley, Simpson, Hartley, Smallpage, Riley, Lord, Wood, Robinson, Cuerdale, Astin, Lane, and Whalley, with Messrs. Foulds and Shuttleworth on trial.

According to a plan of 1837 the following places had been given up:—Burnley Lane Head, Read, Haggate, and Huncoat; whilst the following had begun to be visited in the intervening years:—Burnley Moor, Dineley, Timber Hill, Fur Barn, and 'Simon-Stones.' There also appear to have been considerable changes amongst the preachers. Of the names on the list of 1830 there remain only Smallpage, Lord, and Astin, all of Burnley. There had been received during the seven years, Hopwood, Holden, Crossley, Owen, Thompson, Riley, Moore (Higham), Platt (Higham), Robinson, Close, Smith (Wheatley Lane), Emmett, and Holgate. "On trial" were Messrs. Scarr, Taylor, G. Heys (Lowerhouse), Fletcher (Padiham), Bradshaw (Higham), Hargreaves (Worsthorne), and Kay. Where no residence is given it may be assumed the preacher lived at Burnley.

The Local Preachers' Minute Book, extending from 1818 to 1829, is still in existence. Under December 24th, 1818, occurs one of the earliest entries. The question is asked, "What is the opinion of this Meeting respecting local preachers abetting the cause of combinations, and encouraging revolutionary measures?" The answer given is, "We are unanimous in our opinion that, as preachers of righteousness and followers of Christ whose Kingdom is not of this world, we ought to respect every ordinance of man for the Lord's sake, whether of the King, as Supreme Governor of this Realm, or of Magistrates, acting under his authority." With the exception of a few records of alterations in place or time of preaching, and of occasional instances in which brethren had to be admonished for neglecting their appointments, the book contains but two matters of any general interest.

Down to 1828 a man had no examination to pass before being received as a "fully accredited" local preacher. A satisfactory trial sermon and a favourable report of his work during the time he had been on trial were evidently deemed sufficient. The truth of the first part of this statement is clear enough from a resolution passed on the 25th of September, 1828, "That no person be admitted into full connexion, who is absent from the Local Preachers' Meeting at the termination of his probation."

During the superintendency of Mr. McKitrick, several "Watch Night" services were held at the quarterly meetings. The local preachers met at three, and after transacting their ordinary business considered some theological subject. After an hour for tea, the Watch Night service began at 7-30 ; but at what time it concluded we are not told. At various meetings the subjects discussed were the Fall, Repentance, Justification by Faith, while amongst the evening preachers were William Moon, James Hartley, James Greenhalgh, William Simpson, David Floyd, Thomas Scarr, Reuben Langstaff, and Gilbert Holden. The last entry in the book is dated June 1st, 1829, and states that Joseph Moore, Robert Dugdale, and David Platt were to be heard by Mr. Phillips at Higham.

The following is a list of ministers who have travelled in the Burnley circuit since its formation to the present time, with the number of members as reported to the Conference each year.

| Year | Ministers | Members |
|---|---|---|
| 1810. | Thomas Rogerson, Thomas Davies | - |
| 1811. | Thomas Rogerson, Lawrence Hargreave | 560 |
| 1812. | James Needham, Lawrence Hargreave | 700 |
| 1813. | James Needham, Isaac Keeling | 700 |
| 1814. | James Needham, William Catton | 710 |
| 1815,-16. | William Leach, Thomas Stead | 580, 620 |
| 1817. | John Stamp, William Vevers | 635 |
| 1818,-19. | William Welborne, Joseph Roberts | 590, 650 |
| 1820,-21. | William Bird, John Bowers | 652, 650 |
| 1822,-23. | Thomas Stanley, George Manwaring | 670, 670 |
| 1824,-25. | William McKitrick, Samuel Crompton | 710, 720 |
| 1826,-27. | Thomas Garbutt, William Binning | 720, 650 |
| 1828,-29. | John Phillips, Charles Hawthorne | 1000, 1000 |
| 1830. | John Phillips, Richard Heape | 900 |
| 1831,-32. | Richard Heape, Joseph Rayner | 824, 843 |
| 1833. | Philip Garrett, Joseph Rayner | 839 |
| 1834. | Luke Barlow, Samuel Allen | 986 |
| 1835. | Luke Barlow, Benjamin Slack | 1000 |
| 1836. | Robert Heys, Benjamin Slack | 1110 |
| 1837. | Robert Heys, William Pemberton | 1074 |
| 1838,-39. | James Heaton, William Pemberton | 990, 1035 |
| 1840. | James Heaton, Thomas Powell | 990 |
| 1841. | Thomas Powell, John Griffith | 1027 |
| 1842. | Benjamin Firth, John Griffith | 1080 |
| 1843,-44. | Benjamin Firth, John Lambert | 1118, 1125 |
| 1845. | Abel Dernaley, John Lambert | 1138 |
| 1846. | Abel Dernaley, John Relph | 1148 |
| 1847,-48. | Thomas Dunn, John Relph, John Clulow | 1147, 1148 |
| 1849. | Thomas Dunn, John M. Kirk, John Clulow | 1294 |
| 1850,-51. | Jonathan Bates, John M. Kirk, John H. Lord | 1298, 1121 |
| 1852. | Alexander Strachan, John Watson, William R. Rogers | 1027 |
| 1853. | Alexander Strachan, William R. Rogers, John G. Cox | 1078 |

## THE BURNLEY CIRCUIT.

1854. Alexander Strachan, John G. Cox,
          William Brailey  1060
1855. John Kirk, John G. Cox, William Brailey - 1053
1856. John Kirk, Levi Waterhouse, William Brailey 1202
1857. John Kirk, Levi Waterhouse, John Lyth - 1215
1858. Joseph Lawton, Levi Waterhouse, John Lyth 1242
1859. Joseph Lawton, William Bond,
          George C. Taylor, Peter Mackenzie 1436
1860. Joseph Lawton, William Bond,
          George C. Taylor, Robert Posnett 1526
1861. Isaac Keeling, Joshua Mason, Robert Posnett 1582
1862. Isaac Keeling, Joshua Mason, Robert Posnett,
          James Daniel 1076
1863. John Randerson, Joshua Mason, Stephen Cox,
          William Bunting 1088
1864,-65. John Randerson, Stephen Cox, William Bunting,
          Thomas H. Lomas  1132, 1148
1866,-67,-68. Wilson Brailsford, Edward Stokes,
          Joseph Rippon  1163, 1254, 1365
1869. James Findlay, John M. Bamford,
          Charles W. Prest 1278
1870,-71. John G. Cox, John M. Bamford,
          Charles W. Prest  1204, 1185
1872. John G. Cox, Joseph Webster, Joseph Howard 1168
1873,-74. James Nance, Joseph Webster, George Charter
          1166, 1248
1875. James Nance, George Charter, Josiah Mee - 1313
1876. William Davison, James F. Broughton,
          Josiah Mee 1350
1877. Henry Hastling, James F. Broughton,
          Josiah Mee, William W. Walton 1403
1878. H. Hastling, J. F. Broughton, R. Waddy Moss,
          W. W. Walton 1423
1879. H. Hastling, R. W. Moss, Samuel Owen Scott,
          W. W. Walton 1385
1880. William Ford, R. W. Moss, S. O. Scott,
          G. Beamish Saul 1420
1881. William Ford, Charles D. Newman, S. O. Scott,
          James Critchison 1294
1882. William Ford, Charles D. Newman,
          J. Critchison, William J. Fowell 1279
1883. Simpson Crump, C. D. Newman, J. Critchison,
          W. J. Fowell 1329
1884. Simpson Crump, W. J. Fowell, William Brooks,
          Clement Stuchbery 1325
1885. Simpson Crump, William Willey,
          William Brooks, Clement Stuchbery 1328

| | | |
|---|---|---|
| 1886. | W. Willey, W. Brooks, C. Stuchbery, | |
| | Nicholas W. Tomlinson | 1337 |
| 1887. | W. Willey, Walter Briscombe, John W. Blackett, | |
| | N. W. Tomlinson | 1318 |
| 1888. | G. Holbrey, Walter Briscombe, J. W. Blackett, | |
| | N. W. Tomlinson | 1410 |
| 1889. | G. Holbrey, W. Briscombe, J. W. Blackett, | |
| | Thomas Pitt | 1385 |
| 1890. | G. Holbrey, John Clegg, James Dixon, T. Pitt | 1397 |
| 1891. | J. Clegg, G. England Sheers, B.A., J. Dixon, | |
| | T. Pitt | 1424 |
| 1892. | J. Clegg, G. E. Sheers, B.A., J. Dixon, | |
| | S. Bingham Beattie | 1540 |
| 1893. | Bamford Burrows, G. E. Sheers, B.A., | |
| | William Brookes, S. B. Beattie | 1572 |
| 1894. | Bamford Burrows, Thomas Rodgers, | |
| | William Stevinson, B.A., S. B. Beattie | 1548 |
| 1895. | B. Burrows, T. Rodgers, W. Stevinson, B.A., | |
| | F. Stuart Kirkness | 1551 |
| 1896. | James R. Berry, T. Rodgers, W. Stevinson, B.A., | |
| | F. S. Kirkness, T. Akrill Pye | 1562 |
| 1897. | J. R. Berry, John Thackray, B.A., | |
| | Jonathan Chapple, F. S. Kirkness, T. A. Pye | 1559 |
| 1898. | (*Wesley*)—J. Chapple, Alexander Mayes, T. A. Pye | } 1467 |
| | (*Fulledge*)—J. Thackray, B.A., W. Barlow Brown | |

The following ministers have also resided in the circuit as supernumeraries:—Charles Tunnicliffe, from 1816 to 1827; John Phillips, from 1833 to 1846; John Wesley Barritt, in 1838; Alexander Strachan, from 1858 to 1865; Richard Allen, in 1862 and again from 1871 to 1873; John Randerson, from 1866 to 1869; James Wilson, from 1864 to 1879; and Joshua Priestley, in 1879 and 1880. Mr. Barritt's health had completely failed through his sleeping in the damp beds, with which it was in those days too often the misfortune of Methodist preachers to be accommodated. So great was the mischief that, as early as 1810, the following note was inserted in the Minutes of Conference at the close of the obituaries: "It is much to be desired that all our friends would take due care to have the beds in which they put the preachers perfectly dry."

To the above list may be added the names of ministers, who have served in the circuit as temporary supplies: W. Illingworth, H. J. Robinson, and G. B. Austin.

To some of the above names a few notes may fitly be added, though silence must be the rule concerning most of the ministers who are still living.

Lawrence Hargreave was appointed to the circuit in 1811.

He was in the habit of preaching in the Market Place, and among his hearers was frequently a youth, named James Howorth, of Baptist parentage, who had come as an apprentice to Burnley. The preaching and conversation of Mr. Hargreave led to his conversion, and he joined the Methodists. Mr. Hargreave died of fever on the 10th of April, 1813, and was interred in the ground attached to the old Hall Hill Chapel, Padiham. He was the first of the two ministers, who have died in the active work during the eighty-eight years of the existence of the circuit.

Isaac Keeling was born on February 12th, 1789. His first appointment to Burnley was made by the Conference of 1813, and on account of his youth and shyness was not altogether satisfactory. His biographer describes[1] him as "at first painfully conscious of being more wondered at than appreciated in his pulpit efforts"; but two years later the young minister wrote in a letter of humiliation that several ascribed their conversion to his ministry. Already he had given promise of great ability, and been singled out by Dr. Beaumont's mother, a woman of clear discernment, as "a remarkable man." In 1855 he was elected to the presidency of the Conference; and in 1861 was appointed for a second time to Burnley. After two years' service he was invited, notwithstanding his age and feebleness of health, to remain a third, but with some natural hesitation wisely declined. His decision was communicated to the quarterly meeting in a kind of pastoral letter, in which the old man expressed his opinions with much more than his ordinary vigour or picturesqueness. He did not want the choice of a successor to be determined by the meeting on several grounds. "Names may be mentioned of popular men who are not yet engaged. But many of this class tantalize and vex their circuits by being elsewhere for a great part of their time . . . Again some men are praised for energy; but it is material to ask what sort of energy. Some have a fussy energy. They are great in little things, delight in noise and bustle, keep up a continual racket; but all the dust and stir is about as meaningless and mindless as the hammering in a tinner's workshop." He did not believe in circuit committees, which he regarded as "superfluous and objectionable," as minifying "the most important lay office in a circuit by putting it in commission"; but if such committees were not abolished, they should be strengthened and made fairly representative of the weightiest interests. The ministerial office he was evidently disposed to magnify, but not at the cost of greater

---

1. In a Memorial Sketch prefixed to "Isaac Keeling's Sermons," edited by W. Willan.

things. "I have a long settled conviction," he wrote, "that no man can act aright as a ruler in Christ's house, who does not himself 'walk humbly with God'; that no man does or can walk humbly with God who walks proudly with man. I know some think otherwise; but I cannot conceive of a man, who is haughty, harsh, and rude to his fellow men, as being humbled at the throne of grace at the same time as a penitent sinner. I am convinced that no amount of talent will qualify a man to be a safe and useful superintendent, if he has not firmness to stand calmly in the gap when principles are assailed, and at the same time a tender concern for the peace of Jerusalem." Mr. Keeling retired to the house of his son-in-law at Earby, where he continued, as he wrote to a daughter, to enjoy "the kindness of Burnley friends." In the spring of 1869 he removed to Ripon, where in the August following he died in peace.

Thomas Stead married Sarah, the sister of Messrs. George and Richard Fishwick. One of his sons, Mr. J. Fishwick Stead, still lives at Southport: and the others rendered good service to Methodism.

John Bowers was born on July 19th, 1796. He spent two years in the circuit from the Conference of 1820; and there is a tradition, which his age at the time renders extremely unlikely, that he had been employed in it before as a supply after the decease of the Rev. L. Hargreave. On which of the occasions the incident occured, is a matter of little importance. He was very young, and he looked still younger. His first services in the circuit were conducted at Worsthorne and Mereclough. After the afternoon service at the former place, he was engaged in renewing the members' tickets, when he asked an old lady, "What is the state of your mind?" and received the unexpected and disconcerting answer, "I am not beawn to tell thee." The youthful preacher however soon showed himself a capable man. He was elected to the presidency of the Conference in 1856, acted for twenty-one years as governor of the Institution House at Didsbury, and died in honour at Southport on May 30th, 1866.

Samuel Crompton does not appear to have been a very brilliant or conspicuous man, but the opinion entertained of him by James Montgomery, the poet, is worth preserving. In conversation with the Rev. James Everett, Mr. Montgomery referred incidentally to Mr. Crompton, and continued, "Mr. Everett, I love that worthy man: he is a real hedger and ditcher in the Lord's vineyard, doing the work while others are running away with the praise. His reward will be great."

John Phillips was three years in the circuit. On one occasion, as he was returning from an appointment at Wheatley

Lane, he broke his leg by a fall at the bottom of Greenhead Lane. His place was supplied by William Illingworth, who greatly endeared himself to the societies. In 1833 Mr. Phillips returned to Burnley as a supernumerary, but in 1847 he removed to Southport, where he died on Nov. 17th, 1858, at the ripe age of eighty-eight. His son, Mr. Peter Phillips, was a highly esteemed local preacher; and his grandson, Mr. John W. Phillips, still resides in Burnley.

Philip Garrett was an earnest student of astronomy, and frequently made use of its teachings in his sermons. The dial still to be seen on the Court-house, formerly the chapel, at Keighley Green, was fixed under his direction. It will be noticed that he was in Burnley only one year. For some reason, not now apparent, the leading people did not desire him to be appointed for a second year. When it was understood that he was to leave, a petition to Conference was prepared, asking that his appointment might be renewed. This petition was taken round for signature by Mr. John Nowell. Among other places he visited Higham. After he had succeeded in obtaining a considerable number of names, he proceeded to call upon Henry Wilkinson, "Old Henry," as he was called. The old man listened to what Mr. Nowell had to say, looked at the petition, and at some of the signatures, and then, folding it up and putting it in his pocket, remarked, "We don't want anything of this sort at Higham." Some seventy members were alienated by Mr. Garrett's removal, worshipped for a time in a room in Lane Bridge, and ultimately joined the Free Methodists. The old body however prospered, and the next year reported a slight increase of membership. The wife of Mr. Garrett died in Burnley, and is said to have been buried in the Keighley Green chapel yard—the only burial that ever took place in that ground.

During the ministry of the Rev. Alexander Strachan occurred a revival, which is described by one who witnessed it as "unexampled in the range of its influence and the permanence of its results." Mr. Strachan cannot be characterised as a revivalist. He was a gifted and philosophic expounder of Scripture, fond of Jewish history and of texts from the Prophets, always earnest in a quiet way, but rarely rousing, and with his emotions under strict control. He had moreover in the pulpit a certain peculiarity of manner, generally somewhat diverting but on this particular occasion an addition to the impressiveness of the service. He was in the habit of using a small bible of his own, and when reading discarded his spectacles; but as soon as he had announced the text, he would put his spectacles on, stretch forth his right hand with the forefinger directed towards the front galley, and proceed with great deliberation to open his message. In the spring of 1853 Wesley chapel was one Sunday evening crowded as usual, and the earlier parts of the service proceeded as usual. When the preacher had given out his text, " These shall go away into everlasting punishment, but the righteous into life eternal" (Matt. xxv. 46), he paused, and seemed too full of emotion to proceed. Recovering himself, he took off his spectacles and announced the text again, but could go no farther. With his eyes dim with tears he made a third attempt, with the same result. At length he was able to say, "My friends, when I read out to you my text the first time, there was given me such a vivid and terrible conception of the sufferings of the lost that I was struck dumb." In a moment he added, " I cannot preach, I can only pray that this may not be the doom of any one of us," and sat down. The effect was electrical. "Suddenly there came a sound from heaven as of a rushing mighty wind." The people were stricken down on every side, and the glory of the Lord filled the place. The service was turned into a prayer-meeting; and the good work thus begun continued for many weeks, and extended through the whole circuit. "We have heard with our ears, O God, our fathers have told us, what work thou didst in their days, in the times of old." "Turn thou us unto thee, O Lord, and we shall be turned ; renew our days as of old."

Amongst the converts were included almost all the elder scholars in the Sunday school, men like Mr. W. Tattersall, of Blackburn, and some three or four youths who afterwards entered the ministry,—Peter Hargreaves, W. J. Wilkinson, and G. Latham. William Halstead, too, a doffer in Barnes' factory, had his heart touched, and began to read and think. When the cotton famine came, with his parents he left England for America. There he soon found his way into the ministry of the Canadian Methodist Church, and for many years spent himself in the Christian care of destitute and needy children. Not long ago he visited the scenes of his early life, and showed in himself what personal religion can do for a man, just as in his daily work he shows what a man can do under the inspirations of religion.

In 1859 the Rev. William Bond was stationed at Burnley. In a recent letter he states that Methodism in the town was " even then a strong and flourishing cause, and after its infancy had attained a ripe manhood. In our noble Hargreaves Street chapel, especially on Sunday evenings, we had I should think the largest congregation of any Methodist chapel in the whole of the Manchester district, not excepting Manchester itself." He adds, " I have a vivid and grateful memory of the noble men, who then took a leading and active part in carrying on the work of God in the circuit." Mr. Bond writes with special interest of the two Bible classes he conducted, and of a battle royal between one of the members and an infidel lecturer. The former is described as studious, acute, argumentative. Hearing of the proposed visit of the lecturer, he announced his determination to take up the cudgels, and refused to be dissuaded. When the evening came, the town had been well placarded, and a great assembly gathered in the hall of the Mechanics' Institute. The lecturer spoke for an hour, and members of the audience were invited to reply to him in ten minutes each. Up jumped the young Methodist, protested against the limitation of time, but soon found his minutes gone. When the chairman sought to silence him, the audience cried, "Go on, lad;" and the lad went on. The lecturer thereupon rose, and laid his hand on his opponent's shoulder, when instantly some strong fellows leaped on to the platform, and the next moment the lecturer was thrown headlong into the body of the hall. The police interfered, and gradually the people were persuaded to go home. What became of the lecturer, is not said; but the proposed series of lectures was brought thus to an abrupt conclusion.

The same year witnessed the commencement of a ministry, the like of which in its earlier years has rarely been known. At the June quarterly meeting it was resolved that the services as fourth minister of Peter Mackenzie, who had been accepted by the Conference of the preceding year largely through the pleading of the Rev. William Arthur, and sent to Didsbury for a training that proved impossible, should be secured, if a sum of £250 could be raised to cover the cost of his house and allowances. The amount was carefully apportioned to the various societies, as though the effort to raise it involved deliberation and strain. In six months the total of the subscriptions received was £336 11s. 0d.; and when the year was over, the circuit found itself with £38 10s. 5d. and a houseful of furniture in hand.

Mr. Mackenzie had become known through conducting mission services at Padiham and Barrowford, and preaching at five o'clock in the morning before the district meeting which was held that year in Burnley, and at Park Hill when the evening congregation was so large that an adjournment had to be made from the chapel to a field adjoining. His sermons are described by one who heard him often in Bolton, as "remarkable for their striking originality, but most of all for the unction and power, often overwhelming, which resulted night after night in the conversion of many souls." A gentleman, who claims to have been present at one hundred and thirteen services conducted by Mr. Mackenzie during the year of his residence in Burnley, writes that "his career, so far as popularity as a preacher is concerned, was an ecclesiastical triumphal march from the day he entered the circuit to the day he left": and he adds, "I doubt whether he ever preached, on Sunday or week-night, without the chapel being full."

His work in the circuit commenced a week earlier than usual with a couple of memorable services in connection with the opening of a new schoolroom at Higham on August 28th. The congregations were so large that the panes were taken out of one of the windows, in order that the preacher's voice might reach the people outside; and the heat within was so intense that the preacher doffed his coat, and set to work in his shirt sleeves. On Monday week following his first public appearance as one of the resident ministerial staff took place in Burnley itself, and the congregation reached the abnormal limits for a weeknight of about a thousand people. The Sunday School anniversary at Wesley fell that year on the 2nd of October, and the secretary of the Conference, the Rev. John Farrar, was expected to preach. He however was prevented by sudden illness in his family, and in the emergency the services were distributed amongst the circuit ministers. In the morning the Rev. William Bond preached from Ruth ii. 12; in the afternoon the Rev. G. C. Taylor delivered an address based upon some incidents in the history of Moses; and in the evening the Rev. Peter Mackenzie preached from Eccl. xii. 1. The collections for the day reached the unprecedented amount of £173 12s. 3d. Thus it continued throughout the year. Wherever Mr. Mackenzie preached, crowds were attracted to hear him, crowds followed him from place to place, he was in demand for every anniversary, the excitement and enthusiasm were infectious. The following August 20th, a Monday evening, he conducted his last service in Wesley Chapel as one of its ministers, and it has been said that probably there have never been more people in the chapel at one time than on that occasion. The last services of all were held six days later at Higham, where once more a window had to be taken out, and the preacher stood on the sill and addressed an audience of some two thousand people. He concluded by giving out a hymn that closes with the couplet,

> For, lo! the everlasting Rock
> Is cleft to take us in;

and the congregation took up the words, repeated them again and again, until emotion and endurance were alike exhausted. A few days afterwards the man of great gifts started for his new circuit, Monmouth, bearing with him many a substantial token of goodwill, leaving behind him a people torn with the conflicting feelings of indignation at his removal and gratitude for his consecrated powers.

James R. Berry was the last superintendent of the undivided Burnley circuit. He was just completing his second year of service, had succeeded in arranging a much-delayed scheme of division, and was looking forward to attending the Conference in Hull, and returning for a third year, full of plans for increasing usefulness, when he was seized with typhoid fever, and died on the 19th of July, 1898. He was interred in the cemetery at Burnley.

From the circuit have passed into the ministry, though not in all cases directly, some score of men, who have served their generation well. Philip B. Wamsley was the first, at least in later times. In 1857 he was accepted as a candidate; and when he died in 1886, his brethren in the ministry concurred in the opinion[1] that "sincerity in all the relations of life was a striking feature of his character." His brother, J. Maydew Wamsley, was the next. He had come from a Christian home in Leek, and was apprenticed to a Methodist tradesman in Burnley. Some three years before the revival that commenced under Mr. Strachan's ministry, he consecrated himself to God, and in his own words "felt in duty bound to sever his connection with his old companions who feared not God, resolving to be without a companion unless he could find one who was godly, and who would be helpful spiritually to him. Some eighteen months after, hearing that a youth who was a member of the Wesleyan society had come from Snaith, in Yorkshire, he found him out, and invited him to class. The invitation was accepted, and a lifelong friendship was then formed. In the course of time they were introduced to two other young men, whom they induced to join the same class." All four subsequently entered the Wesleyan ministry. The youth from Snaith is better known as the Rev. George Latham, who was actually sent out by the Doncaster circuit; and the other two were William J. Wilkinson, who after seventeen years' service as a missionary in the West Indies passed into the home-work, and Peter Hargreaves, who again was actually sent out by the Northwich circuit, and has spent his life in effective Christian work in South Africa.

In 1864 John Swain Heap entered the ministry, but retired after a few years' service. The following year Thomas Hargreaves was accepted as a probationer; he died September 12th, 1890, and the record[2] concerning him is, "A beautiful example of Christian virtues: while bold and firm in the maintenance of right principles, he was singularly amiable and conciliatory

---

1. See the obituary notice in *Minutes of Conf.*, 1887, p. 14.
2. See the obituary notice in *Minutes of Conf.*, 1891, p. 17.

in spirit." In 1871 the name of Crawshaw Hargreaves was enrolled; and six years later Robert Matterson entered the ministry of the South African Conference. Preston actually sent him out; but that was because in his modesty he ascribed the good opinion of Burnley to friendship rather than to unbiassed judgment, and determined to put the question to a test in a place where he was comparatively a stranger. The list may be completed by the addition of the names of Samuel Chadwick, whose ministry dates from 1886, and of George H. McNeal, who began ten years later—both of them skilled workmen in regard to the needs and dangers of closely-packed populations.

Of missionary careers few can be compared in quiet thoroughness, or in the value and permanence of the results, with that of Peter Hargreaves. In 1857 he was sent to Clarkebury to work amongst the Tembus, and thenceforward for a dozen years and more may be said to have been almost forgotten. Meanwhile he was teaching the people not only to read and write, but to plough and build, to clothe themselves and make their own tools, and was himself the creating and ruling spirit of a great technical school. In influence he became the chief of the chiefs of the land. When war broke out, and Kreli was ravaging the country with fire and sword, Mr. Hargreaves started with two or three local preachers to stop him. As the missionary drew near to Kreli's encampment, the chieftain in amazement went forth to meet him. "I hunger, Kreli," began the missionary; and the wild passions of the savage were stayed, while he entertained his guest. When the meal was over, Mr. Hargreaves said, "The government of England will be surprised to find you here." Kreli nodded a sullen assent, and the missionary continued, "I am surprised to see you here; Kreli, go home." Mr. Hargreaves withdrew, and so did the Kaffirs at the mere bidding of the upright man in whom they had learned to trust.

Some years after another war was prevented by the intervention of the missionary. He was living at Emfundisweni in Pondoland; and in 1886 the Pondos became restless, and their young men thirsted for blood. The mischief done on the frontiers was so great that the Cape Government mustered a force of several thousand men, and sent to Mgikela, the Pondo chief, an ultimatum requiring him to withdraw his army and discuss conditions of peace within fifteen days. On the last of the days the Pondo chief appealed to Mr. Hargreaves to act as intermediary: and then followed several weeks of intense anxiety, with the Colonial soldiers on the one hand impatient of delay and the natives on the other angry, distrustful, and afraid. It was the influence of Mr. Hargreaves alone

PETER HARGREAVES.

that secured the peaceable settlement of the dispute, saving a tribe from destruction and establishing a just system of border control. A church that has missionaries of that kind can fairly claim to rank amongst the most important factors in the spread of civilisation, and in the promotion of the interests of the race. Mr. Hargreaves is described as showing some of the signs of old age, but as still hale and vigorous, and as not unlikely to extend still further the work in which he has been so long and nobly engaged.

A passing glance at the number of members in the circuit at various times reveals considerable fluctuations. An explanation of some of these can be given.

The decrease in 1815 was due to the separation of Accrington and Oakenshaw from Burnley, to help in forming the Haslingden circuit, of which the other parts were separated from Bury.

When the superintendent was making his return to the Conference of 1818, he wrote in the register with regard to the previous return, "This account of members is incorrect, there being only 625 names entered in the preceding list." It will be borne in mind that it was then a rule for each superintendent to leave a list of the names of the members to whom tickets had been given in June, arranged in their classes, for the use of his successor. These lists have been preserved from 1811 to 1828, when they were discontinued. After each list is a summary. In the summary for the year in question the separate societies are given with the number of members in each, and the total is 640. In this summary Worsthorne appears with 13 members, though the names were not entered in the list, and this Mr. Stamp had not noticed when he wrote the above note.

Shortly after there appears in the register the following letter from Thomas Stanley to his successor: "My dear brother, I went to Leeds Conference with a full expectation of being returned to this circuit a third year. This prevented me, after the June tickets were given, entering the names of every member in this book. I can only now give you the number in each class." This he proceeds to do, making a total of 775; but he adds, "I have returned to Conference 710."

Two further notes on the numbers in the register may here be given. In 1825 the number of the names is 785; the appended note is, "Returned to Conference 720, allowing for school children and contingencies." Next year, 1826, there was a falling off: the names in the list were 745, and in a note the superintendent says that he "returned to Conference the same number as last year, 720." The society was certainly at this time declining, for the following year the return was 650;

but in the two succeeding years the number returned is 1000. This number is suspiciously round, and we are quite prepared to find that the full number of members, who had received tickets, and whose names are recorded, was not returned. There are actually 1109 names in the register, with a note, "Returned to Conference, 1000." This was repeated the following year; and then in spite of the large reserve for contingencies, decreases are reported, till the number appears in 1831 as 824. Several causes contributed in various degrees to cause this decrease. There was possibly a re-action following the 'Great Revival' of 1828; then there was great political excitement in the country in connection with the first Reform Bill, and this was unfavourable to personal religion; and lastly, the agitation carried on by the men who left Methodism on account of the erection of an organ in Brunswick chapel, Leeds, though it did not prevent the growth of Methodism generally, wrought great harm in several localities, of which Burnley was one.

A decrease again of 120 followed the 'Warrenite' agitation in 1836, and another of 271 was sustained in the more calamitous disruption of 1850. In connection with this last disturbance the following resolution, moved by Mr. Samuel Smallpage and seconded by Mr. Butterworth, was carried unanimously at the quarterly meeting, December 27th, 1849:—"That this meeting deeply regrets the unholy and mischievous course which Messrs. Everett, Dunn, Griffiths, and others have pursued, and are still pursuing; cordially approves of the disciplinary acts of the late Conference; and having entire confidence in the wisdom, integrity, and impartiality of our beloved ministers, resolves to support Methodism as it is, and to employ every effort for its preservation and extension." The meeting also directed that this resolution should be inserted in the *Watchman* newspaper. At the next quarterly meeting, March, 1850, as efforts were still being made "to disturb the peace of the body," the representatives felt themselves "called upon to repeat the sentiments expressed in the resolution of the last quarter-day." One more reference to these disastrous incidents occurs in the quarterly meeting Minute book, in Sep., 1850:—"The resolutions of the late Conference having been read by the secretary, it was unanimously resolved that this meeting cordially approves of those resolutions, and hopes that they will be the means of promoting the peace and prosperity of the Connexion."

The next decrease appears in 1861, when the societies at Padiham, Sabden Bridge, Higham, Lowerhouse, and Hapton were formed into a new circuit. A committee to consider this question was appointed in September, 1860, and met on October 8th. The quarterly meeting in December recommended the report of the committee for adoption by the March quarterly meeting. Padiham was to take upon itself the redemption of the minister's house for the benefit of the new circuit, Burnley contributing £100. The amount was not paid for some time, as neither were the Burnley finances flourishing, nor was the new Padiham circuit prepared to entertain a scheme for the purchase of property. At length by the autumn of 1866 the debt on the Burnley current account had increased to £162 17s. 4d. A sum of £301 was raised by subscription. Burnley circuit wrote off its own debt, met its liabilities to Padiham on November 30, 1867, and the two places, associated in Methodist work so long, parted company at last.

At the Conference of 1866 the Rev. Joseph Rippon was appointed to the circuit. He describes it in a letter as "in a very depressed condition, as it had not recovered from the terrible cotton famine, and everything wore a gloomy aspect. It had just given up its fourth preacher," and was generally dull and lifeless. The new superintendent, the Rev. Wilson Brailsford, at once took the debts in hand, and by Christmas announced that sufficient had been promised to clear them off. "Meanwhile," continues Mr. Rippon, "a remarkable revival had commenced in the circuit." Its outbreak occurred on the occasion of his second Sunday evening service in Wesley chapel, when twenty-three persons publicly accepted Christ as their Saviour. "That was the beginning of a revival, which lasted through the whole winter, and extended to nearly every place in the circuit. Nearly four hundred new members were added to the society ; and yet there were no special services, no undue excitement, nor any strangers employed. The whole work was done through the instrumentality of the circuit ministers, ably seconded by a large proportion of the local preachers, leaders, and other members of the church. The second winter was an encouraging and prosperous one, and we were looking forward to similar times of refreshing during the third, but unfortunately our hopes were blighted by the general election of November, 1868. Burnley was a newly created borough, and party spirit was very high. Our leading members were ranged on different sides, and in addition to the absence of unity their minds were completely diverted from the great work of saving souls, so that we had a loss on the year. This was not caused by the falling away of the new converts, but the removal of many from the class books who had ceased to be members in everything but the name."

Finally in 1872 Brierfield, at which a school and chapel had been built in 1859, and which now had a membership of seventy-eight, was transferred to the Nelson circuit.

The following have occupied the office of circuit stewards,

so far as can be ascertained :—

| | |
|---|---|
| 1815. | Thomas Kay. |
| 1825,-26. | E. Pollard. |
| 1828. | Thomas Wood, John Dewhirst. |
| 1833. | James Howorth, Wm. Hopwood, sen. |
| 1836,-37. | Wm. Hopwood, jun., G. Barnes. |
| 1838. | Wm. Hopwood,[1] sen., Jas. Howorth. |
| 1839,-40. | Jas. Howorth, Wm. Hopwood, jun. |
| 1841. | Wm. Hopwood, G. Barnes. |
| 1842. | G. Barnes, John Butterworth. |
| 1844. | John Hargreaves, John Butterworth. |
| 1845. | John Hargreaves, Jas. Howorth. |
| 1846. | W. Hopwood, Jas. Howorth. |
| 1847. | W. Hopwood. S. Smallpage. |
| 1848,-49. | S. Smallpage, John Butterworth.[2] |
| 1850,-51. | J. Butterworth, G. Barnes. |
| 1852,-53. | G. Barnes, Jas. Howorth. |
| 1854. | Jas. Howorth, S. Smallpage. |
| 1855,-56. | S. Smallpage, Wm. Hopwood. |
| 1857. | W. Hopwood,[3] Jno. Barnes. |
| 1858. | John Barnes, James Hopwood.[4] |
| 1859,-60. | John Barnes, John Butterworth. |
| 1861. | John Barnes, Dr. Brown. |
| 1862. | Dr. Brown, Saml. Smallpage. |
| 1863,-64. | Saml. Smallpage, Peter Phillips. |
| 1865. | Peter Phillips, George Howorth. |
| 1866,-67. | George Howorth, John Barnes. |
| 1868. | John Barnes, Adam Dugdale. |
| 1869,-70,-71. | Adam Dugdale, John Howorth. |
| 1872. | John Howorth, William Lancaster. |
| 1873,-74. | William Lancaster, Adam Dugdale. |
| 1875,-76,-77. | Adam Dugdale, John Butterworth. |
| 1878,-79,-80. | John Butterworth, John Thornton. |
| 1881,-82. | John Butterworth, William Lancaster. |
| 1883,-84. | William Lancaster, H. D. Fielding. |
| 1885. | H. D. Fielding, B. Moore. |

---

1. Mr. Hopwood died during the year. At the midsummer quarterly meeting, his son was elected in his place, so that for the second half of the year, the stewards were James Howorth and William Hopwood, jun.

2. John Barnes was elected in December, 1847, but afterwards declined to serve, and John Butterworth was therefore elected in his stead in March, 1848.

3. W. Hopwood, being about to leave the town, resigned, and his son, James, was elected to take his place.

4. James Hopwood resigned, and John Butterworth took his place from June.

1886.     B. Moore, William Nowell.
1887,-88. B. Moore, J. W. Thompson.
1889,-90. J. W. Thompson, John Thornton.
1891.     John Thornton, E. Jones.
1892,-93. E. Jones, James Lancaster.
1894,-95. James Lancaster, John Butterworth.
1896.     John Butterworth, Francis Scowby.
1897,-98. Francis Scowby, T. P. Smith.
1899.     *(Wesley)*—W. T. Fullalove, H. J. Robinson.
          *(Fulledge)*—John Butterworth, Robert Simpson.

A few miscellaneous resolutions of the quarterly meeting may here be given in due chronological order, and will show the various matters in which the meeting interested itself. On March 29th, 1838, it was resolved unanimously, "That it is the opinion of this meeting that the society at Sabden Bridge ought to bring to the quarterly meeting the sum of 2s. 1d. per member according to our rules, and that a letter to that effect be addressed to them." The letter seems to have led to a gratifying improvement; for when, under date March 26th, 1846, it is stated that "Sabden Bridge needed more chapel accommodation," it is added that "in consideration of the very satisfactory manner in which they have exerted themselves, they should be allowed to canvass the circuit for subscriptions, under the inspection of the superintendent, and if they can comply with the conditions of the building committee, they be allowed to proceed with the contemplated erection." Sabden Bridge appears again with a request for enlargement in June, 1849. The quarterly meeting agreed to the proposed enlargement and alterations of the Sunday school, but decided that no application should be made for financial help except in Sabden Bridge, till the debt on the Mereclough chapel had been reduced. Whether the proposed alterations under these conditions were carried out or not, does not appear; but in March, 1860, an enlargement of the school at a probable cost of £200 was agreed to, on condition that there should be no addition to the debt.

On March 26, 1839, it was resolved, "That a committee for carrying out the objects to be advocated at the Centenary meeting consist of the travelling preachers, the circuit and society stewards for town and country, with power to add to their number, and that a public meeting be held in Burnley some time in June." The latter part of this resolution was not adhered to, for at the autumn quarterly meeting, held October 4th, 1839, "it was agreed that at the religious celebration of the Centenary of Wesleyan Methodism, on Friday the 25th of October, a collection be made after preaching in the evening, that a copy of the Centenary volume be presented to each of

G

the local preachers ; that a tea be provided at Burnley (and the same be recommended to the country places) on Saturday afternoon, and that the tickets be sold or given to the members as each may prefer; that Friday, the 11th of October, be observed as a day of special humiliation and fasting, and that prayer meetings be held in each country place at 8 o'clock in the evening, and in as many places as possible at twelve o'clock at noon." A list of persons to be invited to this Centenary meeting, with a *p* to indicate those who were actually present, and *s* to show who at the time were prevented by sickness from attending, is still in existence. The total amount raised by the circuit was £891 10s. 6d., the largest contributions being Mr. William Hopwood £210, Messrs. George Barnes & Sons £100, Mr. Edward, Miss, and Miss Sarah Pollard £100, and Messrs. Spencer and Moore £100. The circuit treasurer was Mr. George Barnes, Jun., and the secretaries Mr. James Howorth and Mr. Henry Kay.

On March 25th, 1847, it was determined to ask for the appointment of a third minister, to reside at Padiham, the circuit pledging itself to provide a house for a married man at the end of four years. In June of the same year, however, the stewards were authorised to engage at once a house that was offered at Padiham, and to purchase furniture at a cost of not more than £100. In September, the stewards were instructed "to borrow £75 on interest toward the furnishing" of this minister's house. From an entry at the Christmas quarter, it appears that the money had been borrowed from the Wesley chapel trustees. Twelve months afterwards, "taking into consideration the present and prospective financial circumstances of the circuit," the meeting earnestly requested the trustees "to present to the circuit the borrowed sum. To this request the trustees acceded at their next annual meeting, and thanks were accorded them for their gift by the quarterly meeting of June, 1849.

On June 22nd, 1848, it was resolved "that petitions from the principal chapels in the circuit be presented to the House of Commons, requesting the closing of public houses on the Lord's Day." More than fifty years have passed, and in greater number than ever the houses are open still.

"In accordance with a resolution of the September quarterly meeting" this year, "a meeting of the local preachers, leaders, and stewards was held in the school-room at 6 o'clock on Friday evening, October 6th. Nearly seventy sat down to tea. The evening was spent in spiritual conversation and prayers. A very gracious influence pervaded the meeting, and all engaged to give themselves afresh to God and His church, and in the performance of that engagement to use every possible prudential effort, each in his sphere, to promote the interests of the Church of God and the conversion of men to Christ. It was good to be there."

On March 30th, 1854, it was resolved "that a memorial to the magistrates against Sabbath-breaking, and other forms of immorality, read by Mr. Strachan, be signed by the ministers and stewards, and duly forwarded."

Under the date of December 29th, 1859, is an entry that recalls old-world usages. An attempt had been made to charge ministers and local preachers with toll in going to and from their appointments on the Lord's day; and the superintendent, having brought the matter by a summons before the magistrates at Burnley, had obtained a decision in favour of exemption. It was unanimously resolved that the best thanks of the meeting be given to Mr. Lawton for the great attention and labour he had paid to the case, and to Mr. Holmes, solicitor, and Messrs. Southern and Ormerod for the legal ability with which they had prepared and presented the case to the magistrates.

Of the liberality of Burnley Methodists and Methodism many notable instances have occurred. About 1875 or 1876 it was decided to raise a fund of £7,000 for circuit extensions. Donations of £1,000 each were at once made by Mr. John Butterworth, of Springfield House, and Miss Barnes, of Spring Hill: and it is not necessary to add that the enterprise was soon brought to a successful issue. In 1878 the trustees of Whittlefield School met in consternation to face a debt of £870, but parted in gratitude and relief, Mr. Butterworth having presented them with a cheque for the whole amount. In April, 1880, when the circuit was feeling somewhat pressed, a little bazaar was held, which realised £584 2s. 7d. The following year a current debt upon the quarterly meeting of £48 was cancelled by the junior steward, Mr. William Lancaster, whilst his colleague, Mr. Butterworth, undertook to pay the cost of furnishing a fourth minister's house. In September another bazaar was designed to complete the scheme of extension, upon which the circuit had entered a short time before. The sum of £1,800 was asked for, but the total proceeds amounted to no less than £2,308 6s. 3d. So the story proceeds. In October, 1890, a bazaar yielded £725 9s. 1d.; and in April, 1894, another produced £1,319 19s. 2d. Whenever in the history of the circuit any well-considered attempt at progress or consolidation has been made, occasionally of course there has been heard a little grumbling, but in the end the funds have been forthcoming and the desired result has been attained.

A document is available from which a general view may be obtained of the capital value and income of the plant of the circuit at a comparatively recent date. On April 9th, 1886, a Trustees' meeting was held, at which Mr. Thomas Nowell presented and read an abstract of the accounts of all the trust estates in the circuit. The estates numbered eighteen, thirteen in the town and five in the country, and included chapels, schools, and minister's houses, all of which were settled on the approved terms of the Connexion. The entire property was valued at £56,959, and the entire debt was only £3,540, or about six per cent of the value, and arrangements were then being made for its gradual extinction. The total net income for the year was £1,959. Pew rents yielded £1,070, including Wesley £465, Fulledge £246, Accrington Road £157, and Colne Road £77. Other income, such as annual collections and rents of houses and schools, yielded £889. The total expenditure, including £204 paid to the quarterly meeting, amounted to £1,247. And the net sum of the balances in the hands of the various treasurers was £810, of which a portion was to be applied forthwith to the reduction of debt on security. It was a balance-sheet at which any man of business might be abundantly satisfied, and which was a clear evidence of the solvency and financial prosperity of the circuit.

The circuit regularly noted the loss of its more prominent members by death or removal, and in the former case its sympathy with the survivors. Thus Mr. William Fishwick was singled out for honour; and at later dates Mr. George Barnes, Mr. Procter in whose memory a tablet was put up in the Wheatley Lane Chapel, Mr. James Howorth, Mr. Thomas Fowler, Mr. Thomas Walmsley, of Padiham, Mr. James Dugdale, and many others. This Mr. Dugdale came to Burnley from Rimmington. He was a local preacher of great pathos and power. The Sunday before his death he had preached at Wesley Chapel on, "Follow peace with all men, and holiness, without which no man shall see the Lord." On the 9th of September, he with James Nowell and others met to have supper together, as a kind of farewell to Philip Wamsley who was going to the Institution. After supper they talked about the best ways of winning souls. During the conversation, Mr. Dugdale complained of sickness and had to retire. Two of the young men carried him home, one remaining till midnight and the other till six in the morning. At nine he passed away.

From 1810 to 1831 the Burnley circuit was in the Halifax district. In the latter year there was a general re-arrangement of districts throughout the Connexion, and Burnley was placed in the newly constituted Bolton district. But four years later, in 1835, the Manchester and Bolton districts were combined into one that was known for more than thirty years by the joint names of both towns. At length it became so large that to facilitate the despatch of business, in 1869, the union was dissolved; and since then Burnley has remained in the Bolton district.

It has not often been that the chairman of the district, in which the circuit was included, has been stationed in Burnley, the earliest instance is that of John Stamp in 1817, and the latest that of Henry Hastling in 1877 to 1880. Only on two other occasions has the honour been given to Burnley: in 1823 when the chairman was Thomas Stanley, and in 1833 when the office was held by Philip Garrett.

The following Tables will show how the new circuit recognized its obligation to the Connexion, and contributed to its funds.

AN ACCOUNT OF THE YEARLY, KINGSWOOD AND MISSIONARY COLLECTIONS FROM THE DIFFERENT PLACES IN THE CIRCUIT FOR THE YEAR 1811.

| Members. | | Yearly. | | | Kingswood. | | | Missionary. | | |
|---|---|---|---|---|---|---|---|---|---|---|
| | | £ | s. | d. | £ | s. | d. | £ | s. | d. |
| 218 | Burnley | 6 | 16 | 3 | 2 | 16 | 0 | ...... | | |
| 120 | Padiham | 3 | 9 | 6 | 1 | 17 | 8 | 2 | 6 | 2 |
| 94 | Accrington | | 13 | 3 | 1 | 2 | 2 | 1 | 0 | 0 |
| 15 | Mereclough | | 5 | 6 | ...... | | | ...... | | |
| 26 | Lowerhouse | | 7 | 0 | ...... | | | ...... | | |
| 9 | Gannow | | 4 | 6 | ...... | | | ...... | | |
| 24 | Higham | | 4 | 6 | | 17 | 0 | ...... | | |
| 16 | Worsthorne | | 2 | 0 | ...... | | | ...... | | |
| 12 | New Laund | | 2 | 3 | ...... | | | ...... | | |
| 50 | Warren Lane | | 7 | 6 | | 8 | 0 | ...... | | |
| 11 | Oakenshaw | | 2 | 3 | | 4 | 2½ | ...... | | |
| 14 | Whalley | | 5 | 10 | | 6 | 6 | | 7 | 0 |
| 609[1] | | 13 | 0 | 4 | 7 | 11 | 6½ | 3 | 13 | 2 |

1. The total number of members in the circuit was 637: Sabden with thirteen and Little Moor End with fifteen, appear to have made no contribution whatever.

In addition to the above there are in the same year records of "Collection for the debt of the Connection, £8 8s. 0d.;" and also "Public collection and private subscriptions for preventing Lord Viscount Sidmouth from carrying his obnoxious Bill into execution, £10 0s. 0d." This Bill was intended to stop the growth of Dissent, and would have been most injurious to the Methodists. Its ministers would have been seriously cramped, and its local preachers, exhorters, prayer-leaders, Sunday school teachers either silenced or thrown into prisons. Petitions were signed and presented against it; and it was ultimately defeated without a division. See Stevens' *History of Methodism*, ii. 147-8, and *Life of Dr. Bunting*, ed. 1887, pp. 342-347.

In succeeding years, the amounts contributed by the circuit as a whole were as follows:—

|  | Yearly. | | | Kingswood. | | | Missionary. | | | Preachers' Fund. | | | Members. |
|---|---|---|---|---|---|---|---|---|---|---|---|---|---|
|  | £ | s. | d. | £ | s. | d. | £ | s. | d. | £ | s. | d. |  |
| 1812 | 14 | 6 | 6 | 8 | 13 | 9½[1] | 18 | 1 | 7½ | 6 | 12 | 0 | 776 |
| 1813 | 17 | 18 | 0 | 13 | 17 | 9 | 27 | 13 | 4[2] | 7 | 4 | 0 | 700 |
| 1814 | 21 | 3 | 6 | 17 | 3 | 4 | 106 | 16 | 9[2] | 8 | 8 | 0 | 726 |
| 1815 | 17 | 0 | 0 | 18 | 14 | 6 | 86 | 18 | 5 | 8 | 5 | 0 | 590 |
| 1816[3] | 20 | 16 | 0 | 32 | 9 | 0 | 109 | 18 | 7 | 10 | 10 | 0 | 635 |

1. Additional for Woodhouse Grove, £17 6s. 6d.
2. Including special contributions or collections.
3. This year appears collection for Contingent Fund, £7 3s. 0d.

After this date the Missionary collections appear to have been paid through circuit and district lay-treasurers, and are recorded in a separate book. The collections in the superintendent's book are continued as follows :—

|  | Schools, &c. | | | Yearly. | | | July (Home Mission and Contingent.) | | | Preachers or Auxiliary. | | | Chapel Fund. | | | Nos. |
|---|---|---|---|---|---|---|---|---|---|---|---|---|---|---|---|---|
|  | £ | s. | d. | £ | s. | d. | £ | s. | d. | £ | s. | d. | £ | s. | d. |  |
| 1817 | 26 | 0 | 0 | 17 | 0 | 0 | 6 | 0 | 0 | 10 | 10 | 0 | …… | | | 640 |
| 1818 | 23 | 4 | 0 | 16 | 3 | 6 | 8 | 8 | 3 | 13 | 16 | 6 | …… | | | 590 |
| 1819 | 22 | 1 | 6 | 20 | 0 | 0 | 5 | 2 | 6 | Not recorded | | | …… | | | 652 |
| 1820 | 22 | 0 | 0 | 18 | 10 | 0 | 5 | 0 | 0 | 13 | 3 | 0 | 5 | 0 | 0 | 662 |
| 1821 | 19 | 18 | 0 | 19 | 0 | 0 | 7 | 10 | 0 | 11 | 13 | 0 | 7 | 0 | 8 | 650 |
| 1822 | 18 | 8 | 0 | 19 | 0 | 0 | 8 | 0 | 0 | 11 | 2 | 0 | 7 | 2 | 0[1] | 670 |
| 1823[2] | 11 | 5 | 8 | 19 | 18 | 0 | 8 | 3 | 0 | 11 | 5 | 6 | 7 | 15 | 6 | 670 |
| 1824 | 13 | 9 | 0 | 18 | 19 | 6 | 7 | 19 | 2 | Not recorded | | | 10 | 1 | 5 | 710 |
| 1825 | 12 | 8 | 0 | 20 | 5 | 0 | 9 | 0 | 0 | Not recorded | | | 10 | 19 | 6 | 720 |
| 1826 | 10 | 2 | 6 | 11 | 14 | 11 | 4 | 3 | 5½ | 5 | 14 | 0 | 7 | 5 | 6 | 720 |
| 1827[3] | 6 | 9 | 0 | 13 | 0 | 0 | 5 | 2 | 6 | 6 | 14 | 0 | 5 | 12 | 0 | 650 |
| 1828 | 6 | 15 | 0 | 15 | 15 | 6 | 5 | 14 | 0 | 6 | 16 | 0 | 7 | 2 | 0 | 1000[4] |

1. Trust subscriptions to Chapel Fund first appear: Burnley, 21s., Padiham, 21s., Higham, 21s.
2. Private subscriptions to connexional Funds first appear:—Chapels (Trustees) £3 5s. 0d., Auxiliary £6 13s. 6d., Schools £7 0s. 0d.
3. The year of great distress.
4. Year of the "Great Revival."

The circuit has always contributed largely to the Foreign Missions of its church. In 1863 the Jubilee of the Missionary Society was celebrated, when a sum of £157,431 11s. 5d. was raised in Great Britain alone. The Burnley circuit contributed £1,273 17s. 3d., the largest donation being £500 by Miss Barnes. In 1878 followed the Thanksgiving Fund of £297,518 3s. 4d., in commemoration of the tranquillity with which a great change in ecclesiastical order had been effected. The Burnley contribution amounted to £2,451 6s. 9d., and included such items as Mr. J. Butterworth and family £1,000, Miss Barnes £500, Mr. J. Howorth £100, Mr. and Mrs. G. Cowgill and family £100, Mrs. Adam Dugdale £100, and the Misses Dugdale £100. What it will do for the still greater Twentieth Century Fund now in course of being raised, has yet to be seen.

The circuit was divided at the Conference of 1898 according to the following scheme.

## WESLEY CIRCUIT.

| Ground Rents. | Debts on Securities. | Members. | Local Preachers. | INCOME. | Class Contributions and Collections. | Trust Contributions. |
|---|---|---|---|---|---|---|
| £ s. d. | £ s. d. | | | | £ s. d. | £ s. d. |
| ...... | ...... | 257 | 8 | Wesley .............. | 228 7 11 | 120 0 0 |
| ...... | 250 0 0 | 283 | 5 | Accrington Road..... | 108 0 7 | 40 0 0 |
| ...... | ...... | 38 | 2 | Park Hill............. | 24 17 1 | 10 0 0 |
| ... - | ...... | 16 | ... | Ighten Hill........... | 9 1 6 | ...... |
| ...... | ...... | 52 | 3 | Lane Bridge ......... | 22 0 11 | ...... |
| ...... | ...... | 5 | ... | Rose Hill ........... | 2 10 11 | ...... |
| 11 17 0 | ...... | 56 | ... | Whittlefield ........ | 28 11 5 | ...... |
| ...... | ...... | 34 | 1 | Wood Top ........... | 10 5 5 | ...... |
| 11 6 2 | 87 10 0 | 47 | 2 | Stoneyholme ........ | 25 14 3 | ...... |
| 17 9 2 | 260 0 0 | 30 | 3 | Piccadilly Road ..... | 14 11 8 | ...... |
| | | | | Int. on Investment... | 32 12 0 | ...... |
| | | | | Deficiency .......... | 10 12 11 | .. .. |
| 40 12 4 | 597 10 0 | 818 | 24¹ | | 517 6 7 | 170 0 0 |

### EXPENDITURE.

| | Present. | Additional in two years. |
|---|---|---|
| | £ s. d. | £ s. d. |
| 3 Ministers............................................... | 490 0 0 | 60 0 0 |
| Assessments² ........................................... | 63 0 0 | |
| Children – special ................................... | 13 13 0 | 2 2 0 |
| House Bills............................................... | 6 2 2 | 3 1 1 |
| Rates and Taxes ...................................... | 24 19 3 | 12 9 6 |
| Furnishing ............................................... | 40 0 0 | 20 0 0 |
| Sundries .................................................. | 16 9 6 | 8 4 9 |
| Ground Rent (Palatine Square) ................ | 3 2 8 | ...... |
| Rent—Padiham Road ... .......................... | 30 0 0 | 30 0 0 |
| | £687 6 7 | 135 17 4 |

Estimated Value of Property £38,443.
This Circuit is pledged to provide a furnished house at the Conference of 1900 at a cost of about £400.
Prospective deficiency—after 1900=£135 17s. 4d. + £10 12s. 11d. = £146 10s. 3d.
1. 6 of whom take no work.
2. Assessments fixed by District Synod. This is five-ninths of the present assessment.

## FULLEDGE CIRCUIT.

| Ground Debts. | Debts on Securities. | Members. | Local Preachers. | INCOME. | Class Contributions and Collections. | Trust Contributions. |
|---|---|---|---|---|---|---|
| £ s. d. | £ s. d. | | | | £ s. d. | £ s. d. |
| ...... | ...... | 269 | 4 | Fulledge ............ | 177 9 0 | 60 0 0 |
| ...... | 450 0 0 | 193 | 5 | Colne Road............ | 99 15 0 | 30 0 0 |
| ...... | 200 0 0 | 56 | 0 | Wheatley Lane ...... | 38 13 8 | 5 0 0 |
| 17 6 6 | ...... | 96 | 6 | Brooklands Road ... | 52 16 8 | ...... |
| 6 14 0 | ...... | 19 | 0 | Mereclough ......... | 8 14 6 | ...... |
| 13 3 0 | ...... | 23 | 1 | Worsthorne ......... | 9 5 9 | ...... |
| | | | | Deficiency ............ | 81 14 5 | ...... |
| 37 3 6 | 650 0 0 | 656 | 161 | | 468 9 0 | 95 0 0 |

### EXPENDITURE.

|  | £ s. d. |
|---|---|
| 2 Ministers ............................................................. | 380 0 0 |
| Assessments[2] ......................................................... | 50 10 0 |
| Children — special ................................................ | 13 13 0 |
| House Bills ............................................................ | 6 2 2 |
| Rates and Taxes .................................................. | 21 17 8 |
| Furnishing ............................................................ | 40 0 0 |
| Sundries ................................................................ | 16 9 6 |
| Ground Rent of Todmorden Road House.. ............ | 4 16 8 |
| Rent of Bank Parade House................................... | 30 0 0 |
|  | £563 9 0 |

Estimated Value of Property £27,104.
1. 3 of whom take no work.
2. Four-ninths of present circuit assessment.

The Wesley circuit possesses also a site (presented by Miss Barnes, and of the estimated value of £790) for a new chapel in Manchester Road, and the Fulledge circuit one adjoining the present school chapel in Brooklands Road. Each circuit also owns the house in which its superintendent resides. The circuits have lived honourably together for three generations, and exerted a notable influence upon the religious and civil life of the town. They are divided now in name only, and not in good-will or helpfulness; loyalty to evangelical truth and method will make the course of each as beneficent as has been the career of the whole.

### KEIGHLEY GREEN CHAPEL.

The leaders in connection with the old chapel when the Burnley circuit was formed in 1810 were:—John Ashworth, Abel Bridge, James Dent, Benjamin Fielding, George Hargreaves, Thomas Kay, William Lancaster, William Moon, James Whitaker, Thomas Whitfield, James Winterbottom.

## EXPENDITURE BY THE STEWARDS.

Leaders' meetings continued to be held, as they had been from 1788, once a fortnight, after the week evening service. At these meetings the leaders paid to the stewards the moneys they had received from their respective classes, and the stewards paid to the preachers the sum that was allowed for their board, reserving what remained for the circuit stewards, who in their turn paid the preacher his quarterage, and met all other expenses that fell on the circuit. These meetings seem to have been well attended for above fifty years. There was an occasional omission on account of some special services in the chapel or a missionary meeting in the country; now and again the entry is simply "no preacher"; and only once or twice did the meeting lapse because no leaders attended.

For some time after the formation of the circuit, the society stewards continued to meet charges which are now always met by the trustees, the reason no doubt being that the latter found it as much as they could do to pay the interest on the debt, and once at least the stewards had to help them with that. The chapel was still cleaned at their cost, the payment being a shilling a week, which was doubled in 1815. Six years later "Susy" Astin appears as cleaner with an allowance of 3s. 6d. per week. In 1824 the trustees after passing a resolution about the pews resolved "likewise that a regular chapel keeper shall be appointed." Whether they proceeded to make the appointment or left it to the society stewards does not appear, but the latter paid him. His name was Henry Goom, and the remuneration five shillings per week. The stewards provided also for the lighting of the chapel, and in 1812 appointed Benjamin Fielding to light the candles and probably also to snuff them for a yearly allowance of thirteen shillings, which three years later was increased to a guinea. In this connection it may be noted that the candlesticks, which were cleaned in March, 1806, at a cost of three shillings, were sixteen years later cleaned again at a cost of eleven shillings and sixpence. Candles continued to be used for ten years after this. It was not till March, 1831, that the trustees resolved that gas should be introduced into the chapel "before another winter." The reader will probably ask, "What about the warming of the chapel?" The answer is that the chapel was not warmed at all. There is no record of any payment for coal till October 15th, 1814. Later entries show that the coal was purchased "for the vestry," and was such as to need for its ignition the application of bellows. On two occasions at any rate bellows had to be provided, the cost being 3s. 4d. in each case.

About the time of the introduction of coals to the vestry, appears another official in the person of Thomas Farrar, who received for some time a quarterly payment of a pound "for playing." On making enquiry of the two members of the choir who survive, we learn that he was the leading singer and played a double-bass. He was very strict in his ideas of female attire. One spring, one of the girls in the choir went so far in the way of adornment as to put a little bow of ribbon on each side of her newly cleaned bonnet. After the morning service the leading singer followed her home, and freely expressed his opinion of her worldliness. At the end of 1825 Thomas Farrar's salary was increased. The society stewards paid him only £2 that year, but added this note, "The school to allow £2, and the chapel trustees £2 in addition, making in all £6 per year."

Soon after Wesley's death there arose a controversy as to the administration of the sacrament of the Lord's Supper, and the holding of service "in church hours" in Methodist chapels. The Colne circuit sent from its quarterly meeting, held at Padiham, July 9th, 1795, a letter (see pp. 39, 40), in which among other things it was stated, "We have not the Lord's Supper administered, or preaching in church hours, in any of our chapels, nor do we at present desire it." The "Plan of Pacification," by which the controversy was settled, was accepted in 1797: and it was not until 1815 that the following communication was sent to the Conference from Colne—"To the Methodist Conference: The trustees, stewards and leaders at Colne unanimously request to have the Sacrament of the Lord's Supper. William Midgeley." The request was endorsed: "Granted. Barber." William Midgeley was the superintendent of the Colne circuit, and John Barber the President of the Conference for the second time in 1815. This document was "sealed to the back of the circuit book, September 9th, 1815, by his [Midgeley's] successor, Thomas Vasey." The same year a similar application to Conference seems to have been made from Burnley: for the society stewards on the 6th of May, 1816, paid 5s. for "two books for the Sacrament."

A few other interesting entries from the stewards' book of this period may be given : " for yard mowing, 4s. 6d. "; "for cleaning snow, 2s."; these occur only once each in the thirty-eight years over which the accounts extend. The following also is found but once, "bad money in the collection, 4s. 7d."

In the year 1810, the society stewards seem to have had some suspicion that the candles were disappearing more rapidly than might be expected, if their disappearance was caused by legitimate consumption. They therefore had a lock placed on the candle box, at a cost of 8d. Whether this lock was found defective, or was tampered with, does not appear, but two years later another had to be provided. The suspicions may not have been groundless, as witness the following entry in the beautiful handwriting of William Fishwick: "Paid for redeeming the old chapel bible which was stole (sic) from the vestry by —— and pledged with the pawnbroker in Bridge Street, 6s." Soon after to ensure the safety of the books and other articles, a lock was placed on the cupboard at a cost of half-a-crown.

In 1826 dark days came to the town. Within two years before, above four hundred new houses had been built, and the town was considered fairly prosperous. But now its prosperity was rudely checked. First of all occurred the failure of Holgate's Bank, and several manufacturers and shop-keepers were ruined. Then came a long-continued drought. In 1826 no rain fell from the beginning of March to the end of September; a hot sun shone every day, and as there were no reservoirs, the mills, which were driven by water power, were compelled to stop, the weavers were without work, and there was practically a famine in the town.

Sir Walter Scott in his Journal thus refers to the great heat of this year, the stoppage of the mills, and the consequent distress. "Nov. 23rd. Breakfasted at Birmingham, and slept at Macclesfield. As we came in between ten and eleven, the people of the Inn expressed surprise at our travelling so late, as the general distress of the manufacturers has rendered many of the lower class desperately outrageous. The people talk gloomily of winter, when the distress of the poor will be increased. Nov. 24. Breakfasted at Manchester. We again pressed on, and by dint of exertion reached Kendal to sleep: thus getting out of the region of the stern, sullen, unwashed artificers, whom you see lounging sultrily along the streets of the towns in Lancashire, cursing it would seem with their looks the stop of trade, which gives them leisure, and the laws which prevent them employing their spare time."

During this year the celebrated "Sammy" Hick, who had retired from his business as a blacksmith, and had given himself entirely to evangelistic work, came to the town, and remained some three months, preaching in Burnley and the surrounding villages. Mr. Lancaster, then a boy, went with him to Mereclough, where he preached from "Rejoice evermore." One day, having been supplied with some money by Mr. Hopwood, he went out to relieve the suffering poor. On his return, having distributed all that he had, he exclaimed, "Master, I could have done with much more." Another day, whilst he was out on his errand of mercy, he saw a boy eating some potato peelings from a heap of rubbish, and another attempting to satisfy the cravings of hunger with the grains that had been thrown out of a brew-house. His sympathetic heart was deeply moved, and he asked, "Is there no one with any money in the town?" He was told the manufacturers and shopkeepers were in great distress but that there was one wealthy gentleman who was able to help, but was a Roman Catholic, and might not be willing to give at the request of a Protestant. 'Sammy,' nothing daunted, set out for Towneley Hall alone. He reached the Hall, rang the bell, and was met by a smart footman, who asked his business. "Are you Mr. Towneley?" asked Sammy. "No," answered the footman, "go into that room, and I will send him to you." When Mr. Towneley entered the room, he was so plainly dressed that Sammy had to ask, "Are you Mr. Towneley?" When he was assured he was in the presence of the gentleman he had come to see, he told him his business, described the distress of the town, and pointed out the need of immediate help. The result of the interview was that a committee was formed, and a subscription list opened, which Mr. Towneley headed with a gift of £150. Meal, bacon, and potatoes were bought and distributed, many families relieved, and doubtless a considerable number of people saved from death.[1]

Another characteristic story is told of Sammy during his sojourn in Burnley. He was visiting in Sandygate. Finding in one of the houses a woman who had evidently met with an accident, he said to her, "Bairn, what's t' matter wi thi arm?" She told him she had bruised it; on which he said, "Tha mun fin t' good Physician an' t' balm of Gilead, if tha wants to be cured." Continuing he added, holding up his thumb, "Looks ta hëar; aw bruised this i't' stiddy: t' doctor sed it wod ha' to come off. One day he browt his instruments to tak it off. Aw went up t' stairs, an' aw sez, 'Lord, this is thy member, this is thy member; what mun aw do with it?' Then aw went doon, an' aw sez to t' doctor, 'Tha can tak' thi instruments away; it's goin' to stop on', an' hëar it is."

To return to the financial position of the Keighley Green society, it is not at all surprising to find that its contributions to the circuit funds had to be reduced, and that, in spite of this reduction and a special effort which realised £15 1s. 0d., the stewards found themselves with a balance against them of £36 19s. 1½d. at the end of 1826. The income of the society fell by almost twenty-five per cent. in three years, from £207 11s. 7d. in 1824 to £155 17s. 8d. in 1826.

After this year, the charges paid by the society stewards for the trustees gradually declined in number, and in a little while finally ceased. Candles for the year 1827 cost £6 1s. 6½d.

---

1. See *The Village Blacksmith*, by James Everett, pp. 119, 120. The same book contains several other stories of Hick's visits to Burnley and the neighbourhood.

The chapel-keeper appears to have been paid to the end of 1828, when with his brushes, dusters, and sundries he disappears from the accounts. The last payment for candles was in December, 1828, and for coals March 2nd, 1829, and the trustees on the 19th February resolved "to defray the expenses of lighting and cleaning the chapel for the ensuing year." The last payments made by the society stewards, which should properly have been made by the trustees, were for a new Bible and Hymn Book, £2 12s.; for a new Register Book, 16s.; and to Mr. Owen for writing over again the Register of Baptisms, £1. These payments are entered in the accounts of 1837.

Thomas Farrar continued to be the leading singer till 1834, and then followed in quick succession Mr. Bracewell, Mr. Hartley, Mr. James Lord and Mr. J. Whitham. About the year 1837, stringed musical instruments seem to have been introduced into the choir, and the cost of keeping these in repair fell on the society stewards. There are several entries referring to these repairs, and to the purchase of bows and strings, a bow for the smaller instrument costing 4s. 6d. and for the largest £1 12s. 0d. It may be considered worthy of note that one steward writes of 'fiddles,' where his predecessor spoke of 'violins.'

The first society stewards were Thomas Driver and Christopher Hartley, who were appointed (see page 60) by Charles Atmore in December, 1788. No change was made till September 25th, 1815, when Christopher Hartley was re-elected, with William Fishwick "as joint steward," and the accounts were henceforth kept by the latter gentleman. At the time of Mr. Fishwick's appointment occurred the first audit of the society's accounts; the certificate reads, "The above accounts have been regularly examined, and settled to this day, and the balance paid into the hands of the circuit steward, as above. Burnley, 2nd November, 1815. Examined by us, William Leach, William Fishwick." The balance was £35 13s. and was paid to Thomas Kay "for furniture for preacher's house." Thomas Kay being the first mentioned circuit steward. Mr. Fishwick retired from the stewardship at the end of 1827, his last entry being dated 25th February, 1828, "Cash received from new stewards, being amount collected by them for that purpose, £14 0s. 1½d. Settled, William Fishwick." The following is a list of the society stewards from the beginning to nearly the middle of the century:—

1789. Thomas Driver, Christopher Hartley.
1815. Christopher Hartley, James Winterbottom.
1816. William Fishwick, James Winterbottom.
1821. William Fishwick, James Howorth.
1828. William Hopwood, Junr., James Smallpage.

1830. James Smallpage, John Arminson.
1831. William Chaffer, J. Arminson.
1832. J. Arminson, Joseph Hargreaves.
1833. J. Hargreaves, George Barnes.
1834. George Barnes, Samuel Smallpage.
1835. Samuel Smallpage, John Butterworth.
1836. J. Whitworth, John Butterworth.
1837. John Butterworth, Peter Phillips.
1838. John Arminson, Henry Kay.
1839. George Barnes, Henry Kay.
1840. G. Barnes, John Whitworth.
1841. James Smallpage, J. Whitworth.
1842. J. Smallpage, John Barnes.
1843. J. Barnes, S. Smallpage.
1844. S. Smallpage, Joshua Lord.
1845. J. Lord, H. D. Fielding.
1846. H. D. Fielding, Peter Phillips.
1847. James Smallpage, Oates Sagar.

In the early part of its history, the society does not seem to have appointed any stewards for the poor. The only references to money for the poor are on the cover of the first society stewards' book, 25th April, 1803, the sum being 4s.; and on the 29th of August, 7s. 1d. The probability is that the money contributed at the lovefeast was distributed amongst the needy members by the leaders at its close. This was at least at that time the practice at Colne.

Immediately after the formation of the circuit, attention was paid to the Keighley Green trust. No minute book seems to have been kept before, or indeed for several years afterwards. Whether the deed required the trustees to meet annually or not, cannot be determined; but there is no reference to any meeting from the formation of the trust in 1788 to October 24th, 1811. The proceedings on this occasion are recorded in the superintendent's Register; and those of some later meetings, invariably signed by the superintendent, in the Seat-Rent book. No trace of any other book can be found; and as a matter of fact there was no need for one, since the society stewards, as we have seen, made the payments usually made by the trustees.

The original trustees of the Keighley Green chapel were:—Robert Riding, Jeremiah Spencer, John Ashworth, William Pollard, William Lancaster, Christopher Hartley, John Eltoft, Richard Bertwistle, John Farrer, Thomas Driver, Joseph Marshall, William Kay, Benjamin Booth, John Tuble, James Wood, John Wood, and John Nuttall. The deed was made between them and John Dewhirst.

The first recorded meeting of the trustees was in 1811,

and was held principally for the renewal of the trust. The record is—"We, Robert Riding, John Ashworth, Christopher Hartley, John Eltoft, William Kay, John Tuble, James Wood, John Wood, and John Nuttall, the major part of the trustees appointed by a trust deed for the Methodist chapel in Burnley in the county of Lancaster, bearing date the 16th day of July, 1788, and enrolled in his Majesty's high court of Chancery, have this 24th day of October, 1811, unanimously elected, chosen, and appointed Thomas Eloft (*sic*), of Burnley in the said county, cotton manufacturer, to be trustee in the place and stead of William Lancaster, deceased. Also Thos. Kay, cotton manufacturer, of Burnley, aforesaid, to be trustee in the place and stead of Joseph Marshall, deceased. Also William Hopwood, of Burnley aforesaid, joiner, to be trustee in the place and stead of Thomas Driver, deceased. Also John Moore of Burnley, aforesaid, dealer and chapman in flour, etc., to be trustee in the place and stead of Benj. Booth, withdrawn from the said society and resigned. In manner and form as is required by and according to the tenor and effect of the said deed, as witness our hands the day and year above written." Then follow the names of twelve "old trustees" and five "new trustees." It will be noticed that only four new trustees were appointed in 1811. The fifth name seems to have been added in 1812, when a trustee who was not present at the first meeting resigned. Appended to the above entry is the following: "I, Wm. Pollard, resign my trust to Mr. Edward Pollard. Aug. 23, 1812."

The next meeting of which a record has been preserved was held in the vestry on the 4th of March, 1819, when "it was thought proper to appoint Thomas Farrer (preacher)[1] to superintend and collect the moneys arising from the bottom pews; and in order to facilitate and establish a regular mode of managing them," it was "likewise ordered that John Farrer" should assist him until a proper system is attained.

From the minutes of the meeting held on February 22nd, 1821, we learn the cost of the sittings in the gallery. The gallery, it should be observed, was considered the most desirable part of an old Methodist chapel; the floor was either almost or altogether free. The prices fixed by the trustees were "fronts and second sittings 2s. each, thirds 1s. 8d., fourths 1s. 7d., fifths 1s. 3d." At the same meeting it was decided that "the chapel should be whitewashed, and afterwards well cleaned,

---

[1] The addition of the word 'preacher' was to distinguish the Thomas Farrer from the official of the same name who played the bass viol and led the singing. They were colloquially distinguished as 'preacher Tommy' and 'fiddler Tommy.'

and a person paid, so as to enable such person to keep it regularly clean." It will be remembered that the first who 'cleaned' the chapel had a remuneration of four pence per week; this was raised to sixpence, and then to a shilling. The trustees did not fix the amount that was to be paid, as they did not pay it; but the society stewards paid Susy Astin 3s. 6d. per week for this work.

At their meeting on February 1st, 1822, Mr. William Hopwood was appointed treasurer. It was also agreed that "a couple of pews" should be made in the bottom of the chapel on the south side of the pulpit, and that blinds should be provided for the bottom windows. Up to this time the floor of the chapel had evidently been supplied only with 'forms,' whether with or without a supporting rail for the back does not appear.

In the minutes of the meeting held February 27th, 1824, there is a further reference to the price of sittings, to the placing of pews in the body, and to other matters tending to the comfort of the worshippers. It was then determined also that the two corner pews in the gallery were to be let at six shillings a quarter. Three pews were ordered to be made opposite the pulpit steps, and eight under the front gallery; each side of the bottom floor was to be boarded, a spout made and put up at the back part of the chapel, and "a regular chapel keeper appointed." This first "regular chapel keeper" was named Henry Goom, and was paid by the society stewards at the rate of five shillings a week (see page 105).

There is no hint of any other meeting till the 21st of February, 1828, when Messrs. James Howorth and John Hargreaves were appointed "joint stewards of the trust concern." Mr. Hopwood was authorised to improve the entrance into the chapel yard, and make "a fence sufficient to mark the boundaries of the trust land now unenclosed at the front gates;" and Mr. William Pollard was empowered to "conclude the purchase of the house adjoining the chapel from the assignees of Christopher Hartley upon the best possible terms."

At the meeting held on February 19th of the following year the stewards were re-appointed, the trustees took upon themselves to defray the expenses of lighting and cleaning the chapel, and increased the rent of the superintendent's house from £8 to £16 a year. The following concise record of the decisions of the meeting held March 4th, 1831, may be given in full. "Agreed at a trustee meeting that John Hargreaves and William Fishwick be re-elected as stewards. Empty pews and aireay (sic) to be attended to. William Moon's preaching at all not approved of. The alterations to be done as early as possible. Painting and repairs to be attended to. Gas to be introduced before another winter. All the deeds to be examined into. The stewards with Mr. Hopwood to attend to the above. A subscription to be entered into to defray the whole expenses."

The particulars of the next and last recorded meeting of the trustees are contained in the register of the deeds of the circuit. The meeting was held in the vestry of the chapel on Monday, October 29, 1838. Three of the original trustees, William Pollard, Christopher Hartley, and John Farrer, were present, with two appointed by a lost deed of 1816, William Fishwick and Edward Pollard, and the superintendent, the Rev. James Heaton, in the chair. The principal business was the appointment of new trustees, and the following were chosen—William Fishwick, John Spencer, William Hopwood, William Pollard, Edward Pollard, William Winterbottom, John Hargreaves, Henry Kay, John Moore, George Fishwick, James Howorth, John Robinson Kay, George Barnes, John Butterworth, Thomas Hudson, Joshua Lord, and David Shuttleworth. Since it had been resolved in September, 1837, to build a new chapel as soon as fifteen hundred pounds were raised, it is probable that this final renewal of the Keighley Green trust was made in view of the sale of the chapel and the erection of another.

A Sunday school was opened in connection with the Burnley society soon after the formation of the circuit. These schools were now rapidly springing up in various parts of the country. The first connected with Methodism was established at High Wycombe in 1769 by Hannah Ball, who afterwards became the wife of the Rev. Samuel Bradburn. Possibly schools of the same sort were commenced at other places, but it was Robert Raikes of Gloucester, who first brought the subject before the public in the *Gloucester Journal* of November 3rd, 1783. John Fletcher began one at Madeley in 1784; three hundred children were soon gathered together, and Fletcher himself acted as superintendent until a week before his death. Wesley's first notice of these schools occurs in his Journal under the date of July 18th, 1784: "I preached morning and afternoon in Bingley church . . . Before service I stepped into the Sunday school, which contains two hundred and forty children, taught every Sunday by several masters, and superintended by the curate. . . . I find these schools springing up wherever I go. Perhaps God may have a deeper end therein than men are aware of. Who knows but some of these schools may become nurseries for Christians?"

Again under the date of April 16th, 1786, he records that he preached at Bolton. "The house was crowded the more because of five hundred and fifty children, who are taught in our Sunday schools. Such an army of these got about me when I came out of the chapel, that I could scarce disengage myself from them." Under the date of July 27th, 1787, he writes: "Thence we went to Bolton. Here are eight hundred poor children taught in our Sunday schools by about eighty masters, who receive no pay but what they are to receive from their Great Master. About a hundred of them (part boys and part girls) are taught to sing; and they sang so true, that, all singing together, there seemed to be but one voice. . . . In the evening, many of the children still hovering round the house, I desired forty or fifty to come in and sing 'Vital spark of heavenly flame.' Although some of them were silent, not being able to sing for tears, yet the harmony was such as I believe could not be equalled in the King's chapel." Of Sunday, April 20, 1788, he writes: "At eight and at one the house [at Bolton] was throughly filled. About three I met between nine hundred and a thousand of the children belonging to our Sunday schools. I never saw such a sight before. They were all exactly clean, as well as plain, in their apparel. All were serious and well behaved. Many, both boys and girls, had as beautiful faces as I believe England or Europe can afford. When they all sung together, and none of them out of tune, the melody was beyond that of any theatre; and, what is best of all, many of them truly fear God, and some rejoice in His salvation." In a letter to the Rev. Charles Atmore, dated March 24th, 1790, he writes: "I am glad you have set up Sunday schools in Newcastle. This is one of the best institutions which have been seen in Europe for some centuries, and will do more and more good, provided the teachers and inspectors do their duty. Nothing can prevent the success of this blessed work, but the neglect of the instruments. Therefore be sure to watch them with all care, that they may not grow weary of well-doing."

The general practice was for the schools to begin at one o'clock, the children being taught the three $r$'s—"reading, writing and religion." At three they were taken to their respective churches, then conducted back to school, where a portion of some useful book was read, a psalm sung, and the whole concluded with a form of prayer composed and printed for that purpose. Boys and girls were kept apart; the masters were mostly pious men, and were paid from one to two shillings a Sunday for their services according to their respective qualifications. Each had a list of his scholars' names, which he was required to call over every Sunday at half past one and half past five.

But it was not always that the children were welcomed in the church. When the first Sunday school in Rochdale was formed in 1784, Mr. James Hamilton marched his three hundred and twenty children in procession to the Parish church.[1] The beadle met them at the door, and refused to admit them. James Hamilton told him that it was a Sunday school, and must be admitted. At this the beadle was enraged, and got ready the hand-cuffs. One of Hamilton's assistants then took to his heels, and ran down the one hundred and twenty-two steps by which the church is approached; but Hamilton stood his ground. Thereupon the beadle shut and locked the door, and ran to tell the vicar that two men had brought a lot of dirty children that they called a Sunday school, and were determined to get them into the church, and that he was determined to keep them out. The vicar, evidently somewhat puzzled, said, "Put them in some corner out of sight."

It is supposed that at the beginning of the century there were not less than two hundred thousand children receiving instruction in the Sunday schools of the country. In this district Bolton and Rochdale led the way; Blackburn followed in 1787, and Burnley in all probability shortly after. No exact account of the method pursued in the Burnley schools has been preserved, but it cannot have differed greatly from the plan followed elsewhere.

The Methodists opened their first Sunday school in a hired room in Exmouth Street, Lane Bridge, in November, 1811; and this school was the first in the town, in which the teachers were not paid. The scholars, of whom the late Mr. John Butterworth was one, were taken every Sunday to the service at Keighley Green Chapel.

It will have been observed that writing was one of the things taught in these schools. At that time the school days of children were very few. They began to go to the mills at a very early age, and they remained at their work from early morning till late at night. Boys had then few opportunities of learning, except such as were afforded by the Sunday school; and it was considered a great boon to teach them on the Sabbath day to read and to write. But this question of writing soon gave rise to a very warm contention. Dr. Bunting was strongly opposed to it, and many ministers refused to preach the "Charity Sermons" unless the practice of teaching writing was discontinued. The Rev. Philip Garrett was asked to secure a man to preach the school sermons at Rochdale in 1821; and writing,[2] evidently from Conference, he says, "I waited on Mr. Newton yesterday; he wanted me to present his respects to you, and to inform you that he would have

---

1. See *Strange Tales*, by John Ashworth, p. 251.
2. This letter is in the possession of Mr. John Howorth, of Park View.

endeavoured to have met your desires, but for one circumstance, viz., your teaching writing on the Sabbath day. He absolutely denies every application, where writing is taught on the Lord's day." Conference finally pronounced against the practice, as a breach of the fourth commandment. It was held that while it was clearly a religious duty to teach children to read, that they might have access to the word of God, it was just as clearly a secular duty to teach them to write.[1] Some years however passed after the decision of the Conference on the subject had been given, before the practice was entirely discontinued.

Soon after the formation of the Sunday school in Exmouth street, the premises at Keighley Green were enlarged by the erection of a Sunday school. We are indebted to a paper written by the late Mr. James Howorth, and published in a little journal called "The Reporter," for April, 1842, for the following particulars. The building was commenced in the spring of 1812, and completed on the 28th of February, 1813. The country was then engaged, as it had been more or less for five and twenty years, in a continental war, so that building materials were very costly, and the erection of such premises as were deemed desirable was attended with a large outlay. The entire cost of the premises, inclusive of furniture and apparatus, was above £1,600. An appeal was made to the public for help, and gentlemen of all creeds subscribed, Mr. P. E. Towneley giving £30. Still only a little over £500 was raised, and two-thirds of the outlay, according to the easy habits of those days, was allowed to remain as a debt. The deed was dated February 21st, 1814.

Mr. John Ackroyd, a local preacher, appears to have taken a leading part in the organisation of the schools on the new system of voluntary and unpaid teaching. In this work he was supported by many willing helpers, and especially by Mr. William Fishwick. Other active workers in the school were Mr. James Howorth, Mr. Hopwood, Mr. John Hargreaves who kept the Old Brewery, and Mr. William Chaffer. There were at that time four superintendents in each school-room, who attended, with a sufficient staff of teachers, in rotation, each once in four weeks. Outside the school, a large sign-board was hung up, with the inviting inscription, "Sunday school for children of all denominations."

For twelve or fourteen years writing was taught in this

---

1. The resolution to that effect is emphasised in the Minutes of 1823 by an unusual *nota bene*, "This minute was passed by an unanimous vote of the Conference." In 1873 the principles on which Sunday schools should be conducted were formulated by the Conference, and the seventeenth reads, "Neither the art of writing, nor any branch of merely secular knowledge, shall be taught on the Lord's day."

school on the Lord's day in what was called the "Sand Class." Paper was very dear, being about a shilling a quire, and every possible economy had perforce to be practised. Fine sand was therefore obtained and placed in long, shallow boxes, which, when the surface had been made smooth, served in place of a copy book. With a pointed iron rod or piece of wire, the scholars copied the letters that were held up by the teacher on a card in front of the class. After the letters thus formed had been examined, the writing was easily erased, and the surface smoothed again for further use by running over it a ruler or piece of wood. These sand classes were probably conducted in many of the schools of the neighbourhood. References to them have been met with at Honley, Huddersfield, and Heywood, where the sand is said to have been obtained from the neighbouring churchyard, and to have been spread out on a flat stone.

The earliest Minute book of the Sunday school committee has been lost; and it is not until 1823 that any further details of its arrangements can be confidently described. In December of that year, the library was commenced; and in 1826 the plan of monthly teaching was rejected in favour of a plan according to which all the teachers were to attend every week, or at least every fortnight. In the same year it was resolved "to discontinue the practice of teaching writing on the Sabbath day, and to substitute a week-day evening for the same purpose." This was carried out without delay, the boys being assembled each Saturday and the girls each Monday evening for instruction in writing. The Saturday evening was chosen for the boys, because on that day the mills closed at six o'clock. About this time paper was provided instead of sand, and quill pens in place of the iron rods, and the time of one man was entirely taken up in making and repairing these pens. Mr. W. Witham, for long one of the town missionaries, became a scholar in 1825, and says that it was Mr. Thomas Riding who taught him and other boys to write. About the same time the custom of having a prayer meeting in the school every fifth Sunday was established. In 1830 the present Lesson system was introduced into the school, and the following year the first attempt was made to combine all the Wesleyan Sunday schools throughout the circuit into a Union.

The schools prospered and were well supported from the beginning. Up to 1834 the collection at the anniversary amounted only on a single occasion (1815, when the Rev. Richard Reece was the preacher) to £100, but the annual average to that date was no less than £76 11s. In 1831 the teachers numbered thirty-four, with an increase of two the next year, and the scholars 508, with a corresponding increase of forty-five. The population of Burnley is estimated as having been at that time about one-eighth of its present number, and it is obvious that a fair proportion of its children and young people were under religious instruction at Keighley Green.

The attention of the Methodists was early directed to the value and need of Day schools. The first action was taken on December 26th, 1834, when a deputation was appointed by the School committee to visit Liverpool with a view "to collect information in reference to the establishment of week-day schools." Accordingly the deputation waited on Mr. John Davies, the teacher of the Jordan Street school, Liverpool, who gave them all necessary information and urged them to proceed with their intention. An infant school was thereupon added to the other premises at a cost of about £300; and in June 1835 the day schools were opened. The first teachers were Mr. Thomas Owen for the boys, Miss Johnson for the girls, and Miss Lewis for the infants. The charges were 1½d. a week for each boy or girl, and 2d. for each infant. In 1842 the number of scholars in the Day school was 395, whilst in the Sunday school there were 649. At that time there was no Government grant, the income being derived entirely from the school pence and an annual collection. The cost of the school in 1841 was £240 9s. 10d., and the collection at the anniversary was £126 2s., the preacher being the Rev. G. B. Macdonald. The Day and Sunday schools were both worked financially from a common fund, which was rarely allowed for long to be inadequate for its purposes.

In 1836, a Sick Society was established for the benefit of the scholars, the contributions of the members being 1d. per week, and the allowance in case of sickness 4s. per week; and so great was its popularity that, at the end of six years, it reported 143 members in its books, with an accumulation of £35 7s. 0d. in the bank.

The annual missionary meetings at Keighley Green, dating from about 1817, were great events. The Methodist employers closed their mills either at noon that their people might get to the sermon which was preached in the afternoon, or at least soon after tea, that they might be in good time for the meeting in the evening. On such occasions the chapel was crowded, for a returned missionary was generally expected to speak, or a converted chief of some wild tribe to tell of what had been done by the Gospel in his land, and to exhibit the gods which his people had been accustomed to worship. Two men, however, who had not been missionaries were always sure to draw large congregations, Robert Newton and "Billy" Dawson. People used to come for many miles, and, as there were no public conveyances, they had to make use of their own, which were generally put up at the Bull, the best place of entertainment in what was then but a small country town. Seeing so many conveyances about the inn one day in 1828, someone said to the ostler, "What's all this about?" "Nay," said the ostler, "I'm lost with this lot; but I believe the Methodists have got so much religion that they are going to export some of it." This was told to Newton and Dawson, and it gave them both a good text for their speeches in the evening.

The Sunday evening prayer meetings were always a great institution in connection with Keighley Green. It was found that many people who would not attend public worship could be got into a cottage. At the close of the service, which began at six o'clock, bands of "prayer-leaders" used to go to different parts of the town, and hold meetings, wherever a house was placed at their disposal. The following is a copy of a printed notice, now in the possession of Mr. William Lancaster, which was read out at the chapel every Sunday in the year 1830. "Prayer meetings to commence at 8 o'clock this evening will be held at the following places: viz., Foundry Street, Peter Hargreaves'; Gannow, Thomas Halsteads'; Pickup Croft, John Balderstone's; Exmouth Street, Ann Hutton's; Thorney Bank, James Herd's; Cable Street, George Tattersall's; Burnley Lane, Thomas Boothman's; St. James's Street, John Nowell's; Dawson's Square, James Spencer's; Union Street, Mary Ingham's; near Rake Head, Benjamin Bell's; Curzon Street, Sarah Simpson's; and in the chapel vestry." Dr. Bunting and other leading ministers regretted the gradual giving up of these cottage prayer meetings; and the superior benefit that was anticipated from one united meeting in the chapels has not been secured.

## WESLEY CHAPEL.

The Keighley Green chapel was used continuously for over half a century. At length the congregation had so completely out-grown it, that a new and larger one was absolutely necessary. The quarterly meeting, held September 25th, 1837, at which the matter was first formally discussed, declared its approval of the project, but resolved that it should not be commenced until the sum of fifteen hundred pounds was actually raised. In June, 1838, a plot of land in Hargreaves-street was purchased of Mr. Waddington[1] for £510 16s. 0d. The site had previously been used as a drying ground, the posts upon it being the property of Mrs. Coates. Concerning the choice of this site an interesting story is told. Mr. James Howorth, at

---

1. The agreement for sale is dated September 25th, 1837, the day of the quarterly meeting just referred to. The deeds are dated February 14th, 1839, and May 2nd, 1840.

that time a provision dealer in St. James' Street, had built himself "a house in the country." The house was the one now occupied as offices by Messrs. J. Sutcliffe & Sons in Hargreaves Street, and before it and on either side fields stretched uninterruptedly. When Mr. Howorth gave up this house, it was taken by the circuit for the superintendent minister, and so used for many years. One Sunday afternoon Mr. William Hopwood was taking tea at Mr. Howorth's house, when the conversation drifted, as was then usual, to the subject of the site of the proposed chapel. Mr. Howorth, seeking to elicit Mr. Hopwood's opinion, asked where the chapel was to be built: and Mr. Hopwood in reply immediately pointed through the side window to the plot on which the chapel now stands, and said, "That is the place." The suggestion was adopted; and its wisdom has been sufficiently proved. The arrangements however progressed slowly, the death of Mr. William Hopwood, one of the trustees, and the depressed state of trade interfering with the project. In the autumn the society and the town were carefully canvassed for subscriptions, and the promises were so large that it was resolved to proceed with the building at once. Mr. Simpson, of Leeds, who was then engaged in the erection of chapels at Keighley, Boston, and York, was selected as the architect, and the following, among other tenders, were accepted for the work:—for the stone work, Messrs. R. Smith & Sons, £1,145; for timber work, Mr. Robinson, £1,800; for plastering and painting, Messrs. Radcliffe & Sons, £226 5s. 0d; and for plumbing and glazing, Mr. Lancaster, £279 12s. 6d. On Good Friday, March 29th, 1839, in the presence of more than five thousand people, the foundation stone was laid by Mr. Wm. Fishwick, who died in the same year on the 26th of December.

As the work proceeded, it was found that the site was hardly large enough, and more than one addition seems to have been made, including a plot bought of Mr. Hamerton for £74 17s. 4½d. At length on Friday, July 17th, 1840, the building, which supplied 1,600 people with comfortable seats, was opened for public worship, the Rev. Thomas Jackson preaching the first sermon. The other preachers who took part in the opening services were Mr. W. Dawson, of Leeds, the Revs. Dr. Beaumont, G. B. Macdonald, John McLean, and John Bowers. On the first Sunday all the chapels in the circuit except that at Padiham were by resolution of the quarterly meeting closed. The amount received in the collections was a little over £600. When the accounts were balanced after the completion of the chapel, it was found that the total cost, inclusive of land, had been £5,656 5s. 5d., and that the trustees were burdened with a debt of £2,490 7s. 1d.

The principal contributors to the fund for the erection of the chapel were as follows:—Messrs. William Hopwood & Son, £400; Geo. Barnes & Sons, £500; James Howorth's family, £200; Wm. Fishwick, £200; Geo. Fishwick, £100; J. Robinson Kay, £100; Miss Kay, £105; Geo. Fishwick, "in memory of a beloved daughter, whose highest enjoyment was to promote the cause of the Redeemer," £100; James Winterbottom & Son, £100; Smallpage & Bracewell, £100; John Hargreaves, £80; James Smallpage, £70; Lord & Whitworth, £60; James Pollard, £50 18s.; John Butterworth, £50; John Bailey, £30; Peter Phillips, £30; Mrs. Phillips, £30; Messrs. Henry Kay, £20; Thomas Eagin, £20; Thomas Eltoft, £20.

The original trustees were George Fishwick, John Robinson Kay, William Hopwood, James Howorth, John Hargreaves, George Barnes, Peter Phillips, James Smallpage, Samuel Smallpage, Joshua Lord, John Whitworth, Henry Kay, John Butterworth, David Shuttleworth, Charles Astin, Henry Marsden Ormrod, and James Heaton, superintendent minister. The Rev. William Pemberton, father of Mr. William Pemberton of this town, was the second minister at the time, and he, along with Mr. Joseph Lord, was appointed secretary of the Building committee. His great interest in the work was manifested by his invariable attendance at the numerous meetings of the committee and trustees, and by the copious minutes that he made of their proceedings.

Both Keighley Green and Wesley chapels seem to have been used for some time; but it was decided on May 27th, 1841, that the Sunday afternoon and Monday evening services should be held in Wesley chapel only from the 12th of the following June. The next year the trustees after serious deliberation considered it advisable to close the Keighley Green chapel and to offer it for sale on condition that, if purchased for religious purposes, it should only be by "some denomination of Protestant Christians, holding the Divinity of Christ as an article of their creed." In 1843 Wesley chapel was duly licensed for the solemnisation of marriages.

A new trust was appointed by deed dated May 22nd, 1869, the trustees being as follows:—John Robinson Kay, John Hargreaves, Peter Phillips, Samuel Smallpage, Joshua Lord, John Butterworth, senr., William Hopwood, Henry M. Ormrod, all of whom were trustees before, with George Howorth, John Howorth, John Barnes, Adam Dugdale, George Hopwood, John Southern, John Thornton, Henry D. Fielding, William Lancaster, John Taylor, Richard Thomas, John W. Phillips, James Holland, James Nowell, James Pollard, John Butterworth, junr., William Pemberton, and John Lewis

Ormrod. Wilson Brailsford was the superintendent mnister.

The list of gentlemen who have occupied the position of treasurer, and the period of their office are as follows. William Hopwood, junr., seems to have been treasurer in 1839 in the preliminary stages of the erection; and George Barnes succeeded him probably about the time of its completion, and remained in office till March, 1846. Henry Kay served from 1846 to 1848; James Howorth from 1848 to his death in March, 1858; John Butterworth from 1858 to 1864; Peter Phillips from 1864 to 1870; Henry M. Ormrod from 1870 to 1875; John Thornton from 1875 to the present time. It would be difficult to name seven gentlemen with more honored memories, or more suitable for the important office they held. Mr. Thornton is the only survivor of the seven.

It is somewhat singular that in nearly sixty years there have been only four chapel keepers. The first was Lawrence Collinge, who entered upon his duties in September, 1840, and continued to discharge them to the satisfaction of the trustees, till failing health compelled him to resign. He left the chapel house on the 9th of November, 1862, having faithfully served the trustees for over twenty-two years. The same day John Hargreaves, the second chapel keeper, took possession of the house, remaining in it till July 1st, 1872. The third was George Ashworth, of Stacksteads, who continued in the office for only eighteen months. He was succeeded in January, 1874, by James Crompton, who had for some time previously been acting as school-keeper.

On the 6th of December, 1839, the trustees "after considerable deliberation" decided by a large majority to provide an organ to be ready for the opening services. This first organ was but a small instrument, with only some half dozen stops. It was played at the opening services by Mr. Henry Stott, brother of Mr. John Stott, of Haslingden. When the building was thoroughly dry a somewhat larger instrument was substituted, which appears to have cost £100. It was built by a Mr. Lonsdale, of Burnley, and as part of the contract was for a time gratuitously played by his son. This in its turn was sold for £60 and replaced by a more powerful instrument, supplied by Gray and Davison, of London, at a cost of £450. The new organ was opened on Christmas Day 1845, the service being confined to simple psalmody. At that time it was by far the finest organ in the town. About the year 1876 it was rebuilt with many additions and improvements by its original constructors at a cost of £580. The organists, succeeding Mr. J. Stott, were Mr. Grundy, Mr. G. E. Fielding, Mr. Jas. Pollard, Mr. John Ashworth, and Mr. Jos. Pickles, who still holds the office.

## WESLEY CHAPEL.

In the year 1853 about £1000 was raised by subscription, as the commencement of a scheme for extinguishing the debt. The following were the principal contributors :—Mr. Hopwood, £200; Mr. Butterworth, £150; Mr. James Howorth, £150; Mr. G. Barnes and H. Kay, £210; Mr. J. Barnes (in memory of a daughter), £90; Mr. S. Smallpage, £75; Mr. Hargreaves, £30; Mr. Fielding, £20; and Mr. Luke Collinge, £10. Two years later a final effort was made, the following being the chief contributors :—Mr. George Barnes, £100; Mr. John Barnes, £50; Mrs. John Barnes, £50; Mr. James Howorth, £50; Mr. Wm. Hopwood, £50; Mr. John Butterworth, £50; Messrs. Spencer and Moore, £50; Mr. Samuel Smallpage, £30; and Mr. Henry Kay, £20.

Since its opening in 1840, the chapel has undergone various modifications and changes. The principal of these are as follows. In 1843 the interior was newly painted and decorated by Mr. Veevers at a cost of £170. At the same time the vestries were supplied with tables and forms. In 1849 a house for the chapel keeper was built on a plot of land behind the chapel. In 1853, a defect having been discovered in the title of the trustees to the land on which the chapel was built, a new conveyance and trust deed were made. In the following year, with the consent of the Conference, a plot of land behind the chapel was sold to Mr. Holroyd at 7s. 6d. per yard on condition that he should erect a boundary wall, and make and maintain the streets adjoining. In 1861 the chapel was again painted throughout by Mr. Veevers at a cost of £217 10s. 0d.; a defect in the roof was repaired, book-boards placed in the large pews, &c., by the executors of Thomas Chaffer at a cost of £58 10s. At the same time the organ was cleaned at a cost of £12. In 1862 certain excavating and flagging work was carried out by Mr. William Duckett for £69.

On Thursday evening, February 7th, 1877, a meeting was held in Red Lion Street School, presided over by Mr. John Butterworth, in furtherance of an extension scheme, which involved a total outlay of £7,000, and was to be extended over a period of five years. The objects contemplated were the renewing of Wesley Chapel, and the provision of a new chapel in Burnley Lane and new premises in the Whittlefield district. The subscription list was headed by Mr. John Butterworth and Miss Barnes, each of whom promised the handsome sum of £1,000. Other subscriptions promised were :—Mr. A. Dugdale, £500; Mr. John Howorth, £200; Mr. W. Lancaster, £200; Mr. H. D. Fielding, £200; Miss Howorth, £100; Mr. Richard Thomas, £100; Mr. J. Butterworth, Junr. £100; Mr. P. Rylands, M.P., £50; Mr. Peter Phillips, £50; Mr. J. W. Phillips, £50; and Mr. John Thornton, £25.

The most costly alterations were those carried out in connection with the enterprise just mentioned. The chapel was repewed, new vestibules front and back with convenient vestries were provided, and many other important improvements effected under the direction of Messrs. Waddington & Son. The total expenditure was £3,368 6s. 1d. The re-opening services

WESLEY CHAPEL (EXTERIOR).

yielded £800. In connection with this movement the name of the late Mr. Adam Dugdale must ever be honourably associated. His great interest in the work was evidenced by the pains he took in the initiation and carrying out of the scheme, and the amount of time and help he gave to it. After the repewing the chapel was left with its present number of 1,300 sittings, of which 50 are free, 120 set apart for children, and the rest available for letting.

WESLEY CHAPEL. (INTERIOR).

The Jubilee of Wesley chapel was celebrated by a large public meeting on July 17th, 1890. Mr. Geo. Howorth, of Bowdon, presided; Mr. B. Moore read an interesting paper on the Growth of Methodism in Burnley; and the speakers were Messrs. W. Lancaster, John Thornton, W. Tattersall, John Howorth, and the Rev. Geo. Holbrey. On such occasions Methodists like "good, old tunes"; and on this occasion the lovers of the old must have been highly gratified, for all the hymns were sung to such tunes as might have been heard in the former sanctuary at Keighley Green:—Ascension, Calcutta, Comfort, Diadem, Cranbrook, Simeon, &c. In anticipation of the Jubilee celebration the chapel had been re-decorated, the organ thoroughly overhauled, a new boiler connected with the heating apparatus, and other improvements made. At the re-opening services held on May 29th, June 1st and 8th, when the preachers were the Revds. F. W. Macdonald, S. O. Scott, and John Jeffries, the sum of £351 5s. 9d. was contributed, about sufficient to cover the liabilities that had been incurred. In 1896 the electric light was introduced, and in 1899 the chapel was re-decorated and the organ overhauled at a cost of £200.

The trust was renewed in the year 1893, when the following gentlemen were appointed:—Messrs. John Howorth, George Howorth, John Thornton, William Lancaster, John William Phillips, John Butterworth, William Pemberton, James Lancaster, Benjamin Moore, Francis Scowby, Henry James Robinson, Angelo Waddington, William Lupton, Frank Ernest Thornton, Brian Cowgill, William Lancaster, Junr., John Hargreaves, Thomas P. Smith, William Nowell, James Whitham Thompson, Robert Simpson, Edward Jones, William Whittingham, and J. S. Horn.

In Wesley chapel there are mural tablets on either side of the organ, and the following are the inscriptions.

Sacred to the memory of Mr. William Hopwood, senior, of Oak Mount, who died on the eighth day of June, A.D. 1838. Aged 73 years. By the instrumentality of Methodism, he was brought to a saving knowledge of God in the vigour of his youth: and for five and forty years, whether as private member, leader, steward, or trustee, he endeavoured to maintain the doctrines, uphold the discipline, and exemplify the spirit of Methodism, and thus promote its purity and extension. In all the relations of life, in the interest he took in Sabbath and day schools, in his generosity to the poor, and sympathy with the afflicted, and especially in his prayers and liberalities for the conversion of the world, he was eminently a man of God. This tablet is erected as a memento of his great worth. "The memory of the just is blessed."

Sacred to the memory of William Fishwick, Esq., of Longholme, formerly of Burnley, who died December 26th,

1839, aged 48 years. In early life he was truly converted to God, and for upwards of twenty-six years he was a most influential member and officer of the Wesleyan Church. For catholicity of spirit, affability of manners, integrity of conduct, kindness to the poor, and all the virtues of domestic life, he was indeed pre-eminent. He took a deep interest in the establishment and success of Wesleyan schools, and supported the great cause of missions both by liberal contributions and an eloquent advocacy. He laid the foundation stone of this chapel, and gave largely towards its erection. This tablet is raised as a token of grateful and affectionate respect. "The righteous shall be in everlasting remembrance."

In memory of Mr. George Barnes, of Burnley, who was a member of the Wesleyan Methodist society 42 years, sustained in that body various offices with fidelity and prudence, and rendered to the cause of God important service in connection with the erection of this sanctuary and of Red Lion Street school premises, and also in the management of the trust estate and of the week-day and Sunday schools. He was sagacious and diligent in business, just and kind in all the relations of life, unassuming and blameless in his deportment; and after a course of unostentatious piety and usefulness, he entered into rest on the 23rd day of August, 1855, in the 58th year of his age, and was interred at St. Peter's church, Burnley, on the 30th of the same month. "The righteous shall be had in everlasting remembrance."

Sacred to the memory of James Howorth, of Park House, Burnley Wood, who died on the 9th day of January, 1858, in the 65th year of his age. He was the sincere, the gentle, unobtrusive, yet firm and faithful Christian. During the course of more than forty years, as class leader, Sunday school superintendent, circuit steward, treasurer of the Benevolent and Strangers' Friend Society, and trustee of this chapel, he rendered invaluable service to the cause of Christ.

## RED LION STREET SCHOOLS.

After the opening of the premises in Hargreaves street, the female scholars were transferred from the Sunday school at Keighley Green to the basement under the new chapel. But the arrangement was not a success. The rooms that were used were ill adapted for the purpose; and there were constant difficulties in conducting the male scholars from Keighley Green to the services of public worship at Wesley. In June, 1849, the quarterly meeting gave its sanction to a proposal of the trustees "to purchase ground for the erection of new school premises." Owing however to "the agitated state of the society," to quote an old minute book, the scheme was found impracticable at the time, and had to be deferred.

Two years later the agitation had so far subsided, that efforts could be renewed to carry out the proposals. A large plot of land at the corner of Red Lion Street and Parker Lane was bought of Mr. Grimshaw for £1,180, so large indeed that part of it was afterwards resold to Mr. Joshua Sutcliffe for £398 12s. 0d. Mr. James Simpson, the architect of Wesley chapel, was selected as the architect of the new buildings; and the following amongst other tenders, were accepted:—for stonework, Mr. Robert Smith, £1,100; for wood-work, Mr. Thos. Hird, £510; for plastering and painting, Mr. Wm. Clarke, £148; for slating, Mr. James Walters, £175, and for plumbing and glazing, Mr. John Lancaster, £45.

The foundation stone was laid by J. Robinson Kay, Esq., of Summerseat, on Good Friday, April 18th, 1851; and the school was opened on July 19th, 1852, with 344 children in attendance. On the 30th of the May preceding sermons were preached in anticipation of the opening by the Rev. Philip Hardcastle. The total cost of the premises, including land, and furniture, was £3,701 19s. 4d., toward which, as the premises were for day as well as Sunday school purposes, a Government grant amounting to £807 was made. The old premises[1] at Keighley Green were sold, but the debt on them was so considerable, that a surplus of only £50 remained. The rest of the expenditure was nearly, if not quite, covered by the subscriptions of the friends of the schools, and by the proceeds of the opening services.

The Sunday schools were successful from the beginning. The congregation at Wesley is composed largely of those who have been trained in them; and workers soon began to be drafted off elsewhere—to Wood Top, Sandy Gate, Lane Bridge, Colne Road—in quick succession to found new schools or strengthen bands of Christian teachers. In 1852 the first annual tea-meeting was held, with an attendance of eight hundred persons. In 1871 the schools were re-arranged; and whenever alterations or enlargements have been required, there has been but little delay in effecting them, and no serious difficulty in raising the necessary moneys. The school is provided with an excellent free library, replenished annually with new books, and open to all scholars, to the local preachers

---

1. The premises have been used since 1851 as the County Police Court. The dial on the front of the building was designed by the Rev. Philip Garrett.

on the circuit, and to the members of the Wesley congregation.

In September, 1880, the centenary celebration of the foundation of Sunday schools took place. On this occasion the Red Lion Street school displayed a new banner of mediæval design. Upon the centre in tapestry appeared a life-size portrait of John Wesley, represented as preaching with a bible before him, while his right hand is stretched out as if in the act of exhortation. Surmounting the portrait are embroidered flowers on a scarlet border, and below it is an elegant fringe in four colours. On the back is the name of the school, with the date of its foundation, upon a scarlet ground in green. The cost was £26.

The following year the school had 650 names of scholars on the books, with an average attendance of 324. The teachers and officers numbered 111.

In 1884 the school was enlarged by the addition of two rooms over the infant school for the use of the young men's and the young women's classes, a new staircase, etc. The cost of the alterations and furnishing was £750, towards which £572 was raised by a bazaar opened the following Christmas by Sir Ughtred Kay-Shuttleworth, M.P.

The Band of Hope society was founded in 1869, and is an auxiliary association connected with the Sunday school. It is governed by its own committee, of which the constitution is subject to the approval of the Sunday school committee. Its membership numbers at present about three hundred, and its services are tending powerfully to the promotion of temperance amongst the young.

A mission school was commenced in 1885. Mr. Clayton, one of the town missionaries, visited the homes of the poor people in the neighbourhood in order to get the children to attend. The school was opened on the first Sunday in April, 1885, from nine o'clock to ten in the morning, when there were present ten boys and ten girls with two male and two female teachers, and Mr. Lupton as superintendent. In the afternoon, from two o'clock to three, there were twenty-five boys and thirty-five girls present, with seven teachers. The second Sunday there were eighty-two scholars present, with Mr. Kennerley as superintendent. The school has been carried on ever since, and is still making progress. Mr. Lupton held the office of superintendent for twelve years, and Mr. W. H. Nuttall for nine. Mr. Caleb Lancaster taught the first class of boys from the beginning to 1895, when he succeeded Mr. Lupton as superintendent. After holding that office two years, he retired, having been a worker in Sunday schools—Lane Bridge, Burnley Lane, and Red Lion Street—for over sixty years. Mr. James Holt and Mr. W. B. Potter have also been workers in the school since its formation, and are the present superintendents. The school is in a prosperous condition with twenty-two officers and teachers. In 1898 the average attendance of officers and teachers was seven in the morning and nine in the afternoon, and of scholars thirty-six in the morning and fifty-eight in the afternoon.

The trust of the schools was renewed under Fowler's Act in 1896, and the following gentlemen were then appointed:—Messrs. John Howorth, John Thornton, William Lancaster, John Butterworth, James Lancaster, Benjamin Moore, Francis Scowby, Frank Ernest Thornton, Brian Cowgill, John Hargreaves, Thomas P. Smith, James Whitham Thompson, Edward Jones, William Whittingham, Joseph S. Horn, E. Houlding, T. Nowell, and R. Simpson.

## LANE BRIDGE.

Although the cradle of Methodism in Burnley must be sought in the district of Lane Bridge, yet for a number of years prior to 1865 the place was almost entirely neglected, not only by Methodists, but also by most other Christian churches. In 1865, a band of devoted men, amongst whom were Mr. John W. Phillips, Mr. Joseph Smallpage, and Mr. T. H. Smith, commenced preaching services, and opened a Sunday school and a night school (now known as the 'Jerusalem school,' and included in the gas-works premises) for the benefit of the population. A small room, which had formerly been used for worship was taken, and within a very short period, owing to diligent and earnest labour, was filled. Notice to quit was moreover soon given, and it became necessary to establish the mission in premises of its own. A plot of land was obtained, and the foundation stones of the present chapel laid by Mr. John Butterworth, senr., on April 25th, 1868. It was mainly indeed through his warm interest and generous support, seconded by the patient and self-denying efforts of Mr. James Kelly, the recently appointed town missionary, that the cause prospered. The subscription list for the building of the chapel is a remarkable one, and shows the great interest taken in the enterprise by all classes. It contains the names of 279 persons, and the amounts vary from £100 to sixpence. Amongst the contributors were many belonging to other churches, such as General Scarlett, the Rev. William Thursby, Sir James Kay-Shuttleworth, and Mr. Richard Shaw. The total cost of the building and land was £1,000.

The chapel was opened on October 22nd, 1868, by the President of the Conference, the Rev. S. Romilly Hall. The opening services were continued by the Revds. Peter Mackenzie, George Dickenson, T. H. Lomas, and Mr. John Dawson, of

Bacup. At first the work was carried on against great opposition The doors and windows were cannonaded night after night with stones and peas. Occasionally a rush was made through the door, and every light in the place extinguished; or the

LANE BRIDGE CHAPEL.

disturbers took their seats, and waited until a hymn was given out, when they insisted upon singing a song to a tune of their own. But such was the perseverance of Mr. Kelly and his co-workers, and the blessing of God upon their labours, that the disturbances eventually ceased; and the neighbourhood has in every way considerably improved.

The chapel was renovated and enlarged in 1886, the gallery being so altered that it could be used for Sunday school purposes, and a new harmonium was obtained. In 1889 it was again enlarged at a cost of £300, by the erection of a wing of four class rooms, the re-opening services taking place on May 19th. A bazaar was held in December, 1894, by means of which the premises were cleared of debt. There is also a small endowment, created by the generosity of one or two benefactors, by which the current expenses of the mission are partly met. As far as is known, there is no other endowment on Wesleyan Methodist property in Burnley.

The name of James Kelly will always be associated with the founding and early history of the mission. He was a man of strong personality, unceasing in his devotion to the sick and destitute, and for twenty-one years he went in and out amongst the people until his name became a household word in the district. He died, January, 1888, and in the following year a marble tablet to his memory was placed in the chapel.

## STONEYHOLME.

After services had been conducted for several months in a room in Regent Street, the room in Railway Street was opened on Sunday, February 8th, 1880, when the Rev. S. O. Scott preached in the afternoon and the Rev. J. Priestley in the evening. This room soon became too small, and the mission was moved to Canning Street in January, 1881. In two years there were 260 scholars in the Sunday school, and two additional society classes had been formed. On Sunday evenings there was a congregation of 150. It was not however until 1887 that steps were really taken towards building a chapel. At that time there were 60 members of society, and 300 scholars. A bazaar was opened in April, 1887, by Mrs. Adam Dugdale, for the purpose of raising £500 towards a building fund, but the net proceeds amounted to £750. The sum of £1,200 was granted from a circuit extension fund. The memorial stones were laid on Saturday, June 18th, 1887, by Messrs. Howorth, Lancaster, and others, the proceeds on the occasion amounting to £232 19s. 2d. The cost of the chapel and site was £2,900. The chapel is in the form of an amphitheatre, and seats four hundred people. The school is on the upper floor, and consists of a central hall, with fifteen class-rooms around, providing accommodation for five hundred. The premises were opened on Thursday, April 12th, 1888. A few years later the chapel was decorated. A bazaar was held in 1895, by means of which the debt was cleared. In 1898 a further debt had accumulated of £162, but by means of a bazaar in December, which yielded £337, this was removed, and a substantial sum left towards the provision of an organ.

STONEYHOLME CHAPEL.

The pulpit used in the Canning-Street Mission Room is said to be one from which John Wesley preached. The amount of truth in this tradition cannot easily be decided. If it be correct, the pulpit will probably be the one that was originally used in the old chapel at Colne, built in 1777, and may have been transferred to Burnley to save expense on some occasion when the Colne chapel was repaired or altered. But it is quite as likely that the tradition has no foundation. Many pulpits of antique appearance and decaying woodwork are credited with the same honour.

## PICCADILLY ROAD.

Early in 1890 a small cottage was rented in the neighbourhood and a Sunday school commenced, preaching services also being held. The room soon became too small for the needs of this rapidly increasing district, and it was thought desirable to erect a school-chapel with larger accommodation. On April 23rd, 1892, the foundation stones were laid by Mr. William Parkinson (the Mayor), Mrs. Adam Dugdale, Miss Barnes,

Mr. John Howorth, Mr. James Howorth (for Mr. George Howorth, of Bowden), Mr. W. Lupton, Mrs. George Cowgill, Mrs. J. Lancaster, Miss L. Moore, Mrs. E. Jones, Mr. T. E. Lancaster, and a representative of the school. The sum of £300 was realised. The chapel was opened on December 6th of the same year, the opening services being conducted by the Revds. M. G. Pearse, Dr. Young, and J. E. Clapham, and £190 being raised. The total cost of the premises, including the capitalised value of the ground rent, was £3,160. The chapel

PICCADILLY ROAD CHAPEL.

seats 350 persons and has accommodation for 300 scholars. The school is already full, and a good congregation in regular attendance. The sum of £1,100 was granted by the Circuit Extension Fund Committee, and by a bazaar held in May, 1897, the balance of the cost was met. The premises are now entirely free from debt.

## ROSE HILL.

A mission was started in 1871 at Rose Hill through the generosity of the Dugdale family whose house is close by. Two cottages were taken, and adapted on a small scale to school and preaching purposes. The school was opened on January 8th,

1878, when there were present seven teachers and forty-one scholars, the superintendents being Messrs. E. Houlding and B. Cowgill.  The mission has been continued ever since as a Sunday school, and public service has been held every Sunday night.  A lady missioner has also been employed for many years by the Dugdale family in visiting the homes of the people and generally promoting their domestic and religious well-being. The present missioner is Miss Laugher.

## ACCRINGTON ROAD.

The earliest reference to Methodism in the Accrington Road district is contained in the Burnley society steward's book under the date of September 5th, 1796,—" Received from 'Abergamhaves' Class 4s."  In 1806 a class was formed at Gannow, then a village or hamlet outside Burnley, with Robert Law as leader, and in the list of members in 1811 it appears, with William Lancaster as leader, with nine members. There was also at the same time a class in Sandygate, where too a Sunday school was carried on.  In 1817 appears Back Lane with seven members.  After the quarterly meeting of September, 1824, it had preaching on Sunday afternoon and evening alternately; and in 1828 its membership had risen to twenty-six, six years later to twenty-nine.  In still another place in the neighbourhood, Bentley Wood Green, a Methodist society was in existence. Here in 1818 were seven members; next year there were fifteen. At what time preaching services were first held cannot be ascertained; but in 1822 it was resolved that

DOROTHY LANCASTER'S COTTAGE.

the preaching should be in the afternoon instead of in the evening, and in 1827 that one service a month should be taken from it and given to Castle Clough. In 1834 the membership was seventeen.

But the society that must be regarded as the actual precursor of that at Accrington Road was the one which carried on its work in Cog Lane, in a house once tenanted by Dorothy Lancaster, in which both preaching services and a Sunday school were conducted. These premises soon became too small, and a larger cottage in the same lane was hired, where a peculiar contrivance was resorted to in order to provide accommodation for the hearers The preacher was stationed in a corner of the room on the ground floor. Above his head a

COTTAGE IN COG LANE.

hole of a suitable size was driven through the ceiling, and protected by a low rail. The scholars, with their teachers, remained upstairs during the time of service. The rest of the congregation filled the room below. Both could partially see and distinctly hear the preacher. It was an arrangement, which perhaps better than any other solved the difficulty of packing large numbers into a small space, but it involved physical inconvenience to all. Not even in this way could the adapted cottage be made to accommodate the congregation that gathered on such a festive occasion as that of the Sunday school sermons; and consequently a barn in the neighbourhood, belonging to a farm occupied by Mr. Benjamin Eastwood, was brought into

BARTLE HILLS CHAPEL.

use. There were also prayer meetings held with some regularity at Gannow House, where Mrs. Fletcher then resided.

The first chapel was built in Cog Lane[1] in 1849, and was

---

1. According to the ordnance map for 1846, the road from Holme Lodge (not then built) viâ the Griffin Hotel to the old pipe shop below the Bull and Butcher inn was Back Lane; and the road from Gannow Lane viâ Haslam's mill, Stoops chapel, and Gretna Green to the Bull and Butcher was Cog Lane.

known as the Bartle Hills chapel. It was a room twelve yards square, and the building still stands. The chapel was opened the following year by the Rev. F. J. Jobson, D.D., and the cause was removed from Back Lane. In June, 1850, the quarterly meeting gave its sanction to the trustees "to proceed with the erection of a vestry, provided they could secure beforehand one-half of the contemplated amount."

The minute book of the teachers' meeting of the Bartle Hills Sunday school has been preserved, and contains particulars of varied interest, some of them relating to the proceedings at Back Lane. In 1846 it was resolved that no copybooks should be sold in the school on the Sabbath, but the superintendents were authorised to give one to any scholar too poor to buy for himself. In 1849 the managers of the Sandy Gate school were thanked for the presentation of their books; and that resolution fixes with strong probability the date when the branch school at Sandy Gate ceased to be. Three years later occurs a painful entry concerning the excursion of the scholars to Goole on July 12th. Ninety-six from Bartle Hills joined detachments from other schools; and "the trip had a melancholy termination: several lost their lives, and many were more or less injured." In 1853 Mr. John Taylor, the superintendent of the school, was requested to prepare a memoir of Sarah Boothman, a pious and useful teacher who died at the age of twenty-three. He wrote a little pamphlet of eighteen pages, full of wise counsel and encouragement; and some two thousand copies were distributed.

In twenty years the congregation at Bartle Hills outgrew its accommodation: and a plot of land in Accrington Road was given in 1871 by Miss Barnes, of Spring Hill, Burnley, for the erection of a new chapel. The foundation stone was laid by Mr. Howorth in her behalf on Saturday, February 4th, and the chapel was opened the following year, the collections amounting to £191. The building was designed in the Lombardic style by the architect, and provided seats for seven hundred people. The cost was £2,700, towards which the sum of £2,147 10s. was raised, including a donation from Miss Barnes in addition to the site of £700, another from Mr. John Butterworth, senr., of £400, and a share of £500 in the proceeds of a circuit bazaar. A few years later a further sum of £650 was expended in decorating the chapel and erecting an organ.

On August 29th, 1874, it was decided to build schools adjoining the chapel, and to transfer to them the work that had been carried on so long on the Bartle Hills premises, now entirely inadequate for the purpose. An extension of the site was again generously given by Miss Barnes, with the sole stipulation that the trustees must be sure to take enough land for their requirements. The building was at once proceeded with, and completed in August, 1876, at a cost of about £2,000. In 1883 enlargements were effected, which involved a further expenditure of £1,840, and made the premises capable of accommodating about a thousand scholars. A large part of

ACCRINGTON ROAD CHAPEL.

this expenditure was met by the proceeds of a successful bazaar. There remained a small debt, which after several fluctuations stood on May 5th, 1898, at £400. A committee was appointed to deal with it. Instead of holding a bazaar it was decided unanimously to appeal directly to the people for contributions in money. Messrs. A. Cowpe and F. Robinson volunteered to undertake the task of solicitation, and on September 27th reported that the sum of £411 12s. 2d. had been collected. The premises were thus entirely freed from debt.

## WHITTLEFIELD.

In 1873 Mr. John Greenwood was engaged by the Town Mission committee, and located for a time at Whittlefield. A room over a blacksmith's shop in High-street was opened for preaching, and a Sunday school established on the 22nd of June in that year. Four years later, a large site was secured, and the foundation stones of a school-chapel were laid on August 4th by Mr. John Butterworth, senr., and the Misses Barnes, Dugdale, Lancaster, and Waddington. The chapel was opened for public worship on Wednesday, June 17th, 1878. The need of such a place had been keenly felt on account of the rapid growth of the locality. The building consists of a chapel, 55 ft. by 26 ft., and a schoolroom, 40 ft. by 28 ft., with vestries. The two are connected by an arch, so equipped with sliding shutters that they can be thrown together, and thus provide accommodation on special occasions for five hundred. The building is of stone, and the style is a modified Romanesque. There were at that time between two and three hundred scholars in attendance, with thirty teachers, and fifty members of society.

The entire cost of the premises was £2,786 2s. 4d. A grant of £1,500 was made from a circuit chapel extension fund, and the stone-laying and opening services yielded £431 0s. 7d. In December at a meeting of the trustees it was announced that a debt of £832 17s. 8d. remained. This was at once defrayed by a cheque for the full amount from Mr. Butterworth, who had previously cleared off a debt on the old blacksmith's shop formerly used, and to whom the trustees presented on behalf of the congregation a massive and handsome timepiece as an expression of gratitude. Slight alterations were made in the interior fittings in 1880, and the chapel redecorated in 1892. Four years later several structural improvements were effected, and a new organ obtained; the whole expenditure was covered by the proceeds of a bazaar and the re-opening services, with the generous help of friends. The premises are free from debt, surrounded by a large population, and ought to become a powerful Methodist centre.

## WOOD TOP.

In the autumn of 1878, Mr. Thomas Holden and others succeeded in establishing a mission school at Wood Top, which in December of the same year was formally connected with the Methodist organisation, and worked to a large extent as an offshoot of Accrington-road. Religious services, a society class, a library, and other agencies were added in due course. The work was carried on for some years in a loft over a bakery behind a public house. It prospered to such a degree that in 1880 there were the names of 250 on the school roll. At length in 1891 the erection of a suitable building became practicable through the success of a large circuit extension scheme, and the memorial stones were laid on a site in Florence street on July 4th, the proceeds of the day amounting to £142 1s. Accommodation was provided for three hundred persons at a cost of £1,195 19s. 5d. The chapel was opened by Rev. W. L. Watkinson, on January 28th, 1892; and the mission has ever since been carried on with varying success.

## PARK HILL.

At the local preachers' meeting held September 28th, 1826, it was determined to begin preaching at Cheapside once a fortnight at half-past six. The preaching place appears to have been a large room over the shop and warehouse, subsequently used by Mr. Thomas Whitehead, with steps outside at the gable end leading up to it. A society was soon formed. In June, 1828, Charles Astin was the leader, and he had twenty-three members under his care. In the next four years, however, the society gradually dwindled; and in 1832 the number was six, and the contribution to the 'Yearly' collection, which had

PARK HILL CHAPEL (EXTERIOR).

never exceeded 1s. 6d., fell to 8d. The following year only four members were returned; in 1835 there were seventeen, and in 1836 thirteen, the leader now being Mr. Sagar.

In 1843 a great impetus was given to the Methodist cause by the late Mr. Thomas Dugdale, who built at his own cost the chapel, school, and school-keeper's house. The first service in the new premises was conducted by Mr. Dugdale himself, but they were formally opened on Tuesday, November 3rd, when the Rev. Dr. Hannah preached two sermons. On the following Sunday services were conducted by the Revs. Dr. Osborn and J. L. Posnett, when collections were made on behalf of the Wesleyan Missionary Society. Two society classes were formed, and in a few years three more were added. Three of the classes

PARK HILL CHAPEL (INTERIOR).

were met by Mr. Dugdale in his own house, the other two being led by Mr. and Mrs. Hy. Saunders. A Sunday school was soon after established, Mr. Dugdale being the superintendent for many years, and defraying all the cost of its maintenance. This rendered unnecessary any of those school anniversaries which are such a notable feature of Lancashire Methodism. Mr. Dugdale, however, made a great point of the Foreign Missionary anniversaries, and obtained the services as preachers of such men as Dr. Newton, Rev. John Rattenbury, and others, when the collections sometimes reached £40 or even £50, four or five times the amount that would have been obtained but for Mr. Dugdale's generous zeal. At the opening of the school

Mr. Dugdale presented each scholar with a New Testament and each teacher with a Bible.

About the year 1876 considerable alterations were made. The chapel was repewed, two vestries were added, a new organ put in, and a porch erected, at a cost of £1,200. Subsequent expenditure on the decoration of the chapel and schools left a rather large debt, which was gradually reduced by a series of sales of work and other means.

In November, 1893, the jubilee was celebrated by a public meeting, at which there was a large attendance. Mr. Starkie Baldwin, who had been connected with the school for forty years, welcomed the old members, and Mr. Robinson Mercer, who had been connected for forty-four years, the scholars. Structural alterations in 1896 and 1898 involved the expenditure of over £600, which again was covered by the proceeds of various efforts: and the premises are now entirely free from debt.

On the wall near the pulpit, which Mr. Dugdale was always glad to occupy, is a marble tablet with the following inscription :—

'"They who turn many to righteousness shall shine as the stars for ever and ever." In affectionate remembrance of Thomas Dugdale, of Park Hill, who died August 5th, and was interred at All Saints, Habergham, August 9th, 1872, aged 56 years. In 1838 he joined the Wesleyan Methodist society, and was for some time a superintendent of Lowerhouse Sunday school, and afterwards for many years in connection with Park Hill chapel. For upwards of thirty-three years he was a class leader and local preacher, and in 1843 he built this chapel, school, and premises. Also in loving memory of Sarah, wife of Thomas Dugdale, who died on the 20th of June, 1872, in her 52nd year, and was interred in the same vault. "Blessed are the dead which die in the Lord from henceforth: yea, saith the Spirit, that they may rest from their labours: and their works do follow them"—Rev. xiv. 13. This memorial was erected by their nephews and nieces. 1876. He loved Christ—he preached Christ.'

## IGHTEN HILL.

The origin of Methodism at Ighten Hill is somewhat obscure, but there are indications that two of the first generation of members in or about Burnley resided in that township, one at Ighten Hill farm and the other at Top o'th Close farm. The last-named farm was on the Burnley plan early in the century, and the former appears on a plan for 1827. Three years before school sermons were preached in a cottage next door to the present place of worship, and a society class was in existence under the leadership of Mr. James Smallpage. On March 28th, 1828, the local preachers' meeting decided to discontinue the service, and the class too was eclipsed for a few quarters. It re-appears in the register for 1835, as containing six members; and before that date services also had been re-commenced at various farmhouses, the last being an old one at Meadow Top, occupied by Thomas Broughton whose descendants are still connected with the Methodism of the place. It was whilst worshipping there in 1845 that James Smith and James Hartley considered it would be better to have a building specially set apart for public worship. The building now used was accordingly rented from the Gawthorpe estate, and of late years the rent has been reduced to a nominal sum by Sir U. Kay-Shuttleworth. The chapel was opened on September 1st, and worship has ever since been conducted regularly in it. Failure has at times seemed near, but there have always been a few staunch adherents, amongst whom should be mentioned Mr. James Smith, who was the leader of the society for forty-three years. In 1864 the Sunday school which had lapsed was re-established by Messrs. J. Smith, George and Henry Pollard, and T. Pilkington. On September 1st, 1895, the jubilee of the little chapel was celebrated.

Ightenhill is a capital illustration of the vitality of village Methodism. The fact that in a small township with a sparse population and no connexional chapel Methodism has held its own proves this. The descendants of those who in the early part of the century worshipped there still carry on the work. Though small, the influence of the place has been felt in many lands, and in an important sense its "line is gone out through all the earth," and its "words to the end of the world."

## FULLEDGE.

When the idea of building a chapel at Fulledge was first conceived, it is not easy to say, but to Mr. James Howorth the credit probably belongs. In June, 1858, the local preachers sent to the circuit quarterly meeting a communication in which they said that they thought it desirable to commence preaching in Brunshaw road or Fulledge road. On this being read, a conversation arose as to whether the subject of erecting a chapel in the locality indicated should not be "resumed." A committee was appointed to consider the whole matter. This committee consisted of the ministers, the circuit and town stewards, with Messrs. S. Smallpage, George Howorth, John Howorth, Dr. Brown, William Lancaster, and George Taylor, with power to add to their number. To the September quarterly meeting they could only report that they had not met; and they were urged to do so as soon as possible. Stimulated by this direction they entered upon their investigations at once; and the character of their recommendation appears from the fact that in December the sanction of the

FULLEDGE CHAPEL.

quarterly meeting was given to the erection of a chapel and school at Fulledge "to be free from debt."

A suitable site, once occupied by the works of a coal-pit, the shaft of which is beneath the outer vestibule of the chapel, was obtained for £1,457 3s. 8d. First of all the present chapel was built. Its foundation stone was laid on Good Friday, April 22nd, 1859, by Mr. John Barnes. A procession started from Red Lion Street school, in which a thousand persons took part. Mr. John Butterworth presented a silver trowel to Mr. Barnes, and Mr. James Robinson, the architect, on behalf of himself and the contractors presented a rosewood mallet and level. The trustees were the Rev. Joseph Lawton, with Messrs. John Barnes, John Butterworth, William Hopwood, Samuel Smallpage, Henry Kay, George Howorth, Peter Phillips, Henry Deighton Fielding, John Howorth, Thomas Brown, M.D., Henry Marsden Ormrod, Edmund Rawlinson, George Pomfret, William Hargreaves, Luke Collinge, William Lancaster, and Edward Maden. The builders were Messrs. Smith and Watson, and James Wiseman. The chapel is 100 ft. long and 60 ft. wide, outside dimensions, and 40 ft. high in the clear inside. The style is Grecian of the Corinthian order. Comfortable sitting accommodation is provided for 1,200 persons, including 440 seats which are free.

The chapel was opened for public worship on May 30th, 1861, by the Revs. G. B. Macdonald and L. Tyerman. The opening services were continued the two following Sundays, and the total amount contributed at the services was £528.

Two years later the school buildings were erected, at a cost of £2,268 7s. 6d., the entire cost of chapel and schools being £8,050. The whole premises, inclusive of land, furniture, and the school-keeper's house, have cost about £12,000, and are now free from debt. At the opening of the schools on August 2nd, 1863, sermons were preached in Wesley chapel by the Rev. James Clapham, of Hull, and in Fulledge by the Rev. J. W Greeves, of Manchester. On August 9th, the Revs. John McKenny, of Bradford, and G. C. Harvard, of Manchester, preached in the same chapels. The Rev. P. Mackenzie lectured in Wesley Chapel on Wednesday, August 12th.

There is a curious entry concerning the first anniversary sermons preached by the Rev. John Moore, then of Huddersfield, on December 4th, 1864, when the collections amounted to £87 18s. 4d. "Owing," so the entry reads, "to the late period of the year, the committee recommended the female singers to appear in their regular dress and bonnets, suited to the season, and not in white dresses, as is customary on these occasions. Twenty-five young women singers had each $1\frac{3}{4}$ yds. of 4 inch cord ribbon for strings at $13\frac{1}{2}$d. per yard, and a bonnet front at $6\frac{1}{4}$d. Fifteen girls had each $1\frac{1}{2}$ yds. of $3\frac{1}{2}$ inch cord ribbon, same quality, at $10\frac{1}{4}$d. per yard, and a bonnet front at $4\frac{1}{2}$d. The whole of the strings and fronts cost

£4 7s. 7d. Twenty-five singers paid only 1s. 3d. each, and fifteen girls only 10d. each." The remainder was defrayed by a gentleman still living, whose generosity has shown itself in many ways. The entry closes with the following comment, entirely needless, considering the sex and youth of those to whom it refers, "The singers looked remarkably well on the occasion."

The first report of the schools, of which the superintendents were Messrs. John Butterworth, H. M. Ormrod, George Howorth, and John Howorth, shewed that there were 559 scholars with an average attendance of 261, or 46·69 per cent. In 1865, there were 395 scholars with an average attendance of 234, or 59·24 per cent., shewing a decrease during the first twelve months of 164 scholars. This was no doubt owing to the fact that, these being new schools, scholars flocked from others, remained a short time, and then returned to the schools they attended previously.

In 1866 the chapel was renovated at a cost of £350. Re-opening services were conducted by the Rev. G. C. Harvard, of Leeds, and others, when £281 was raised.

On March 24th, 1870, a new organ was opened, which had been erected by Messrs. Foster and Andrew, of Hull. A special service was conducted by the Rev. Charles Garrett of Manchester; the following day two performances were given by Mr. W. T. Best, the organist at St. George's Hall, Liverpool; and on the next Sunday two sermons were preached by the Rev. W. Vercoe of Haslingden.

In 1875 the chapel was closed two months for alterations and decoration. The alterations comprised the connection of the central vestibule with the gallery staircases by means of glazed doorcases, the insertion of wall panelling round the sides of the chapel, the provision of extra seats, and the introduction of book-boards to the scholars' and free sittings. The decorations were based on the Greek type and were executed by Messrs. Preston & Son, Mr. Waddington being the architect. The cost was from £500 to £600. The chapel was re-opened on April 25th, when the Rev. J. H. Beech of Bolton was the preacher; and the following Thursday the Rev. J. Jackson Wray preached and lectured on "John Wycliffe, the first Protestant." The collections amounted to £101.

During the year a young women's Bible class was formed, which met on Saturday evenings, and of which there were 70 members. A young men's class was also formed with 80 members. In 1877 there were 1,123 day scholars and 734 Sunday school scholars. A reading room was opened in October, 1880, and has been conducted with success on the self-supporting principle, the annual subscription of members being 2s. 6d.

In 1880 it became necessary to enlarge the school to provide increased accommodation. The extension consisted of a wing which provides two large teaching rooms, each 37 ft. by 30 ft., and capable of holding 280 scholars, and two class rooms for the young men's class and young women's Bible class respectively. A staircase was constructed at the angle connecting the new building with the old. The work was carried out at a cost, including furnishing, of £1,700, Mr. Waddington being the architect. The re-opening took place on Saturday, February 7th, 1880, when a meeting at which about 700 were present was held, the Rev. H. Hastling presiding. The collections amounted to £59 5s. 6d. The total amount received towards the alterations was £881 2s. 3d., which included subscriptions by Mr. John Butterworth, £200; Miss Whitaker, £100; Mr. John Howorth, £100; Miss Barnes, £52 2s. od.; the Sunday school committee, £100; Miss Howorth, £30; Mr. E. Jones, £100; and Messrs. Brooks and Pickup, £20. The rooms were admirably adapted both by size and ventilation for both Sunday and day-school work.

At Christmas, 1880, there were 887 Sunday school scholars, an increase of seven during the year. The number had risen steadily year by year, with the single exception of 1870 when there was a decrease of two, from 1866 when the total was 419. From the time the school was opened to the year 1880, the names of 1471 boys and of 1387 girls have appeared on the register.

In 1886 the chapel was thoroughly renovated, the ventilation improved, and book rails fixed to the pews in gallery, at a cost of £700. The re-opening services were held on Thursday, April 29th, 1886, when the Rev. R. Waddy Moss, then of Bradford, preached in the afternoon, and the Rev. Sylvester Whitehead, then of Manchester, in the evening. The collections amounted to £63 14s. od. Further services were conducted by the Rev. J. A. Macdonald of Rhyl, and the Rev. Robert Morton.

The Hull Street mission room was opened in January, 1889, and a school was established. At Christmas, 1891, a sale of work was held for various pressing purposes, including the better equipment of the reading room; and £162 was realised. The electric light was introduced in August, 1897.

## BROOKLANDS ROAD.

Reference has already been made to a service at Burnley Wood conducted by a Methodist preacher as early as 1775; but whether the service was held in some house or in the open air is not known. Services were occasionally held for some time afterwards in a house in Hufling Lane, occupied first by Mr. William Pollard and then by Mr. James Schofield; and very early in the present century public worship was regularly celebrated every Sunday afternoon in the Burnley Wood Farm house, occupied by Mrs. Whitaker. This farm house was nearly opposite the Woodman inn. More recently there were also occasional services in a cottage in Hufling Lane, in which it is said the Rev. Samuel Chadwick preached his first sermon. In 1879, a corner shop, which happened at the time to be untenanted, was secured at a rent of 5s. 6d. per week. The rooms in the upper storey were thrown into one, the staircase boarded over, and a new staircase made from the scullery, at a cost of £7 10s. 0d. The room was formally opened on Sunday, August 31st, 1879, by the Rev. R. Waddy Moss and Mr. Wm. Lancaster. A Sunday school was established under the oversight of the Fulledge committee, and it was found that not nine per cent. of the scholars had been in the habit of attending any school on the Lord's day. Religious services were held in the evening, and various other efforts made to benefit the neighbourhood.

This room was soon found to be too small, and early in 1881 steps were taken to provide a suitable building. In March, 1882, it was resolved to purchase a plot of land in Brooklands Road for the erection of a school chapel. The memorial stones were laid on Saturday, September 2nd, 1882,

BROOKLANDS ROAD CHAPEL.

by the Mayor (H. D. Fielding, Esq., J.P.), Mr. John Howorth, Mr. John Butterworth, and Miss E. Butterworth. The following girls each presented a purse containing two guineas or more, the total amount being £53 6s. :—Charlotte E. Butterworth, Lily F. Butterworth, Hetty Butterworth, Ellen B. Butterworth, Edith Smith Cowgill, Sarah Elizabeth Farrer, Amy Hopwood, Louisa Hull, Annie Mary Hargreaves, Annie Holden, Alice Kilburn, Amy Gertrude Kellett, Annie Winifred Lupton, Lilian Moore, Edith Mary Newman, Minnie Rawlinson, Edith Annie Ranshaw, Lizzie B. Sagar, Frances Wharton, Sarah Ann Walton, Mary Maria Williamson, and Clara Walton. The presentation of purses in this way was a novel and successful feature on an occasion of the kind, and the proceeds of the day amounted altogether to £139 8s. 5d. The cost was £1,831, to which must be added £360 for the capitalisation of the ground rent; and in all the sum of £1,000 was raised. The building is in the Elizabethan style of architecture, and provides accommodation for 350 persons in the large room, and 110 children in the gallery.

The school chapel was opened on Thursday, May 3rd, 1883, by Dr. M. Randles, the services being continued on the two following Sundays. At that time there were 160 scholars in attendance, and in twelve months the number increased to 240. A library was opened containing 210 volumes, with 33 readers; and there was established also a Band of Hope society with 70 members.

The accounts were audited in March, 1886, when it was found that there was a balance due to the treasurer of £28 18s. 11½d. The principal contributors were as follows:—Mr. J. Butterworth, senr., £200; Mr. J. Butterworth, junr., £150; Mr. John Howorth, £75; Miss Barnes, £50; a friend, £50; £25 each from Miss Butterworth, Messrs. Brooks & Pickup, and Mr. and Miss Collinge; £20 each from Mr. William Lancaster and son, Exors. of Mrs. Parkinson, Mr. J. S. Collinge, Mr. Geo. Cowgill, Mr. W. Waddington and son, and the Misses Dugdale; Mr. J. Rawlinson, £10 10s.; £10 each from a friend, Cliviger Coal Co., and Mr. H. D. Fielding; Mr. Wm. Goodall, £6; Mr. E. Jones, £5 10s.; £5 each from a friend, Mr. J. W. Phillips, Mr. R. Simpson, Mr. J. Cottingham, Mr. James Collinge, Mrs. Bell, Mr. B. Moore, Mr. William Thompson, junr., Mr. John Thornton, Mr. George Howorth, and Mr. A. Altham. A bazaar in March, 1884, with subsequent efforts in 1885, realised £572 18s. 3d; and the collections at the opening services amounted to £110 2s. 5d. Miss Butterworth, one of the very few female trustees in Methodism, took the greatest possible interest in the work, and to her indefatigable efforts the success of the undertaking is in large measure due.

## COLNE ROAD.

As far back as 1819 Methodist services were commenced in a room near the Black Bull, at Burnley Lane Head, a prayer

COLNE ROAD CHAPEL.

meeting being established about the same time at the house of Mr. Benjamin Bell in Hebrew Road. But though the work at the former place was continued for many years, little progress was made, and the society with a few fluctuations was practically stationary. In June, 1819, there were twenty members, the next year eleven, and in 1824 only nine. In 1825 there were twenty-one members, and in 1833 only six. In 1828 services began to be held on alternate Sunday evenings at Haggate instead of Burnley Lane Head. At length in July, 1863, an earnest Methodist, Mr. John Jackson, began to meet a class at the house of Mr. Abel Riding, in Back Birley Row, where also occasional preaching services were held. In the winter of the same year, a Sunday school was started in a room, entered by a flight of steps outside, over a blacksmith's shop opposite the old Hebrew Road bar, near the Duke of York. This room accommodated about two hundred scholars; but the school increased so rapidly that on May 27th, 1866, it was transferred to a room in Earl Street, afterwards used first as a Reform Club, and then as a private refreshment saloon. Five years later a site was purchased in Colne Road for £700; and upon part of it a school was built at a cost of £1,500, and opened on the 23rd of May, 1872. It was built to accommodate 300 scholars, and designed by Mr. Waddington after the early English type of architecture.

Although school chapels are good helps during the formation and early history of a church, they do not meet the requirements of modern times. The people in the neighbourhood become dissatisfied, largely because of the inconvenience of not being able to obtain family pews. It was decided accordingly to proceed with the erection of a chapel on an adjoining site on the Bank Hall estate. The memorial stones were laid on May 10th, 1879, the collections on the occasion amounting to £195. The chapel was built in the thirteenth century style of architecture, and to-day forms one of the most prominent structures in one of the most flourishing districts of the borough. It was opened on Thursday, June 9th, 1880, when sermons were preached by Dr. W. B. Pope and Dr. James. The entire cost of all the premises inclusive of the land was about £5,700, of which £2,500 was received from a circuit extension fund. In 1888 the school was enlarged at a cost of £1,000, and in 1893 an organ, built by Messrs. Harrison & Harrison, of Durham, and costing £700, was placed in the chapel. Such a provision was in part a recognition of the efficiency of the choir, which two or three years ago took the first prize in a competition of choirs at the Crystal Palace. The money required was raised by several special efforts, culminating in February, 1899, in a large bazaar which yielded rather more than £1,000. The premises are now entirely free from debt; and the church and school at Colne Road are amongst the most enterprising and prosperous Methodist organisations in the town.

## MERECLOUGH.

Methodism was introduced (see page 66) into Mereclough in 1786 by William Banning. In the Burnley stewards' book there are twenty entries of different amounts paid by this society before the formation of the Burnley circuit, amounting to £12 13s. 9d. In June, 1811, the names of seventeen members are recorded, beginning with that of William Halstead. This William Halstead took a very active part in the attempt to establish Methodism in Worsthorne. He lived to be ninety-five years of age, and died about the year 1857. In the latter part of his life he became exceedingly deaf, and being resolved not to lose the benefits of attendance at the chapel, he took his place regularly along with the preacher in the pulpit, and thus managed to catch something of what was said.

After the formation of the Burnley circuit the country societies seem to have paid their moneys to the circuit stewards; but the number of members in society, and generally their names and their contributions to the connexional funds are duly entered by the superintendent in his register. From this it appears that Mereclough had at one time a flourishing society. In 1836 Lawrence Collinge had a class of thirty-seven members, and William Sutcliffe one of twenty-four. Their joint contributions to the connexional funds that year were—to the Schools' fund 5s. 8d., the Chapel fund 7s. 10d., the "Yearly" collection in the classes 4s. 9d., and the Home Mission fund 5s. 2d. Two grandsons of William Sutcliffe were afterwards appointed borough magistrates.

From 1787 to 1824 services were held week by week without intermission in William Halstead's cottage. In 1823 land was leased from the Towneley estate, the deed being dated February 27th. The trustees were William Hopwood, senr., William Hopwood, junr., Edward Pollard, William Fishwick, James Howorth, John Pollard, Thomas Farrer, John Hargreaves, John Higgins, William Sutcliffe, William Halstead, Gilbert Holden, John Simpson, James Crossley, and Henry Sutcliffe. On this site a chapel was built, which was opened in March, 1824, by the Rev. Joseph Roberts. In 1849 the debt seems to have been considerable, for in that year the friends at Sabden Bridge received permission to undertake certain alterations in their premises, but were not to solicit subscriptions in any other part of the circuit except Sabden "till the Mereclough debt was reduced." In March, 1860, the trustees had permission to enlarge the school at a cost of £100 to £120, on condition that they did not increase the debt. In 1865 the school was thrown into the chapel, and the re-opening services took place on Thursday, June 22nd, when the Rev. Peter Mackenzie preached from a window in the new premises, and a collection of £28 was made.

New school premises were at once proceeded with, and opened on August 27th, 1871, a day school being commenced the following year. In 1875 a Young Men's Institute was founded by the Rev. Joseph Webster and others in a cottage which was turned into a library and reading-room; but difficulties soon arose, and the institution was closed. Some years

MERECLOUGH CHAPEL.

later the chapel had to be closed for a time whilst the Cliviger Coal Co. was working the seams beneath. A sum of £187 with costs was paid on account of the damage due to undermining; and the opportunity was taken to extend and improve the premises and to adapt them to modern requirements at an outlay of £800. The chapel was re-opened on August 30th, 1885; and the total amount raised was £460. The centenary of the introduction of Methodism into the village was celebrated in April, 1886; and two years later a bazaar was held, which resulted in the cancelling of the debt, and left the trustees with a balance of £70 in hand.

Mr. Luke Collinge, to whom reference is made in the closing chapter, was closely associated in his early life with Mereclough Methodism. James Crossley first joined the Methodist society at Mereclough, it is said in 1814; his name occurs in the list written out by the superintendent in 1815. His connection with Mereclough however was but brief; for in the list drawn up in 1817 his name appears as the leader of a class at Worsthorne. He took a very active part in the final establishment of Methodism in that village. He and Mr. Astin rented some rooms in what was called the Old Hall, where they opened a Sunday school. He was by trade a warper, and was received on trial as a local preacher in March, 1821. About forty years afterwards he was appointed town missionary in Burnley, and died in 1879 at the age of eighty-four.

## WORSTHORNE.

Extracts from the Burnley Society Stewards' book have already been given, which prove that there was preaching in a house at Worsthorne for three or four years from 1797, and that friends from Mereclough were instrumental in the introduction of Methodism. It would seem, however, that no class was formed at that time, the first contribution to circuit funds being made September 19th, 1807, and amounting to 3s. 6d. The only other separate entry before 1810 is of 8s. 6d., paid on July 29th, 1809. In 1810 there are four entries, amounting together to £1 18s. 6d. The first list of the members of society appears in the superintendent's register in June, 1811, when sixteen persons received tickets of membership. In the 'Recapitulation' for the following year Worsthorne is said to have had twelve members, but only two names are given, George Hargreaves and Hannah, presumably his wife. For two years, 1814 and 1815, Worsthorne does not occur in either the list of members or the summary of numbers. In 1816, however, it re-appears with eight members. For some years its membership fluctuated between seven and twenty-two. In 1817 James Crossley is mentioned as the leader.

As yet there was no chapel, but "Chadwick's House" had been taken by a few earnest men from Burnley, who established a Sunday school and held occasional religious services in it. When that became too small, a room in the Old Hall was taken, and the following agreement was drawn up between the Burnley committee of management and the teachers. Lawrence Redman was a leader at Mereclough; John Simpson, John Higgins, and William Sutcliffe were members at Mereclough; and James Cuerdale a member at Burnley. The foolscap paper, on which this agreement was written, bears a mark indicating that a tax of two shillings per quire had been paid, and on it is impressed a stamp for one pound. At the same time that the school was opened, the room was registered as a place of worship. A copy of the superintendent's request for registration, and of the endorsement are appended. The first document, the Agreement, is possibly unique and of the greatest historical value.

ARTICLES of AGREEMENT, made and concluded upon the

tenth day of February, in the year of our Lord one thousand eight hundred and seventeen, between Thomas Kay, John Moore, William Fishwick, Edward Pollard, John Spencer, Henry Higgin Longfield, and John Pollard, all of Burnley, in the county of Lancaster, the committee lawfully elected and nominated and appointed for the time being of the one part, and William Sutcliffe, John Higgins, James Crossley, James Cuerdale, John Simpson, and Lawrence Redman, teachers of the Methodist Sunday school, situate at Worsthorn, in the said county of the other part.

WHEREAS the Methodists have lately took a room, situate in the Old Hall at Worsthorn aforesaid, the property of Peregrine Edward Towneley, Esquire, for the purpose of converting and using the same as a Sunday school for the educating and instructing poor children of ALL DENOMINATIONS whatsoever, it is hereby agreed mutually and unanimously between the said committee and the said teachers above recited, that the said school shall be denominated "The Methodist Sunday School," but nevertheless shall be free for all denominations to resort unto, who shall subject themselves to the rules and regulations drawn up by the said committee for the observance of the said school, and also that the sole management and government of the said school shall be under the guidance of the superintendent teachers, such teachers being members of the Methodist society. And the said teachers above recited, and all others who may hereafter join or succeed them, do hereby agree with the said committee and their respective successors to submit and faithfully abide to the purport of this agreement. And also the said teachers do hereby promise and agree not to suffer any interference, controul, or management of the said school to be in the hands of any other sect or party whatsoever, but such as shall be lawfully authorised by the committee for the time being. And further that the said school shall be always opened and concluded with singing and prayer by the superintendent teacher appointed for the day, and the children shall join in singing, and shall all kneel down at the time of prayer. And also the said parties do hereby agree for themselves and their several and respective successors, that all kinds of implements requisite to fit up and accommodate the said school, whether benches, forms, desks, tables and so forth shall belong unto, and be the sole right and property of the existing committee for the use of the said school : also all books and other necessary appurtenances relating to the said school, whether purchased by the said committee, or donations given them from any person or persons whatsoever, shall belong to the said committee for the use of the said school as aforesaid.

WITNESS the hands of the parties
Witness to John Spencer, Wm. Sutcliffe, and Jas. Cuerdale signing.

    John Akroyd.

Witness to Messrs. Thos. Kay, John Moore, Wm. Fishwick, Edwd. Pollard, H. H. Longfield, Jno. Pollard, John Higgins, James Crossley, John Simpson, and Lawrence Redman, signing.

    William Leach.

Thos. Kay
John Moore
Wm. Fishwick
Edward Pollard
John Spencer
H. H. Longfield
John Pollard
Wm. Sutcliffe
John Higgin
James Crossley
Jas. Cuerdale
John Simpson his x
Lawrence Redman his x

  To the Right Reverend the Lord Bishop of Chester, and to his Registrar.

 I, William Leach, of Burnley, do hereby certify that a certain room occupied as a Sunday School room, situated in the Township of Worsthorn, in the Parish of Whalley, in the County of Lancaster, and Diocese of Chester, is intended forthwith to be used as a place of religious worship by an Assembly or Congregation of Protestants, and I do hereby require you to register and record the same according to the provisions of an Act passed in the 52nd year of the reign of his Majesty King George the Third, intituled "An Act to Repeal Acts, and amend other Acts, relating to religious worship, and Assemblies, and Persons teaching or preaching therein;" and hereby request a certificate thereof. Witness my hand this 15th day of March, 1817.

      WILLIAM LEACH.

 I, William Ward, Deputy Registrar of the Court of the Bishop of Chester, do hereby certify that a Certificate of which the above is a true copy was this day delivered to me to be registered and recorded pursuant to the Act of Parliament therein mentioned. Dated this 29th day of March, 1817.

     WILLIAM WARD,
      Deputy Registrar.

 In June, 1836, the quarterly meeting resolved that a chapel should be erected at "Worsthorn 9 yards by 11"; and at the Christmas following "that the plan of Worsthorne chapel presented by Mr. Hopwood, senr., be adopted." The Rev. Benjamin Slack thus describes the successful application for help, which he and others made to a landowner in the neighbourhood. "It was our lot," he writes, "in company with the late Mr. Hopwood, and two Sabbath school teachers, to wait upon the wealthy, but somewhat eccentric owner of the township for the purpose of obtaining a site. After the steward had pointed out to the squire the exact place, on a map of the estate which lay before him, the latter very liberally acceded to our request, and fixed the nominal rent of 5s. per annum, on a lease of 999 years. The joy of the venerable man, who was the

WORSTHORNE CHAPEL.

principal party in making the application, was just then full, and his cup running over. Notwithstanding the disparity of circumstances between himself and the lord of the manor (who might be about his own age), and maugré the opposite creed which he professed, Mr. Hopwood exclaimed, 'Bless the Lord! there have been many souls that have gone safe to heaven, even from the old place.' The squire was half fixed by the assertion, and probably believed it; but in his own peculiar and brief manner, merely replied, 'Very well, very well, very well!'" The deed conveying the site thus obtained was dated April 30th, 1838; but the chapel was opened in 1837, and about thirty years afterwards was considerably enlarged.

The memorial stones of a new chapel were laid on Saturday, May 8th, 1875, by Mr. John Butterworth, who gave £125; by Mr. W. Read, of Blackpool, who gave £550; by Mr. James Hargreaves, an active local preacher, who had watched over the society for many years, £125; and by Mr. William Clark, Red Lees, superintendent of the school, £100. Had it not been for the generous help of the above no movement for a new chapel could have been inaugurated with any degree of success. The chapel was built of local stone and in the Romanesque style. It will seat 400 persons. The opening services were conducted on Sunday, August 26th, 1877, by the Rev. Dr. Rigg.

The cost of the chapel, inclusive of site, was about £2800. Its career has been peculiarly unfortunate. No sooner was it nearing completion, than a subsidence of the ground, which had been honeycombed in search of coal, considerably damaged the building, and entailed much anxiety and expense in putting it into repair. A sum of £225 was paid by the exors. of Col. Hargreaves as compensation for the injury. And after various efforts it was announced at a jubilee celebration in October, 1890, that the debt was at last removed. A new organ was introduced in August, 1896; and the society is free from the financial burdens that have pressed upon it for almost two generations.

## WHEATLEY LANE.

A class was formed at "New Lond," midway between Wheatley Lane and Pendle Bottom, as early as September, 1807, and was considered as belonging to the Burnley society. In the four years that elapsed from its establishment to the division of the Colne circuit, eleven separate entries of contributions from this class occur, the total amount paid being £4 19s. In the list of members in the Burnley circuit in June, 1811, are the names of twelve meeting at New Laund, with Richard Dean as leader. In the following year the number fell to nine, and afterwards to six. In the list for 1817 there is no reference to New Laund, but three of the members who had met there are found meeting in the Pendle Bottom class, which had been in existence from June, 1796. Methodism therefore may be considered as having died out at New Laund, though a class, formed in 1814, continued to meet at Laund, a hamlet between Wheatley Lane and Barrowford.

The founders of Methodism in Wheatley Lane were Mr. W. Anderton and Mr. R. Procter. Mr. Anderton was for some time a superintendent of the Sunday school at Higham, and Mr. Procter worshipped at the chapel. Both these gentlemen lived at Wheatley Lane, where, as the class at New Laund had ceased to exist, and Laund, Pendle-Bottom, and Higham were somewhat distant, a class was formed. It was first returned in March, 1824, as having eighteen members; the following year it had twenty-seven, and Robert Procter is named as the leader. In 1828 there were four classes with eighty-nine members. In 1836 Mr. Procter led three classes of twenty-three members, Mr. Anderton one of sixteen, and Mr. Moorhouse one of nine.

A little before this preachers had been invited from Burnley, and the services were held in a room in Mr. Anderton's house. Matters so prospered that in 1824 a little chapel was built on the site of the present one, the land being given for that purpose by Mr. James Hartley, of Ighten Hill Park. It was opened on November 7th, and cost £300, of which £41 17s. 9d. was raised by subscriptions, £13 1s. 8d. by collections at the opening services, and the rest was borrowed. The original trustees were Messrs. H. H. Wilkinson, of Higham; John Robinson, of Higham; John Livesey, of Higham; Robert Procter, of Wheatley Lane; John Whalley, of Wheatley Lane; William Hopwood, James Hartley, Edwin Pollard, William Moore, Thomas Farrer, Thomas Whitfield, William Fishwick, John Hargreaves, Thomas Haworth, and William Hopwood, Junr., all of Burnley. All the sittings were immediately let, and more were wanted. On any special occasion, a barn at Laund in connection with the residence of Mr. James H. Hargreaves, or at Pendle Bottom where the Rev. C. H. Kelly when a student preached the school sermons, was used. The chapel was enlarged first of all about 1853 at a cost of £267; and twice since the process has had to be repeated, in 1868 at a cost of £600, and again in 1878. The trust was renewed on November 2nd, 1856, when the following were appointed—Messrs. J. Butterworth, S. Smallpage, H. Horsfield, R. and J. Procter, H. Wilkinson, G. Howorth, J. Hopwood, Dr. Brown, W. Pollard, W. H. Armistead, W. and C. Waddington, J. Thornton, W. Anderton, J. Howorth, and W. Hopwood.

The land on which the school is built was given by Mr. John Barnes, and adjoins the chapel. The corner stone was laid on Saturday, April 30th, 1859, by Mr. W. P. Wilding, of Montford. The original trustees were the Rev. Joseph Lawton, Messrs. William Anderton, William Hopwood, John Butterworth, Samuel Smallpage, Hartley Horsfield, Robert Procter, Henry Wilkinson, Junr., John Procter, George Howorth, James Hopwood, Thomas Brown, William Pollard, W. Horner Armistead, William Waddington, Charles Waddington, and John Thornton. The school, which cost £428 4s. 6d. was opened by a public meeting on New Year's Eve. In 1881 the managers of the day-school applied to the trustees for permission to convert two cottages into one, in order to provide for a married master, so that the work of the school might be carried on more satisfactorily. The cost of the alterations was £50, and was cleared without burdening the funds of the school.

WHEATLEY LANE CHAPEL AND SCHOOLS.

Further alterations in the chapel were made in 1890, in which year Mr. Barnard Emmott left £50 to the trustees. The same year the trust was again renewed by the appointment of Messrs. J. Thornton, L. Lee, J., W., and H. Procter, R. Ingham, T. Nuttall, T. Ingham, J. Crawshaw, T. Holt, C. Illingworth, B. Moore, J. W. Thompson, E. Jones, F. Scowby, J. Hardwick, Dr. Robinson, and J. H. Blezard. In 1891 improvements were made in the organ, and the premises were re-decorated at a cost of £370. And in 1895 a bazaar was held for the purpose of raising £600, the objects being to extend the burial ground, to improve the day and Sunday school premises, and to clear off a small debt on the trust. The bazaar realised £400.

The district of Pendle Forest is famous for its curious legends and stories. A single one of the many relating to Methodism may be given. One year the Rev. Benjamin Slack was preaching the school sermons, and had amongst his hearers Mr. Thomas Bracewell, of Barrowford, (who will be better recognised under his more familiar appellation of Tommy Bracewell). In the afternoon, Mr. Slack was proceeding with his sermon somewhat slowly and heavily, when the drowsiness was effectually dispelled by the ejaculation, "O Lord, sharpen tools," from Mr. Bracewell. But in the evening, such was the preacher's vigour that Mr. Bracewell could not refrain from publicly announcing a complete change in his opinion, and at a convenient pause in the sermon interjected the criticism, "They call him Slack; but he's not slack, I tell you."

No account, however brief, of Methodism at Wheatley Lane would be adequate that did not refer to the great munificence of Mr. Wilding, and his continuous interest in the village society. Not only did he contribute handsomely towards the enlargement of the chapel, the erection of the school, and its maintenance in thorough efficiency; but his gifts and his ungrudging devotion of time to the work of relief during the years of the cotton famine will not soon be forgotten. Everywhere throughout the Burnley circuit, Methodism in those terrible days took the best care it could of its members. Contributions came occasionally from outside sources, and there is a record gratefully preserved to this effect, "The sum of £80 was sent from London to the superintendent minister, the Rev. Isaac Keeling, for distribution among the distressed poor of Burnley society, 1862." But Mr. Wilding almost exceeded his fellow workers in energy and zeal. He turned the new school premises at Wheatley Lane into the head-quarters of a relief committee, of which he was the treasurer; and the mitigation of the sufferings of the poor in that neighbourhood was due in no small degree to his untiring activity, and that of the ladies of his household.

To Robert Procter and William Anderton allusion has already been made. The latter at the time of his decease in 1879 was reputed to be the oldest inhabitant of the village. He had been a member of society for fifty-seven years, connected with the Sunday school for fifty, a class-leader for upwards of forty, and the day before his death pronounced all to be well. John Procter was a member for forty-five years, "given to hospitality," active in every kind of religious service, but never better pleased than when he was entertaining the preachers. He died in August, 1888, with the assurance upon his lips, "It is all right; it will soon be over, and then I shall be with Christ." Stalwart and devoted men were they and many besides them, like William H. Armistead and Charles Illingworth amongst the dead, Thomas Holt, Lawrence Lee and the Procter brothers amongst the living, pillars of the church in their little village.

PLACES<br>GIVEN UP Reference should be made to one or two places, in addition to those already named, from which Methodism has retired. There was at one time a society with regular religious services at the little hamlet of Dineley, about a mile out of the town towards Cliviger. The place is not mentioned at all in the local preachers' minute book; but it appears in the list which the

Rev. Thomas Stanley left for his successor in August, 1824, as having seven members on trial. In 1825 it was reported as having nine members, but from that time is not mentioned in the register. It is not on the plan for 1830, but had fortnightly service on Sunday evenings on the plan of 1837. The reasons for withdrawing are not known.

For many years there was a Methodist society at Pendle Bottom. There is a reference to a Pendle class on June 16th, 1796, when its contribution to the circuit funds was recorded as 4s. In June, 1816, the class consisted of nine members, and in 1857 there were fifty-one scholars in the school.

For some time the place was visited weekly by the Methodist preachers. The great pillar of the cause there was Jonas Lee, to whom reference has been made more than once. He was a big man, and his kindness to the preachers went so far that he insisted upon fitting them out with his own clothes, whenever their own had been wetted by rain on the walk to their appointment. The smallest man among them had to comply with Jonas Lee's wish in this respect; and it is an open question whether the dampness of their own clothes would not have been a less discomfort than the sense of their ludicrous appearance, as they stood before the congregation clad in a suit "a world too wide for" their " shrunk shanks." For some reason or other the school was closed in 1865, to the regret of many.

**SUNDAY SCHOOL UNION**

An abortive attempt was made in 1831 (see page 117) at the establishment of a Sunday School Union. But on September 16th, 1859, to quote an old minute book, "a tea-meeting of teachers from all the Sunday schools in the then Burnley circuit was held under Hargreaves Street chapel." It was convened for the purpose of considering the condition and prospects of the various schools. The Rev. J. Lawton presided, and the meeting resolved "that the formation of a School Union for the circuit was desirable, and that the various schools and the local committees be desired to appoint representatives who should meet and further consider the question." As a result of this meeting a Union was determined upon, and the committee of the Union held their first meeting on December 10th, 1859, when Mr. George Hopwood was appointed treasurer and Messrs. John Thornton and Joseph Smallpage secretaries. The first annual meeting of the Union was held in September, 1860, when an essay was read by Mr. William Lancaster on "The Best Method of Teaching." A perusal of the minutes of the committee is interesting, in that they record the fact that all the prominent names in connection with Burnley Wesleyanism have been intimately associated with Sunday school work. The following is a list of the different Sunday schools in the Burnley circuits to-day, with the year when each school was established, and the number of scholars as reported at the last meeting of the Union on December 13th, 1898:—

| Schools. | When established. | Number of Scholars. |
|---|---|---|
| Red Lion Street | 1811 | 559 |
| „    „    „ Mission Room | 1885 | 82 |
| Fulledge | 1863 | 888 |
| Accrington Road | 1849 | 730 |
| Park Hill | 1843 | 227 |
| Mereclough | 1824 | 116 |
| Worsthorne | 1815 | 128 |
| Colne Road | 1863 | 705 |
| Lane Bridge | 1865 | 173 |
| Rose Hill | 1871 | 37 |
| Whittlefield | 1873 | 240 |
| Ighten Hill | 1865 | 47 |
| Wood Top | 1878 | 302 |
| Brooklands Road | 1878 | 494 |
| Stoneyholme | 1879 | 450 |
| Piccadilly Road | 1892 | 290 |
| Wheatley Lane | 1830 | 175 |

WEEK-DAY BIBLE CLASSES

Bible classes for young men and young women have been in existence for many years in connection with the principal places in the circuit. They have helped to prolong the influence of the Sunday school, to provide recruits for the teaching staff, and to strengthen attachment to the church on the part of the young. Several have been very popular and prosperous. That at Red Lion St. has been carried on uninterruptedly for more than fifty years, and its jubilee was celebrated in 1896, when all the ministers then living who had taken charge of it were invited to be present.

DAY SCHOOLS

In few towns has more attention been paid by Methodism to secular education than in Burnley.
The erection of large central premises in Red Lion St. has already been described. To those Mr. Murray and Miss Edwards were transferred as teachers from an earlier non-Government school at Keighley Green. They remained only a short time, when their places were taken by Mr. Matthews and Miss Morley, better known in later years as Mrs. J. S. Horn. Mr. Matthews was succeeded by Mr. Edgar,

who died on November 2nd, 1894, after a long absence from Burnley, but whose name is still held in great esteem. His influence was strong and far-reaching, and many of our best known townsmen were brought under it during the fifteen years of his head-mastership. Mr. J. S. Horn succeeded him in the boys' department, but in 1882 after twelve years service became Clerk to the Burnley Union. He had previously been head-master of Fulledge schools, and is indebted to Methodism beyond most men. Miss Fletcher succeeded Miss Morley, and was a most successful girls' mistress. Mr. Midgley, the present head-master, has been in charge seventeen years. In 1889 the schools were re-organised, and a higher grade girls' school was established. The latter was placed under the care of Miss Hargreaves, who was succeeded by Miss Walker, and two years later by Miss Dodgeon. The school reached its zenith both numerically and financially in 1892. Free schools and the establishment of competitive board-schools have made against the attendance, but there are still 700 children on the books, and the efficiency of the schools is well maintained.

The Fulledge day schools were opened on January 11th, 1864. Mr. Horn was succeeded at the beginning of 1870 by Mr. E. Jones, under whose care the school became the largest Wesleyan day school in the country. It was visited by the Right Hon. A. J. Mundella, when Vice-President of the Council, and he expressed great satisfaction with what he saw. In 1896 Mr. Jones was elected to the clerkship of the School Board, and succeeded at Fulledge by Mr. L. Walton. At the present time over a thousand children are in daily attendance. Mr. George Birtwistle, the senior wrangler in 1899, commenced his education at this school, and passed thence with the Howorth scholarship to the Burnley Grammar School. The head mistresses of the infants' department have been in succession the Misses E. Beetham, A. K. Pritchard, S. Herald, E. Grace, A. Roberts, and M. E. Newton. By the extension of the premises that took place in 1880 (see page 148), the accommodation according to Government requirements was increased from 802 to 1,062.

The Accrington Road day school was opened in 1876, when the small school conducted by Mr. James Thompson at Bartle Hills for a couple of years was transferred to the new premises. The teachers of the infants' school have been in succession Miss Ascroft (now Mrs. E. Jones), and Miss Robinson. The Accrington Road school was the first to feel the competition of free Board Schools, and eventually was handed over as far as day school purposes are concerned to the Burnley School Board. An infants' school was established in Whittlefield in 1878, and has been conducted by Miss S. Sharpe from the beginning. There are also two successful country schools at Wheatley Lane and Mereclough respectively. The former is conducted by Mr. Platt, and the latter, which was founded in 1872, by Mr. Tueart.

The Wesleyan day schools in Burnley very soon rose to a high state of educational efficiency, as the particulars of the Government grants for 1880 prove. At that time the grants were made exclusively according to merit, as shown in examination. The national average of the grants that year was 15s. 8¼d. per head, the borough average 19s. 10d. per head: but at the Red Lion Street school the grant averaged 20s. 1½d. per head, and at Fulledge 21s. 8½d. per head. Any one who is familiar with the public life of Burnley will be aware in some degree of the extent to which the educational work of Methodism has assisted in promoting the social and the religious well-being of the people.

THE TOWN MISSION

As far back as 1812 a "Benevolent Society for the relief of the industrous poor in time of sickness or accidental distress" was founded. In the ninth year of its existence it reported an income of £28 14s., and the visitation of nearly a hundred of the sick or needy. The writer of the report availed himself of the opportunity to indulge in a little philosophy. "The wisdom and goodness of God," he wrote, "appear in the continuance of indigent persons. Were they to cease out of the land, the feelings of compassion, tenderness, and mercy would be greatly contracted, and a stoical insensibility pervade the human mind. On the other hand, to diminish the numerous evils attendant on the present state of man . . . affords peculiar pleasure to the generous and humane." This pleasure showed itself in the establishment of a variety of auxiliary but loosely associated institutions. In February, 1840, a Dorcas society undertook "to provide clothing for the industrous or afflicted but necessitous poor"; and its second annual report, after describing trade as "extremely depressed" and the winter as "more than ordinarily severe," congratulated the members that one hundred and ninety-nine cases of need had been relieved. About the same time, or even earlier, arrangements were made for the systematic distribution of religious tracts, and a Friendly Sick society was established. The latter escaped dissolution until March, 1890, when its funds were divided, and each of its sixty surviving members received on the average the sum of £9. The former still flourishes in partial independence, and its report for the current year states that some two hundred and seventy persons are regularly engaged in the dissemination of pure literature in the various districts of the town.

In 1857 most of these organisations were amalgamated, and the Burnley Wesleyan Town Mission began to be. Of

## THE TOWN MISSION.

the original committee of eighteen persons only three survive, Messrs. G. Howorth, W. Lancaster, and J. Thornton. The first year two missionaries were employed, Thomas Towler and James Crossley. In 1865 James Kelly entered upon his useful career, and seven years later John Greenwood. Miss Sarah Aspden was engaged as a Scripture reader in 1873. George Clayton was employed in 1879, and after him came A. Douthwaite, H. Higgins in 1882, and Joseph Astin in 1891. The annual cost of the mission for the last few years has averaged about £300, and few will be unwilling to acknowledge that on the whole the money has been well spent.

DISTRICT MEETINGS
The May meeting of the District Synod has been held in Burnley on several occasions. In 1834 is the first recorded instance, followed by 1855, 1859, 1863, 1871, and several subsequent years, the circuit taking its turn in hospitality regularly with the other principal centres in the District.

# CHAPTER V.

# COLNE CIRCUIT, 1810-1899.

IN 1810 the Colne society was discussing a proposal to erect a school upon a site which Col. Clayton undertook to provide for the purpose at a nominal rent. The scheme was to create a body of trustees who would appoint a master, and to make the master responsible for all expenditure, inclusive of the interest on the borrowed capital. But difficulties quickly multiplied in regard to the site and proposed management of the school. Mr. Richard Sagar disapproved of the plan, and it appears to have been found impossible to carry it out at the time. A new chapel however soon became a necessity, owing to the great increase in the number of worshippers.

At a quarterly meeting held at Southfield in June, 1814, it was determined to solicit subscriptions. A year later a plot

WESLEYAN CHAPEL, ALBERT ROAD.

of land in West Parade, containing 2,560 yards, was purchased from Lord Derby for £200; but for some reason the scheme made but little progress. The superintendent died in 1818, and shortly afterwards Mr. Richard Sagar of Southfield passed away. In 1823 the scheme was revived, and it was resolved to build a chapel on the land already purchased, and to use the old chapel as a school-room. At last, on Good Friday, April 1st, 1824, when the ground was covered with snow, and the day was bitterly cold, the foundation stone was laid. The chapel was opened[1] on Good Friday of the following year. When the trustees decided to build, they thought that £100 might be raised by subscriptions and collections, and that the balance of the proposed expenditure of £2,600 might be left as a debt. Their estimate of cost was nearly correct, as the entire cost, including that of the site, was £2,729 16s. 8d.; but they greatly under-estimated the ability and liberality of the Colne Methodists, for £900 had been promised before the building was completed, and the collections at the opening services amounted to £210. In 1827 an organ was added at a cost of £105; but this was superseded in 1872 by one which cost £700.

In 1852 the debt on the two chapels amounted to £2,400, of which nearly £1,000 was paid off in July, 1857, when the chapel was also repaired and redecorated. In 1859 a further reduction of the debt by £200 took place. Improvements were effected again in 1865. In 1871 a bazaar was held with a view to reduce the debt; and after a still more determined effort at the jubilee of the chapel in 1875, the trustees were able to announce that only £500 remained. The chapel was improved in 1885 by the erection of a portico fronting Albert Road, and by other alterations, at a total cost of £1,200. In 1888 Mr. H. Pickles left the trust the sum of £200. A debt of £650 was cleared by a bazaar in March, 1891. In April, 1895, the chapel was re-decorated, and the sum of £262 was raised at the opening services.

The Sunday school was for many years carried on in the old chapel in Colne Lane. The desirability of having a building both better adapted to its purpose and nearer to the chapel led to the erection of the new school-rooms in George Street. The foundation stone was laid by Mr. Asquith, of East Parade, on Good Friday, 1868; and the building was opened for Sunday school purposes in June, 1869, when the Rev. John Rattenbury conducted the services. The site was purchased from Mr. George Bottomley for £211 9s. 6d., and though £725 was collected, including a handsome donation of £200 by Mr.

---

1. For an interesting account of these services see the *Methodist Magazine* for 1825, and Carr's *Annals of Colne*, pp. 45-48.

James Haworth, of Bacup, on the occasson of his marriage to Miss Halstead, of Colne, a very heavy debt was left. On January 9th, 1871, the premises were opened as an elementary day school with Mr. John Dutton as head master, who was succeeded five years later by Mr. Thomas Baldwin. A large bazaar was held in the spring of 1871, and yielded £1,030 towards the reduction of the debt, which has now entirely disappeared. It is calculated that as many as 5,262 children have passed through the school during the twenty-eight years of its existence, and at present the number on the register is 624, with an average attendance of 521. Various organisations were gradually added to the schools, especially a prosperous Friendly Sick Society, and a Reading Association that has contributed to the retention of the interest of the senior scholars.

The following is a list of ministers who have travelled in the circuit since the separation of Burnley, with the number of members as reported to the Conference each year:—

| Year | Ministers | Members |
|---|---|---|
| 1810,-11. | Stephen Wilson, Joshua Fearnsides | 800, 500 |
| 1812. | William Midgley, Thomas Newby | 520 |
| 1813,-14. | W. Midgley, Joseph Worrall | 560, 560 |
| 1815. | Thomas Vasey, jun., Daniel Jackson, jun. | 580 |
| 1816,-17. | T. Vasey, jun., George Tindale | 600, 700 |
| 1818. | Maximilian Wilson, Daniel Walton | 830 |
| 1819. | Joseph Brookhouse, D. Walton | 800 |
| 1820. | J. Brookhouse, William Ash | 700 |
| 1821. | Thomas Gee, W. Ash | 740 |
| 1822. | T. Gee, Robert Pickering | 900 |
| 1823. | R. Pickering, Thomas Catterick | 960 |
| 1824. | R. Pickering, Thomas Eastwood | 962 |
| 1825. | George Thompson, T. Eastwood | 911 |
| 1826,-27. | Hugh Beech, James Hickson | 1000, 980 |
| 1828. | H. Beech, J. Hickson, Andrew Aylmer | 1120 |
| 1829. | Thomas Preston, Thomas Hickson, A. Aylmer | 1030 |
| 1830. | Joseph Gostick, T. Hickson | 1030 |
| 1831. | J. Gostick, Thomas Skelton | 900 |
| 1832,-33. | John Jones, John Bumstead | 868, 875 |
| 1834. | J. Bumstead, Thomas Slugg | 1000 |
| 1835. | T. Slugg, Benjamin Frankland | 1006 |
| 1836. | B. Frankland, John Raby | 1007 |
| 1837. | J. Raby, Samuel Merrill | 950 |
| 1838. | William Levell, S. Merrill | 930 |
| 1839,-40. | W. Levell, Joseph Mortimer | 836, 979 |
| 1841,-42,-43. | James Wilson, William Winterbottom | 1057, 917, 900 |
| 1844,-45. | William Sleigh, William Exley | 871, 790 |
| 1846. | Peter Prescott, senr., W. Exley | 820 |
| 1847. | P. Prescott, Charles Currelly | 804 |

## MINISTERS IN COLNE.

1848,-49. Thomas Turner, John G. Cox - - 749, 753
1850,-51,-52. Benjamin Gartside, John Eaton - 700, 577, 542
1853,-54,-55. Jonathan Barrowclough, Alfred Lockyer
    502, 532, 538
1856,-57,-58. William Ash, Richard Stepney - 584, 625, 651
1859,-60,-61. Samuel Cooke, William Parkinson 672, 729, 747
1862. John Imisson, Jonathan Dent, William C. Williams 799
1863. J. Imisson, J. Dent, Joseph M. Browne - - 875
1864. James Cooke, J. Dent, J. M. Browne - - 927
1865. William Chambers, Frederick Haines - - 950
1866. W. Chambers, Albert J. Popham - - - 550
1867,-68. Joseph R. Cleminson, Andrew I. Wharton 523, 560
1869,-70,-71. William Watson, John Clements 583, 623, 623
1872,-73. Ebenezer Moulton, Matthew C. Pennington 610, 631
1874,-75. Sampson Cocks, Nelson C. Hesk - 613, 600
1876. S. Cocks, Josiah Goodacre - - - 650
1877. J. Goodacre, W. Boswell Lowther - - - 700
1878. J. Goodacre, William Brooks - - - 680
1879,-80. John Pollitt, W. Brooks - - 700, 716
1881. J. Pollitt, Sampson Nicholls - - - 720
1882. George Hobson, Charles Bryant - - 740
1883. G. Hobson, Vetranio Tyas - - - 772
1884. G. Hobson, James Feather - - - 719
1885,-86. Edmund Maden, J. Feather - - 550, 503
1887. E. Maden, James Wakely - - - 501
1888. Isaac Pollitt, J. Wakely - - - 554
1889,-90. I. Pollitt, W. Clement Kendall - 532, 535
1891. George Oyston, B.A., W. C. Kendall - - 567
1892,-93. G. Oyston, B.A., Charles Forrington 533, 554
1894. A. Leppington Barley, C. Forrington - 578
1895. A. L. Barley, Henry Wostenholm - - 617
1896. A. L. Barley, John T. Watts - - 613
1897,-98. Thomas Law, J. T. Watts - - 629, 657
1899. T. Law, J. Wesley Whitmore - - 699

The following ministers have resided in the circuit as supernumeraries:—John Barritt, from 1820 to 1840; John Wesley Barritt, in 1828 and 1829, and again from 1842 to 1845; William McKitrick, from 1841 to 1843; and Isaac Keeling, at Earby, from 1866 to 1868.

The office of circuit steward has been held by the following gentlemen since the division in 1865:—

1865. William Dixon, John Wilson.
1866. Thomas Wiseman, William Bracewell.
1867-1872. Thomas Wiseman, John Catlow.
1873-1878. Thomas Wiseman, James Hudson.
1879-1880. James Hudson, William Bracewell.
1881. John Catlow, Charles Tatham.

1882-1883. C. Tatham, John Hey.
1884-1887. John Hey, William Holmes.
1888.     W. Holmes, Robert Blakey.
1889-1890. Robert Blakey, Daniel Pilling.
1891-1893. James Stansfield, Caleb Duckworth.
1894.     Caleb Duckworth, Thomas Baldwin.
1895.     Thomas Baldwin, W. Wilkinson.
1896.     W. Wilkinson, Joshua Duckworth.
1897.     Joshua Duckworth, Joseph Hey.
1898-1899. Joseph Hey, J. L. Wildman.

## COLLINGWOOD STREET.

A class was started at Primet Bridge in 1886. It was first held in a cottage occupied by one of the friends. This soon became too small, and a larger cottage was taken. A few weeks after a Sunday school was opened, but to accommodate those who came it was necessary to hire a large room in the neighbourhood. This in its turn soon proved too small. At the same time the population of Colne was increasing so rapidly that further provision for secular education was necessary.

At the Christmas quarterly meeting in 1880 it was decided to build a school at Primet Bridge. The stone-laying took place on Saturday, October 22nd, 1881, when the collection amounted to £123. The cost of the new premises was £2,865, towards which £700 was raised. The premises consist of an upper room, 72 ft. by 30 ft. used as a day school, and a lower room 51 ft. by 30 ft. used for public worship. The school was opened on Sunday, April 9th, 1882, when services were conducted by the Rev. W. T. Radcliffe. The following month a bazaar was held in aid of the new school, and the sum of £518 was raised; and by similar means £250 were obtained three years later. A new infant school was opened in 1888, at a cost of £455. In 1893 another bazaar yielded £333.

## LANGROYD ROAD.

This mission was started in March, 1879, by Mr. S. Cork and Mr. W. M. Simpson, as an offshoot from George street. Services were held on Sunday evenings in a room belonging to Mr. Crabtree in Windy Bank. A Sunday school was formed with twelve scholars to begin with. The number increased, and in 1890 there were 163 scholars and 30 teachers. Mr. Higson, who died in May, 1889, took an active interest in the development of the mission. He was superintendent for four years and secretary for four. A new school chapel was built in 1890, the stones being laid on June 7th by Mrs. Cork, of Blackpool, who gave £25, Mrs. J. Catlow £20, Mr. William

Wilkinson and Mr. John Varley £20 each. The teachers and officers gave £50. Accommodation for three hundred persons was provided, at a cost, inclusive of that of site, of £900. The chapel was opened on September 4th, 1890. A debt of £300 was left upon the trust, but £255 was raised by means of a bazaar in the autumn of 1891.

## TRAWDEN.

Trawden, like Colne, has always been strongly attached to Methodism, but prior to 1810 there was no place of worship in the village, and the people were compelled to walk to Colne to attend religious services. In that year a commodious chapel was erected, the Wesleyans being thus the first religious body

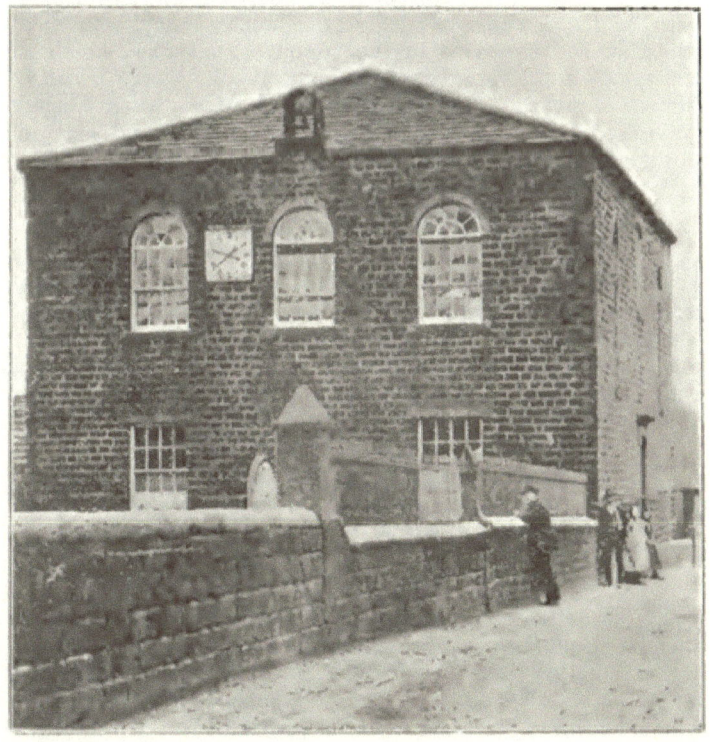

TRAWDEN CHAPEL.

to establish a church in the village. Repeated changes have been made in the village; but owing to the lack of facilities for communication with the centres of industry, the place has grown only slowly, and very few additions have been required to the chapel, though an enlargement took place in 1850. At the time of erection the gallery was pewed, but the area was filled with loose benches which remained until the renovation in 1890, when the desire to build a new chapel was frustrated through the impossibility of obtaining a site. The renovation however was very thorough, and at its completion the chapel was greatly improved. The cost was about £1,600, of which £1,100 was quickly paid off by means of subscriptions and special efforts in the shape of bazaars, &c. But one thing was lacking, an organ to efficiently lead the singing. One was obtained at a cost of about £400, which sum was raised by the time of opening. The chapel has all along been supplied by ministers and local preachers from the Colne circuit.

In front of the chapel is a neat little grave-yard, and here lie the remains of the Rev. Thomas Vasey, who died whilst in active service in the circuit. The stone, which is the oldest in the yard, bears the inscription—"Thomas Vasey, Methodist preacher, who departed this life May 5th, 1818, aged 39 years, in the 18th year of his public ministry and the 3rd in the Colne circuit.

> This mouldering dust shall here repose in peace
> Till that great day when time itself shall cease.
> His spirit is with God ; and this its plea,
> My Saviour lived, my Saviour died for me."

Previously to the alteration of the chapel in 1890, a tablet to the memory of William Hartley and his children, relatives of Mr. W. P. Hartley, of Aintree, occupied a place on the walls ; but during the renovation it was removed, and has since been lying neglected in the grave-yard. It is now broken in two, and rough usage has erased the date of Mr. Hartley's death, though the year 1848 is still to be seen.

When the chapel was first opened in 1810, a Sunday school was commenced. The schoolroom itself was built in 1871, though the cost was not defrayed until fifteen years later.

## FOULRIDGE.

The chapel was built in 1824, and re-opened after alterations on February 13th, 1859. Thirty years later a new organ, built by Messrs. Laycock & Son, of Crosshills, at a cost of £180, was put in and opened on Saturday, January 6th. The following day services were conducted by the Rev. George Dickenson, and the total collections amounted to £20 18s.

## LANESHAW BRIDGE.

The first Methodist chapel was built in 1822. The foundation of a new one was laid on Saturday, May 1st, 1858, by Captain Sagar, of Southfield House. The plan and specifications were furnished gratuitously by Mr. E. Milnes, of Bradford. The chapel was opened on July 15th, when services were conducted by the Rev. Thomas Vasey. Other services followed by Mr. Robert Walton, of Leeds, and Mr. John Dawson, of Bacup; and the total collections were £22 6s. 3d. On June 10th, 1877, a new harmonium was introduced.

## BLACK LANE ENDS.

A Sunday school was started in a room at Black Lane Ends by William Hartley and John Taylor in 1830. In 1838 an effort was made to build a chapel, towards the cost of which £43 was raised. The money was not sufficient, so that a mere shell was erected and a few forms put in. The cost was £84, and the opening services yielded less than £10. At the close of 1839 there was a debt of £40. In 1851 the chapel was pewed at a cost of £70, and the debt was increased to £80. In 1863 a school was built at a cost of £54, and a day school was started. In 1880 a new chapel was built, the foundation stone being laid on September 11th, by Mr. John Butterworth, of Burnley, who gave £50, and allowed the stone to be taken free of cost from a quarry on his land. The site was given by Mr. Wilkinson, of Colne. The cost of the new building was £600, towards which promises were received to the amount of £370. The collection at the stone-laying yielded £34. In 1897 an organ was introduced.

## COTTON TREE.

At the December quarterly meeting in 1892, it was proposed to build at Cotton Tree a school chapel to seat 300 persons, and the proposal was carried out the following year at a cost of about £400. The cause has so prospered during the succeeding years that a movement is now on foot to enlarge the chapel to the extent of doubling its accommodation.

## CHAPTER VI.

## PADIHAM, 1810-1899.

FROM 1810 to 1861 Padiham was included in the Burnley circuit, and shared its vicissitudes. At the Conference of 1847 the circuit had so grown that the services of a third minister were required, and he was appointed to reside at Padiham. The Rev. John Clulow was the first, and remained for three years. He was succeeded in turn by John H. Lord in 1850 and 1851; by William R. Rogers in 1852 and 1853; by William Brailey from 1854 to 1856; by John Lyth in 1857 and 1858; and by G. C. Taylor in 1859 and 1860.

At the conference of 1861, Padiham became the head of a new circuit, in which the following ministers have since been stationed. The figures in the last column show the number of members in March of each year.

| Year | Ministers | Members |
|---|---|---|
| 1861,-62. | Joseph Binns, William Bunting | 496 |
| 1863. | Joseph Binns, James Spensley | 504 |
| 1864. | Thomas Brumwell, John E. Pater | 482 |
| 1865. | Thomas Brumwell, W. J. Hedley | 498 |
| 1866. | Thomas Brumwell, A. I. Wharton | 527 |
| 1867. | John P. Sumner, Sampson Weaver | 570 |
| 1868,-69. | John P. Sumner, R. B. Kent | 748, 657 |
| 1870,-71. | William Winterburn, John Mackintosh | 637, 611 |
| 1872,-73,-74. | Thomas Derry, Edward Crump | 608, 645, 625 |
| 1875. | George Smith, Joseph Higham | 590 |
| 1876,-77. | William Shaw, Joseph Higham | 562, 555 |
| 1878,-79,-80. | Isaac Rodgers, Henry Smallwood | 585, 605, 580 |
| 1881. | Samuel Haigh, Joseph Charlesworth | 565 |
| 1882. | John Rhodes, Joseph Charlesworth | 576 |
| 1883. | John Rhodes, John W. Henderson | 550 |
| 1884. | John Rhodes, Edward Crump | 563 |
| 1885,-86. | Edward Crump, Isaac Pollitt | 557, 523 |
| 1887. | Isaac Pollitt, John Judson | 563 |
| 1888,-89,-90. | Amos White, C. Wilfrid Cook | 540, 540, 550 |
| 1891,-92,-93. | Giffard Dorey, James Hothersall | 583, 587, 592 |

1894.   Joseph Hammond, Elias T. Dickinson -   -   526
1895,-96,-97. Samuel Goodyer, Walter Hudson   507, 432, 417
1898,-99. Abraham Pearce, John H. Wilkinson  -   402, 433

The only supernumerary minister attached to the circuit appears to have been the Rev. G. Harvey Smith, who after but a few weeks' residence in it died in 1881. But it has produced at least one minister whose record is blameless and honourable. Starkie Starkie was the son of the late Robert Starkie, and was born at Higham in 1844. His conversion took place when he was in his twentieth year, and was marked and real. From his childhood he had been connected with the Wesleyan Sunday school, and a regular attendant at the public services and at the prayer meetings. But at length he was made terribly conscious that notwithstanding all these outward observances his heart was not right, and he was enabled to trust in Christ as his Saviour. At once he became an earnest worker in his church, and within a year of his conversion began to preach. On the Sunday when he was appointed to take his first service in a neighbouring village, the officials at Higham chapel arranged a service at five o'clock in the morning, that he and Mr. B. Moore might preach their first sermons there. A large congregation was present at that early hour, and sent forth the young men with many prayers. In eighteen months' time Mr. Starkie accepted an engagement as a lay missionary at Charlestown near Shipley, where he remained for two years. He there became a candidate for the ministry, and entered the Didsbury College in 1868. His circuits during the twenty-nine years of his ministry have been Ilkley, Knaresborough, Romsey, Pocklington, Great Yarmouth, Loughborough, Gravesend, Farnworth, Skipton, Batley, and Pateley Bridge, in all of which his labours have been blessed of God.

The following gentlemen have served as circuit stewards:—
1861-1866. Robert Hindle, John Smith.
1867-1869. William Waddington, James Stephenson.
1870.       Robert Hindle, William Waddington.
1871-1874. Robert Hindle, Charles Waddington.
1875.       Charles Waddington, James Stephenson.
1876-77.   Robert Hindle, John Smith.
1878-79.   Robert Hindle, Henry Dean.
1880-81.   Robert Hindle, Wm. Moorhouse.
1882-1887. Robert Hindle, John Blezard.
1888-89.   John Blezard, John Simpson.
1890-1892. John Blezard, Francis Helm.
1893-1895. Richard Cronshaw, Theo. Simpson.
1896-1899. Francis Helm, Theo. Simpson.

A few other memorable names have been preserved, in addition to those mentioned in an earlier chapter. John

Dewhirst, junr., was the only person who lived to attend the services of the three successive chapels. He was eight years old when the second chapel was opened, and survived the opening of the third by three years. He was never a leader, or an active participant in the evangelistic work of the society; but his membership covered a period of sixty years, and in the material and financial parts of the church's work his services were of the highest value. The following were the leaders during the first quarter of the nineteenth century :—James Wood, John Wood, Thomas Wood, John Stout, William Taylor, Henry Thompson, Thomas Wilkinson, Thomas Stead, Thomas Hudson, Thomas Walmsley, senr., and Henry Webster. For the second quarter the list runs :—Thomas Walmsley, senr., Thomas Wood, Henry Webster, Thomas Hudson, Henry Thompson, Reuben Longstaff, John Lord, Benjamin Dean, George Ainsworth, Richard Tattersall, Thomas Walmsley, junr., James Fletcher, James Kelly, John Smith, George Moorhouse, William Haworth, William Hanson, and Joseph Foster.

The following interesting reminiscences have been supplied by Dr. Scurrah, of Birmingham. "I distinctly remember," he writes, "the large gathering of Sunday school children in the park at Huntroyde on the occasion of the coronation of the Queen. Of course we Wesleyans made the largest display. Indeed at that time the Wesleyan might be called the established church at Padiham, as it was by far the largest and most influential congregation in the town. A day school to which I went was commenced in the St. Giles St. rooms by a Mr. Harding from London, and afterwards was conducted by Mr. John Stephenson in the present school. Two names stand out prominently in connection with the Padiham Methodism of that date, those of my grandfather, Mr. John Dewhirst, and of Mr. William Howorth. Mr. Dewhirst, or 'old John Dewhirst' as he was colloquially called, was for years the main stay and buttress of Methodism in Padiham. Mr. William Howorth was a singularly useful man. He was very reticent and unobtrusive. He knew Methodism well, and was a kind of lay Dr. Bunting, and somewhat like him in person. He was the leader of the choir, and used to give us young folks lessons in singing and music on the Hullah system which was then in vogue. He also used to conduct in the old chapel, Hall Hill, an early morning service at five o'clock every Christmas day, when he read the second chapter of St. Luke from a little flap desk in the gallery just behind the clock. This was a very popular service, but was given up when the new chapel was built, and a resident minister came to Padiham. There were several others who were prominent :—Mr. James Whitaker and family; Mr. Thomas Wood, of the Craggs, at the top of the town: Mr. William

Steward, who was a valuable school superintendent; Mr. James Moorhouse, a good leader; Mr. Thomas Walmsley, a man very gifted in prayer; Mr. John Smith, who built the first organ in the new chapel (there was no organ in the old chapel, but in the square large pew just in front of the pulpit were violas, double bass, fiddles, &c.); his brother Richard; Mr. William Waddington with his brother Charles; and Mr. John Stephenson with his brother James. Then there was James Kelly, an earnest but illiterate local preacher, who, when told he had no business to preach, said 'But I am called.' 'What proof have you?' he was asked. 'Ocular proof,' he replied. 'How so?' 'Why when I preach I've seen people cry and shed tears.'" Of Dr. Scurrah's sisters two married ministers, and of these one is well-known throughout British Methodism as Dr. Randles, theological tutor at Didsbury and an ex-president of the Conference.

The Hall Hill chapel continued to be used for more than a generation after Padiham became a part of the Burnley circuit, but particulars of its early history are not plentiful. In 1839 the trust was renewed by the appointment of the following gentlemen:—James Whitaker, Thomas Wood, Thomas Dewhirst, John Scurrah, Thomas Walmsley, Edmondson Monk, William Howorth, William Hopwood, John Hargreaves, George Barnes, and Peter Phillips. The congregation steadily increased, until it was no unusual thing for every seat to be occupied at the ordinary services; and in the closing months of 1845 a scheme was started for the erection of a new chapel, though only the year before a slight increase of accommodation had been secured by the addition of six pews at a cost of £32 16s. A convenient site was purchased from Mr. John Dewhirst for £257 10s. The foundation stone was laid by Mr. William Hopwood on New Year's Day, 1846, and the premises were opened on July 30th, 1847. Sitting accommodation was provided for 859 persons. The total cost, including that of site, was £3,038 6s. 7½d. By subscriptions was raised the handsome sum of £1,350 0s. 6d., the eight collections at the opening services yielded £248 18s.; and when the accounts were audited, and John Dewhirst had paid for the old Hall Hill chapel which he bought, the trustees found themselves with a debt of £1,150.

Of the musical arrangements at Wesley the history is of some interest. Early in 1863 Mr. John Smith commenced to build an organ, which was intended to supply a pressing necessity. For some time before there had been no musical instrument in the chapel. About 1856 Mr. Smith lent the trustees a small organ of his own, but this he afterwards sold to the trustees of Higham chapel. Prior to 1856 the choir had been assisted by two double-bass and two violoncellos: but after the Higham trustees became possessed of the organ, a flute was used from which the leading singer and the choir took the pitch of the tune to be sung. Mr. John Smith's workshop was in "Th' Fold" up "Th' Rake," on or near the present site of Mr. Cronshaw's residence in Windsor Terrace. The organ

WESLEY CHAPEL.

pipes, the swell, action, pedals, etc., were made mostly by Mr. Hudson. The building of the organ was necessarily slow, as Mr. Smith had but little leisure and desired no assistance; and his progress was watched with keen interest by the members of the congregation. Any one who visited the workshop became quite a centre of attraction and authority, when he related to his friends how many pipes had been made; and when James Hudson had completed the bellows, his achievement became quite a "town's talk." Eventually the work so far progressed that the trustees could make arrangements for the opening services, and the organ was removed by instalments to Wesley chapel. It was opened on the afternoon of Friday, November 5th, 1865. In 1874 Mr. John Smith became the superintendent of Cross Bank Sunday school. He soon foresaw that a chapel would be necessary in the neighbourhood, and with a view to promote its erection promised to give the organ when the premises were ready, and to allow the annual rent of £7 10s., paid by the trustees of Wesley, to accumulate meanwhile in aid of the scheme. The accumulations amounted eventually to £174 12s. 4d. The organ was used the last time in Wesley chapel on October 29th, 1893. It was then removed to Cross Bank, but underwent considerable alteration and enlargement, and was re-opened on Saturday, January 19th, 1894. The same year a fine instrument, built by Messrs. Wordsworth, of Leeds, at a cost, with subsidiary apparatus, of £1,110 7s. 0d., was put into Wesley chapel.

But many changes had taken place in the chapel and its decoration, before it was furnished with this organ. In 1867 the pews were remodelled and the whole premises cleaned and redecorated at a cost of £210, which, with the debts on the chapel and the minister's house, was covered by the proceeds of a bazaar the same year and a smaller one in 1868. Further improvements were made in 1881, when also the old houses that stood in front of the chapel were purchased, and a debt of £350 was left upon the trust. Seven years later this debt was removed by the proceeds of another bazaar, and for it was substituted a balance in hand of £234 2s. 6d. In 1893 still another bazaar yielded £764 0s. 0d., and the trustees were emboldened to purchase the grand organ that replaced Mr. Smith's, and to undertake extensive alterations involving an outlay of £864 17s. 0d. The re-opening services were held in March and April, 1894, and yielded £136 2s. 0d., but left a debt upon the trust of £800. But the Jubilee came in 1897, and collections amounting to £180 were made at the services; and the next year by a bazaar in continuation of the same movement and in aid alike of church and school the sum of £550 was raised.

The school in St. Giles Street soon proved too small to accommodate the scholars that flocked to it. In 1840 a two-storeyed building was erected on another site at a cost of £650. Each room was 56 feet by 30 feet, and over the porch was a small room used as a library. A wing was added in 1861 at a cost of about £400; and ten years later the old part of the premises was taken down and rebuilt on a larger scale, at an outlay of £1,196. In this school Mr. John Smith is said to have worked as teacher or superintendent for fifty successive years. The schools have steadily prospered. In 1866 the number of scholars reported was 700, and the teachers succeeded in clearing off a debt of £380, caused in part by the provision of new vestries. In 1877 the report of the Sunday School Union showed a staff of 165 teachers to 1,884 scholars, and the percentages of attendances were on the part of the former 88·5 and of the latter 62. In 1899 the scholars had increased in number to 2,205, and the teachers to 262. The percentage of average attendance was below that of the date above, but the number of members of society had risen to 191.

The chapel has recently received a bequest of £50 from Mr. Nicholas Helm. In 1889 the circuit received one of £100 from Mr. Robert Hindle, who also left a similar legacy to the trustees of the chapel at Sabden where he lived.

HALL HILL MISSION. The old Hall Hill chapel was bought back from the Dewhirst family, and opened as a mission-room on September 12th, 1883. In 1888 about £90 was spent in painting and refurnishing it, and the following year a bazaar was held with a view to liquidate a debt of £460, left behind in part from the original purchase. In 1890 the school reported an afternoon attendance of 130 scholars, whilst the congregation on Sunday evenings was said to average 250. Mr. R. Cronshaw was an earnest worker in the mission for many years.

CROSS BANK. The Cross Bank school-chapel dates from 1871, the foundation stones having been laid in February of that year and the premises opened for public worship by the Rev. W. O. Simpson on September 8th. The total cost, inclusive of the entire site for chapel and school, was £3,200. Five years later the school was greatly enlarged at a further cost of £1,065. By 1880 the debt had been reduced to £380, which was then removed by another of the frequent bazaars. But the district grew so rapidly that already 350 scholars were reported as enrolled in the Day school and 393 in the Sunday school, and the need of further extension became pressing. In 1891 a start was made in the erection of a new chapel, which was opened by the Rev. W. L. Watkinson in April of the following year. It cost £3,200, and provided accommodation for 750 persons. Bazaars of course preceded and followed, producing £620 in the year of erection, £544 4s. 1d. in 1895, and £351 0s. 5d. in 1897. The history of the organ has already been told.

CROSS BANK CHAPEL.

## SABDEN.

The first introduction of Methodism into Sabden is said to have taken place in 1766, when two Methodists of the names of Moorhouse and Bradley went to live there. The former removed twelve years later to Castle Clough, but about the same time the latter was joined by John Harrison who had come from Accrington; and in 1810 Sabden was put upon the plan of the Burnley circuit, and Harrison's house was opened for the services and class-meetings. The first contribution to the quarterly meeting was made in September of that year, and amounted to 5s. 2d. Mr. Harrison's house was used as the place of worship for a quarter of a century: but in 1835 a chapel, capable of seating 150 persons, was built at a cost of £350, and opened on October 18th by the Rev. Benjamin Frankland. A second chapel, seating 350 persons, was built in 1844 at a cost of £1,130, and opened by Dr. George Osborn. In 1860 the sum of £200 was spent in enlarging the school, the accommodation having proved inadequate through the increase of the population and the thriving condition of the neighbourhood. The third and present chapel,

SABDEN CHAPEL.

seating 500 persons, was built in 1879 at a cost of £2,270, and opened on July 10th by the Rev. W. T. Radcliffe. It is a handsome structure, with a spire rising with the terminal to a height of ninety feet. In 1894 a suitable organ was introduced at a cost of nearly £300, which was met partly by subscriptions and partly by the proceeds of a bazaar in the following year. Land has recently been acquired for the extension of the premises. A Sunday school was established at Sabden Bridge in 1835.

## HIGHAM.

At the time of the formation of the Burnley circuit, public worship at Higham amongst the Methodists continued to be held in the house of H. H. Wilkinson; and his autobiography (see page 53) is the best authority for the history of the years immediately following. In 1812, or possibly the year before, came the opportunity of securing a chapel. Mr. Robert Hargreaves was inclined, so writes Mr. Wilkinson, "to go and live at Burnley, so he gave us the offer of his dwelling-house. He thought we might make the large end into a very good chapel and save the other end for a minister to live in. So we got eight or ten gentlemen of Padiham and Burnley to come up and see the premises, and we decided to make Mr. Hargreaves a bid of £600. He said it was little, but he would rather it was made into a chapel than anything else. Mr. Thomas Kay bought the premises for £630, and Mr. Hargreaves returned the £30 to begin the subscription list. This was a day of rejoicing to us at Higham. They then appointed me and Mr. John Wood to go all round the country where we thought best. We went and told the people that we were going to have both a Chapel and School. Now this was very pleasing to the people for there was not any Sunday School round about. So we got £200, which was all laid out in making the house into a chapel. We got also a local preacher [George Hargreaves] to come and live in one of the cottages and we now had preaching every Sunday. We then got a room for the scholars to write in, and the smaller children were taught in the Chapel bottom. We now went on gloriously, for we soon had two hundred children and plenty of willing teachers. At this time our school served Sabden Bridge, Sabden Hall, Newchurch-in-Pendle, Wheatley Lane and Pendle Bottom." The population of Higham at the time was 742.

The trustees of this first chapel were Messrs. Thomas Eltoft, Thomas Kay, John Moore, Jeremiah Spencer, William Moore, William Hopwood, John Dewhirst, William Taylor, James Stewart, John Robinson, Robert Procter, Henry H. Wilkinson, and J. Livesey. The seat rents for 1813 and the next two years were £14 8s. 4d., £16 2s. 6d., and £14 os. 7d. respectively.

The first baptism took place on January 13th, 1813, when Christiana, the daughter of George and Helen Pollard, was brought, when not quite three weeks old, from Upper House, Barley, a distance of over four miles, and solemnly dedicated to God. Two grand-daughters of this worthy couple are at the present time members of the Higham society, one of them a daughter of the little girl whose baptism has just been recorded.

At their first meeting in 1819, the trustees passed the following resolution:—"Agreed, by the trustees of Higham chapel, that a subscription be made for the purpose of purchasing a violincello [sic] for the accommodation of the said chapel, and that a person be appointed to play on the same: and if the said instrument become any way injurious to the prosperity and peace of the body of people at Higham, the trustees of the said chapel shall have it in their power to stop the said instrument: likewise if any person or persons, players of the said instrument, become any way improper in their conduct, it shall be in the power of the trustees, to dispose of the said instrument to another. N.B. The violincello to belong to the said chapel."

In 1820 the local preacher, George Hargreaves, left Higham, and Mr. Wilkinson was appointed leader in his stead. The same year a graveyard was opened in connection with the chapel, and is said to have been at that time the only burial place within two miles of the village. The first person interred was Margaret, the mother of John Lord. But the progress of the society must have been greatly hindered by the increasing burden of debt, which in 1829 had become so heavy that a special appeal for help was made to the Conference. In the superintendents' register is preserved a copy of the statement presented on the occasion. The debt is put at £903 13s. 5d., and is said to have been caused by "the building of cottages and arrears of interest." After stating that the number of the members was 115, and that the seats were let at the quarterly rental of from 6d. to 1s., there is appended the following hopeless balance-sheet:—

| INCOME. | £ | s. | d. | EXPENDITURE. | £ | s. | d. |
|---|---|---|---|---|---|---|---|
| Seat Rent............... |  | 5 | 2 | 6 | Interest............ | 37 | 2 | 6 |
| Anniversary............ |  |  | 11 | 6 |  |  |  |  |
| Sunday School......... |  | 3 | 0 | 0 |  |  |  |  |
| Funerals & Baptisms |  | 2 | 2 | 6 |  |  |  |  |
| Rent of Cottages...... |  | 8 | 2 | 6 |  |  |  |  |
| Ballance [sic] ......... |  | 18 | 3 | 6 |  |  |  |  |
|  | £37 | 2 | 6 |  | £37 | 2 | 6 |

The Conference directed the Chapel committee to grant a donation of £7 4s. 0d., which, as any one who consults the Minutes of that year will acknowledge, was as much as the distressed condition of the General Chapel Fund would allow.

Better days however soon dawned, and considerable help was obtained from some unknown quarter. In 1832 the society was so far relieved that it was ready to enter upon new enterprises, and a school was built in what was afterwards used as a wheelwright's shop and is still familiarly known as "Proctor's shop." There Edward Starkie was the teacher, in succession to Charles Tunnicliffe, who had used for the same purpose the house opposite the barn of Lowerhouse farm. Eight years later, too, the trustees decided unanimously to enlarge the chapel at a cost of "about £110," but with the wisdom of experience postponed the commencement of the work until three-fourths of the proposed expenditure had been collected. The sum was soon raised, largely through the efforts of Mr. Joseph Calderbank, and in 1841 the "old chapel," as it was long known, was formed by removing the partition walls of the cottages at the back and appropriating the space thus recovered. In 1859 new premises were built for the Day and Sunday schools at a cost of £430, and opened free from debt. Two years later the organ presented by Mr. John Smith, of Padiham, was put in, the opening services being conducted by a man who afterwards attained distinction in another church, Mr. E. Nuttall, of Bolton-by-Bolland. And at length in 1872 the "old chapel" was

HIGHAM CHAPEL.

taken down, and the present one, accommodating 500 persons, was erected on the same site at a cost of £1,700. The opening services in May and June, 1874, yielded £200; almost the same amount was obtained by means of a bazaar the preceding year; and the debt that remained was so small as to cause no serious trouble. The schools were redecorated, and some slight interior alterations were made in 1892. And by means of a bazaar in April, 1898, the sum of £360 was raised, and the entire premises were freed from debt. The bazaar was opened by

Mrs. Varley, a grand-daughter of H. H. Wilkinson, and by Miss Moore, a grand-daughter of Joseph Moore.

Of the Methodist worthies at Higham, in addition to such as have already been mentioned, a long list might be compiled. Joseph Moore was a man given to abstraction and concentrated thought. It is related of him that once, when he was appointed to preach at Sabden Hall, he walked all the way through heavy rain and arrived at the chapel thoroughly drenched, with his umbrella wrapped up under his arm. John Lord in connection with the Sunday school did perhaps more to stimulate a desire for reading and arouse intellectual activity amongst the young than any one else. Edward Starkie was a leader for forty years, and John Tattersall for thirty, walking regularly to and fro from Burnley to Higham that he might meet his class. For the same period Joseph Wilmore acted as choirmaster, and was fruitful in other good works. John Livesey was for nearly half a century an effective local preacher. John Berry, Richard Tattersall, who on his deathbed rejoiced that his life had been prolonged over the day on which his missionary subscription was due, the Roberts family, of Hunter Holme, and many another name, will long be cherished in the traditions of Higham and the memories of good men. The decease in his maturity of Mr. John Starkie, son of the above-named Edward, has taken place whilst these notes were being prepared. His was a typical instance of a useful life in a village community.

Other traditions are of an amusing kind. It is said that a member of the congregation, a working man who was getting on in years, and finding the burden of daily life oppressive, not infrequently gave way to nature's promptings on Sunday afternoons and fell asleep. As soon as he opened his eyes, he would invariably call out, "Hallelujah, praise the Lord!" Sometimes this ejaculation came in inopportunely. On one occasion the preacher was enlarging on "the terrors of the law," and in a most emphatic manner thumped the bible to give emphasis to the words, "If you don't repent, you will have to go to hell to all eternity." The thumping of the bible awoke the sleeper, who according to his custom called out, "Hallelujah, praise the Lord." Another interesting story of Higham village Methodism illustrates how men distinguish in times of sickness between mere professionalism and true Christian character. A man was seriously ill, and the doctor knowing the gravity of his illness suggested to him, as was very common in those days, that if he wished anybody to pray with him, he had better send for the parson at once. The doctor added that if there was any one whom he would prefer for this purpose he would be glad to get him to come. To the surprise of the doctor the sick man replied, that his choice of a visitor would depend upon whether he was likely to get better or not. Whereupon the doctor asked, "Why, what difference does that make?" to which the dying man replied, "Well, you see, if I am likely to get better, I want you to send for the curate, but if I'm likely to die I want you to send to Tummas," referring to a devoted Methodist. The doctor asked again why the difference. "Well," said the sick man, "if I get better I'm afraid I may slip back into my old ways, and if I did I couldn't for shame meet Tummas, but I shouldn't mind meeting the curate."

A Friendly Society was established in the village as far back as October 17th, 1812, and met in the Methodist chapel. It provided not only for temporary help in cases of sickness, but even for old-age pensions. The fourteenth of the original rules ran, "If any member shall arrive at the age of seventy years, having submitted to and performed the rules of the society, he shall receive and be entitled to the sum of three shillings per week during his life, and have liberty to do his best endeavours for himself and family, in aid of the same; and if he become unable to work, no further allowance will be made for him but the three shillings per week during his life." A long table of fines was prepared, from twopence for "sitting in the chair of any of the officers during a meeting," sixpence for "cursing or swearing during a meeting," three shillings for "any member fighting with another member, though not at a meeting," to the climax—"Receiving the benefits of the society under pretended sickness or indisposition, besides being obliged to return the money so received, expulsion." On September 7th, 1845, a Sick Society was established in connection with the Sunday school.

SABDEN HALL

For many years services were held in a preaching room at Sabden Hall. The room was closed for repairs in 1865, and in 1892 was closed altogether for a time, the people having all or nearly all left the neighbourhood. But in August, 1899, the room was re-opened, several young men connected with the Higham school and congregation having undertaken to conduct a weekly service. The first of the new series of services have been very successful, and augur well for the prosperity of the place.

## LOWERHOUSE.

Methodism was introduced into Lowerhouse in 1798 by William Todd, who held a situation at the print works owned by the late Sir Robert Peel. He established a Sunday school at the lower end of the village in a cottage opposite to the present Victoria Terrace: and there services were held for thirty-nine years. When the Dugdales purchased the Lowerhouse estate, they built a large room adjoining what was the new mill, and to this the services and school were transferred in 1837. In 1876 these were transferred again to larger premises, which the Messrs. Dugdale had put up chiefly for the purpose of a day school. But every sensible congregation prefers to worship in a building of its own: and in 1895 the Methodists at Lowerhouse decided to celebrate the centenary of the establishment

LOWERHOUSE CHAPEL.

of Sunday schools by the erection of a school-chapel. A site, containing 3,076 square yards, was readily given by Col. Dugdale, who supplemented his gift with a liberal subscription. On August 28th, 1897, the foundation stones were laid by Mr. William Thornber, and the proceeds of the day amounted to £200. The chapel was opened on Thursday, June 9th, 1898, and the total proceeds of the opening services was £170. The cost of the premises, which provide accommodation for about seven hundred persons, has been £2,800. A debt of £1,500 was left when the building accounts were audited, but was substantially reduced by a successful bazaar in 1899. The society at Lowerhouse reports at present a membership of forty-four, with more than three hundred scholars in the school and an efficient staff of teachers.

Some of the old workers in connection with Methodism in the village still survive. Others, such as George Heys, Moses Altham, Henry Wilkinson, Robert Dawson, William Lambert, are not likely soon to be forgotten. Thomas Sagar's connection is said to have lasted for eighty years, during seventy-five of which his attendance at the school in one capacity or another was regular and unfailing.

## HAPTON.

Up to 1856 there are said to have been no regular religious services of any public kind within the borders of the township of Hapton. A few Methodists resided there, and that year cottage services were begun. The following year a disused warehouse on the bank of the canal was hired, and a Sunday school established. Great difficulty was met with in the attempt to obtain a site for the erection of permanent premises, but at length one was secured from a small landowner, and on Whit-Monday, June 20th, 1859, the foundation stone of the first chapel was laid. It cost £312, and provided accommodation for 130 persons. Through the extension of the works of the late Mr. John Simpson, and Mr. John Riley's chemical works, the population rapidly increased, and the chapel proved too small. After some discussion and much waiting, another site was obtained, and the foundation stones of a second chapel laid

HAPTON CHAPEL.

on October 4th, 1884. The premises were opened in the same month of the following year. Accommodation was provided for 280 persons, at a cost of £1,750. Various bazaars were held in 1875, 1885, 1894, 1897, and probably at other dates, the ultimate result being that at the close of the last mentioned the debt was reduced to £70 or £80. An organ was placed in the chapel on December 4th, 1887.

## ROSEGROVE.

Methodism was introduced into Rosegrove by several families, that accompanied Messrs. Temple and Sutcliffe's business, when it was removed from Padiham. They secured the help of some of the members of the church they had left, and in November, 1863, started a school in a small cottage known as Bowker Fold. At the beginning of the following year they mustered 14 teachers and 47 scholars. In 1866 or 1867 the school was transferred to a newly-built cottage, which was adapted to the purpose by the removal of the partition walls. Amongst the principal workers were Messrs. Paul Helm, John Blezard, James Stephenson, Thomas Moorhouse, and William Riley. This cottage again soon became too small; and on May 25th, 1870, a school-chapel was opened. It provided

ROSEGROVE CHAPEL.

accommodation for 250 persons, and cost £473. In 1883, and again in 1896, the building was enlarged, at a total cost of over £500. Bazaars in 1887, 1891, 1894, 1897, yielded sums that practically covered the expenditure.

## CHAPTER VII.

## NELSON, 1810-1899.

METHODISM was introduced into Marsden about the year 1818. Henry Nuttall of Bradley Row, Robert Halstead of Raikes House, William Halstead and his wife Nancy of Netherfield Farm, William Clegg of Little Clough Head Farm, Robert Parker of Clough Head Farm, with their families, had previously attended Methodist services at Barrowford or Southfield. But at the time mentioned they decided to hold religious service nearer home, and Mr. Halstead lent for the purpose a cottage next door to his own house. In it preaching services were held, and a school conducted for something like eight years.

The population at that time was very small, there being only the little village of Lower Bradley, with its two or three farm houses, a few cottages round Bradley Mill, and Bradley Row in the district now called Nelson, but then known as Marsden. In 1826 the population of Great and Little Marsden together had risen to about four thousand, but trade was so bad and the people so poor that nearly three thousand are said to have been in receipt of parish or other relief. An old book in the possession of Mr. Leonard Marsden gives an account of the relief distributed about this time by Richard Thomas Wroe Walton, Esq., of Marsden Hall, a gentleman who not only found employment for a large number of persons of various trades, but also paid during this period of distress small sums weekly to needy people in the neighbourhood. The book records the amount of the weekly income each such pensioner had, and in scores of cases it appears that an entire family had to be supported on a shilling. Tradition adds that this Mr. Walton was very friendly to the Methodists, attended and contributed to all the anniversary services around his home, entertained the preachers, and when the classes met for the renewal of tickets often asked permission to be present.

But notwithstanding the poverty of the society, its growth rendered larger premises necessary. Mr. Sagar of Southfield offered a suitable plot of land on the old highway from Colne to Burnley at about three farthings per yard. The offer was accepted, though no money seems to have been paid, and no conveyance completed. The chapel was built and opened early in 1827, the Rev. Peter McOwan preaching at Nelson, and the Rev. Jabez Bunting at Colne. The premises were rather curiously planned, the chapel proper occupying about two-thirds of the building, with a gallery on three sides; behind the pulpit was the schoolroom, the floor of which was level with the front pew in the gallery, thus enabling the children to sit in their places and take part in the services. On the back wall,

OLD RAILWAY STREET CHAPEL.

about seven feet from the schoolroom floor, was a pew extending the whole length of the side; and this was used for the girls dressed in white at the anniversary sermons, and for extra accommodation on other occasions when the place was crowded. In the centre of this long pew was hung a bell rope; the bell was rung twenty minutes, and again five minutes, before each service, the ringing in the latter case being continued until the minister entered the pulpit. The property to the right of the illustration is near where the railway station now stands.

While the chapel was being built Thomas Marsden, father of Mr. Leonard Marsden, removed from a cottage near Pasture House, Barrowford, and settled at Marsden. He had met in William Law's class at Barrowford, his ticket on trial having been given to him by the Rev. R. Pickering on March 20th, 1825. On his joining the Marsden society he began to work in the Sunday school, and when the chapel was finished he was appointed the first chapel-keeper. His home was afterwards at Lee, where he cultivated a small farm as well as followed his own craft as a stonemason. In the course of time he became the leader of three classes—one at Southfield on a Sunday afternoon in William Whitaker's house, a second on Monday at Marsden Hall in Benjamin Baxter's house, and a third on Wednesday in his own house. The last he retained until his death in 1855.

The Colne circuit extended at this time from Thirstone on the south to Barnoldswick and Earby on the north; and from Naze End, Wycollar, and Trawden on the east to Barley on the west, with about fifteen preaching places in all. In 1839 the Revs. William Levell and Joseph Mortimer were the ministers, and through their instrumentality a large increase of the society at Marsden took place. But during the next three years many of the members and of the workers in the school for some reason now unknown withdrew, and joined the Primitive Methodists, who were trying to establish a cause in the place. Thus strengthened, they at once built the chapel in the lane leading from the new road to the hamlet of Bradley.

When the Lancashire and Yorkshire Railway was being made from Colne to Manchester, the company wanted the chapel-yard for the entrance to the station at Nelson; and as the land had never been conveyed to any trustees, and the place was burdened with debt, the yard was allowed to go. Thereupon Mr. Sleigh, the superintendent, set to work to form a trust, and thus secure the building. The following gentlemen became the trustees:—Messrs. William Lister Sagar, Ingham Walton, Christopher Grimshaw, Robert Watson, Abraham Robinson, William England, Sagar Kershaw, Thomas Towler, Hargreaves Hudson, Henry Stansfield, Joseph Bracewell, and Edmondson Varley. These gentlemen met to consider the financial position of the trust, and, finding the society of only five small classes was very weak, decided to bring the children into the chapel, to build the schoolroom up to the roof and make it into two cottages, so as to produce a little income.

At this time Methodism in Marsden received great assistance from the family of Mr. Sutcliffe, who carried on the business of a corn miller at the Old Mill, in Bradley. Mrs. Sutcliffe was a very earnest Christian, and, as the result of her training, her daughters grew up like her and did good work in the school, teaching the senior class of girls on Sundays, and classes for writing and other elementary subjects during the week.

About 1849 families began to come from the country districts to Nelson (as Marsden now began to be called, from the sign of the hotel in its centre), the hand-loom giving way to the power-loom. Among them were some from Ickornshaw, in which were several local preachers—Joseph Watson, James Hopkinson, and Leonard Marsden, the son of the Thomas Marsden already mentioned. Joseph Watson was a very acceptable preacher, and through his intense earnestness a revival broke out, in which persons professed to be benefited, and among them the late Mr. Simpson Laycock. Soon after came a time of great uneasiness through the Connexion, on account of the publication of the "Fly Sheets," which were sent out anonymously, and reflected on the character of several leading ministers. The Colne circuit did not suffer as much as many others, though at first some of the local preachers and private members were much dissatisfied, but most of them ultimately decided to remain in "the old body."

Nelson continuing to increase in population, the chapel was found to be too small for both scholars and congregation. The floor was flagged, the place was heated only by an iron stove in the centre, and was altogether very uncomfortable. The school committee and the society met to consider what course to adopt to supply the room that was required. At length it was decided to ask the trustees (who were all non-resident) for permission to take into the chapel the two cottages that had been previously made out of the school-room. To this the trustees agreed, provided that no debt was added to the existing debt of £720. This was in the year 1858. Subscriptions were solicited, and the contract let to the firm of Messrs. Whitehead and Holland, who took down the partition wall, extended the gallery on each side, and prepared a place behind the pulpit for a larger organ than the one that was before in use. All this was done at the reasonable cost of about £400, but according to the agreement the debt was not increased. Amongst those most active in pushing on the work may be named John Elliott, John Smith, Henry Elliott, Thomas Clegg, Lawrence Higgin, Joseph Wilkinson, Simpson Laycock, Leonard Marsden, James Varley, Henry Greenwood, John Sagar, Miss Sagar, and the Misses Sutcliffe. In 1860 a new organ was put into the chapel at a cost of £190, the whole of which was raised by subscriptions with the collections at the opening services.

In the year 1862 it was thought advisable to look out for a site for a new school, and a plot of land was at first selected near the railway goods yard; but it was afterwards decided to build a new chapel, and alter the old one into a school. Ultimately, by the help of Mr. Tunstill, a site of sufficient size for both school and chapel was purchased in Carr Road. As only three of the original trustees were living, viz., Abraham Robinson, Hargreaves Hudson, and Edmondson Varley, a new trust was formed, to which the old chapel as well as the new site was conveyed. The trustees were Messrs. Howarth Sagar, John Sagar, James Stansfield, Lawrence Higgin, Emmott Smith, Henry Elliott, Thomas Clegg, James Hopkinson, Charles Jackson, Simpson Laycock, Leonard Marsden, William Sagar, Joseph Whitham, William Tunstill, John Pilling, Thomas Wiseman, John Catlow, and John Farrar. Subscriptions were solicited, and the list nobly headed by Miss Ellen Sagar, of Carr View, with £200, whilst the sum of £440 was raised by a bazaar. Mr. Tunstill and the Sagar family, along with Mr. Joseph Whitham, contributed very largely to the success of the movement; and the present chapel in Carr Road was opened in the summer of 1865, its cost having been about £3,250. The organ in the old chapel was sold for £150; and when the building accounts were audited, the trustees found themselves with a debt of £1,176, inclusive of £535 on the older premises. For several years no serious attempt was made to reduce the debt.

Meanwhile other matters were being attended to. The circuit quarterly meeting, which was held at Colne, decided that it would be better for the interests of Methodism that the circuit should be divided, and that Barrowford, Nelson, Southfield, Roughlee, and Barley, containing about 320 members, should form a new one under the name of the "Barrowford and Nelson Circuit." To this the Conference agreed, and the first quarterly meeting of the new circuit was held on September 25th, 1865, with the newly appointed minister, the Rev. William Turner Nelson, in the chair. Messrs. Tunstill and John Sagar were appointed circuit stewards.

The following is a list of ministers who have travelled in the Nelson circuit since its formation in 1865, with the number of members as returned each March quarter.

| | | |
|---|---|---|
| 1865,-66. | William T. Nelson | 322 |
| 1867. | Abel Burgess | 374 |
| 1868. | Abel Burgess, Thomas Shepherd | 404 |
| 1869. | Abel Burgess, John Aldred | 405 |
| 1870,-71. | William Allen, John Aldred | 395, 400 |
| 1872. | William Allen, George W. Russell | 411 |
| 1873,-74. | George Russell, George W. Russell, William Henderson | 476, 515 |
| 1875. | John Shipham, John Pogson, William Ellis | 542 |
| 1876,-77. | John Shipham, John Pogson, A. Leppington Barley | 605, 643 |
| 1878. | Thomas Leach, Alfred Wells, A. Leppington Barley | 654 |
| 1879. | Thomas Leach, Alfred Wells, Stephen Harper | 614 |

1880,-81,-82. James Wright, Thomas Dodd, John Fair-
bourne - - - - - 622, 672, 687
1883,-84,-85. Abraham Pearce, George K. Pryor, John
Nayler - - - - - 731, 748, 790
1886,-87-88. George T. Dixon, Edward D. Dannatt, E.
Stanley Shelton - - - 843, 885, 917
1889. Edwin Hayward, Thomas Lawson, G. Beamish
Saul - - - - - - 989
1890. Edwin Hayward, Thomas Lawson, Richard
F. Earnshaw, William May - - - 987
1891. Edwin Hayward, Thomas Lawson, Richard
F. Earnshaw, Arthur Whetnall - - 1019
1892. Charles Swannell, Henry H. Vowles, Philip J.
Cocking, Arthur Whetnall - - - 1070
1893. Henry H. Vowles, Philip J. Cocking, Arthur
Whetnall, Joseph H. Armstrong - - 1037
1894. Henry H. Vowles, Philip J. Cocking, Enoch
Green, Joseph H. Armstrong - - - 1019
1895. H. Owen Rattenbury, John H. Wilkinson,
Enoch Green, Joseph H. Armstrong - 1011
1896. H. Owen Rattenbury, John H. Wilkinson,
Enoch Green, George H. Pickering - - 1012
1897. H. O. Rattenbury, J. H. Wilkinson, Harvey
Field, G. H. Pickering - - - - 1085
1898. J. Rowland Gleave, George Searle, Harvey
Field, George H. Pickering - - - 1125
1899. J. R. Gleave, G. Searle, H. Field, Albert
Wainwright - - - - - - 1162

The only supernumerary who has resided in the circuit appears to have been the Rev. Jonathan Barrowclough, who is so entered in the Minutes of 1872. Of the three candidates for the ministry from Nelson circuit, two afterwards found their way into other occupations, and the third, Thomas Robinson, is now a student at Didsbury College. The increase reported in 1873 is only nominal, as the previous year Brierfield with seventy-eight members had been transferred from the Burnley circuit. But there are probably very few circuits, whose membership returns for a similar period are on the whole better.

Some idea of the growth of Methodism in the neighbourhood may be gathered from the old account book in use by the society stewards. The earliest detailed entry is for the Christmas quarter of 1852, when the sum of £4 4s. 10½d. was sent to the quarter-board. The particulars are :—John Horsfall's class, £2 0s. 3d.; H. Elliott's class, 11s. 0d.; late W. Thornton's class, 7s. 5d.; E. Smith's class, 13s. 6d.; and the quarterly collection, 12s. 8½d. No payment of equal magnitude was made until 1855, when the amount £5 7s. 0d. is entered without details. After that the amount rises for ten years with fair regularity to thirteen or fourteen pounds. But the first quarter after the formation of the circuit, the total leaps suddenly to £22 16s. 1d., inclusive of a grant of five pounds from the encumbered trust of the chapel. The membership in Nelson alone amounted at the same time to 142, and the leaders' names are given as Elliott, Clegg, Laycock, Edmondson, Hopkinson, Marsden, Higgins, and Parkinson.

The following gentlemen have occupied the office of circuit steward, so far as can be ascertained:—

1865-1869. William Tunstill, J. Sagar.
1870-1873. W. Tunstill, Howarth Sagar.
1874-1876. W. Tunstill, Joseph Whitham.
1877-1880. W. Tunstill, H. Sagar.
1881,-82. T. Wiseman, William Hartley.
1883. W. Hartley, John Sagar.
1884-1886. John Sagar, John Greenwood.
1887. J. Greenwood, Joseph Smallpage.
1888. J. Smallpage, Simpson Laycock.
1889,-90. J. Smallpage, Wilkinson Hartley.
1891. W. Hartley, R. M. Prescott.
1892-1894. R. M. Prescott, Samuel Gott.
1895. S. Gott, Henry Atkinson.
1896. W. Hartley, H. Atkinson.
1897. H. Atkinson, Hartley Duckworth.
1898,-99. H. Duckworth, Wilkinson Hartley.

Many of these gentlemen are still living in well-deserved esteem, and of several of the others mention has already been made. Simpson Laycock came to Nelson from Trawden about 1849 at the age of sixteen. He joined the Methodists a year later, and at the age of eighteen was made both a local preacher and a class leader. At first he was employed as a weaver at Lomeshaye Mills, and soon afterwards as a tackler. He then started business on his own account in partnership with Mr. J. Greenwood. He contributed £100 to the Railway Street Chapel, of which he laid a corner stone, and was for some years treasurer of the Worn-out Ministers' Fund. He died on December 9th, 1889.

The minister's house in Carr Road was built in 1867 at a cost of £735, of which £135 was raised by subscriptions whilst the remainder was borrowed for a term of years at five per cent. About the same time a day school was opened with Mr. Blocksedge as master, and there was then no other such school between Lomeshaye Bridge and St. John's church.

In the meantime, as the population continued to increase, the society and especially the Sunday school increased also; and for both greater accommodation was required. In 1872 the trustees were called together and the situation put before them, when it was resolved that a new school should be built on the land already acquired adjoining the chapel in Carr Road. The foundation stone was laid on July 6th by Mr. John Sagar; and when the premises were opened the following

CARR ROAD CHAPEL AND SCHOOL.

year, the entire cost was found to have been £3,007 19s. But meanwhile money had been rapidly accumulating. The old chapel in Railway Street was sold to Messrs. Reginald Elliott and Sons for £840. The teachers and scholars agreed to contribute weekly in their classes for twelve months, and the result was a sum of £389 1s. 3d. A subscription list of £1,112 19s. was headed by Mr. John Sagar with £200, Mr. and Mrs. J. Whitham £200, and Mr. W. Tunstill £105; and the debt after the opening services amounted to only £559 9s. 8d. The first superintendent of the enlarged school was Mr. Leonard Marsden, with Messrs. James Hey and William Croasdale as his assistants, and Mr. Jesse Whitehead as secretary.

The increase of population continued at so rapid a rate that in 1877 it became necessary again to provide further accommodation; and Carr Road chapel was enlarged to its present size. The same year the official name of the circuit was changed to Nelson alone, the name of Barrowford falling out. In 1879 the sum of £2,000, inclusive of the proceeds of a bazaar by means of which the debt on the ministers' houses was reduced by £325, was raised for various purposes. In 1888 the township of Nelson-in-Marsden was divided into the two townships of Nelson and Brierfield, and the suffix 'in-Marsden' ceased to be used. Thenceforwards, as for some years before, the history of the circuit is one of continuous effort to make adequate provision for a population, that grew at a rate exceeded at very few places in the country. The Carr Road chapel itself did not admit of further enlargement. But in 1894 considerable alterations were made. A new organ was introduced at a cost of £850, the electric light was installed, and additional rooms built for the use of the Sunday school, the entire expenditure amounting to £3,000. The town however was overflowing, and rapidly absorbing field after field in every direction; and though in the last dozen years the sum of about £25,000 has been expended in improvements and renovations, it was felt in 1897 that the time was come when an adequate attempt should be made to plant churches and schools in the centres where they were needed. The proposal eventually took the shape of a well-considered scheme to raise £10,000, and to build three chapels—in Fleet Street, at Bradley Hall, and in Temple Street respectively. A great impulse was given to the enterprise by a promise on the part of Mr. William Tunstill to add twenty per cent. to all moneys raised for the purposes of extension; and by March, 1899, the subscriptions exceeded £3,000. In that month a great bazaar was held, which yielded £2865 6s., apart from Mr. Tunstill's contribution. And there is now no doubt that the scheme will be brought to a successful issue, and contribute greatly to the religious opportunities and the well-being of the town.

In regard to the present condition of the circuit, some particulars were given by Mr. W. Hartley in a speech at the opening of the bazaar just named. He said that sitting accommodation was already provided for nearly five thousand persons, which number is now in process of augmentation by fifteen hundred; that the names of 2,300 scholars were enrolled upon the registers of four efficient and well-equipped day schools; and that in the Sunday schools there were nearly four thousand children and young people, of whom a large percentage were members of society. At the last June quarterly meeting the membership was returned as 1,138, and an expenditure of £250 10s. 10d. was reported and was covered by the income of the quarter. The District Synod was held on the Carr Road premises in September, 1893, and again in September, 1897. On August 12th, 1898, five young female members of the society lost their lives in a sad accident on Lake Derwentwater.

<small>RAILWAY STREET</small>   In 1883 the Carr Road chapel was so inadequate that applications for sittings are said to have been compulsorily refused at the rate of fifty a quarter. At the same time the district above the railway was being rapidly covered with houses. But the circuit was committed to so many schemes, chapels at Cooper street and at Barley and new school premises at Brierfield, that it was not able at the time to undertake anything more. In the emergency a few gentlemen were requested to purchase a suitable site, erect upon it a room of moderate pretensions, and hold the whole until the circuit was able to relieve them. The following were the gentlemen in question:—Messrs. Howarth Sagar, John Sagar, Joseph Witham, William Hartley, James Gott, Simpson Laycock, John Greenwood, Wilkinson Hartley, and Leonard Marsden. A mission room was built, at a cost inclusive of land of £1,220, and opened in July, 1884, by Mr. W. Lancaster. During the following year efforts were made to meet the cost of the land and building (£825), and these efforts were so successful that the sum of £575 was raised. In 1886 the premises were placed upon the trust of the model deed, with the following gentlemen as trustees:—Messrs. William Tunstill, J. Sagar, J. Witham, Wm. Hartley, James Hey, John Taylor, Wilkinson Hartley, John Greenwood, Leonard Marsden, Simpson Laycock, Joseph Dyson, Jonathan Greenwood, Hartley Duckworth, Henry Sagar, Joseph Pilkington, John Manning, James Whitaker, and Ezra Sellers.

The next year the need of more room became pressing, and after considerable deliberation it was resolved that the entire premises should be taken down, additional land secured, and a new chapel built to seat not less than 800 people with school accommodation in proportion. In 1889 the scheme was carried out, and a new chapel with schools erected at a cost of about £6,000. The stone-laying took place in July, 1888, when £196 2s. 10d. was raised. The schools were opened in February of the next year, when services were conducted by the Rev. T. Brackenbury; and the chapel in April, 1890. By means of a successful bazaar the sum of £1,780 was raised towards the cost, and handsome donations were contributed—£500 by Mr. W. Tunstill, and £300 each by the trustees and the Sunday school committee at Carr Road. A new organ was erected in 1894 by Messrs. Foster and Andrews, of Hull, at a cost of £450. The opening services realised £77, which with the subscriptions cleared the expenditure.

<small>COOPER STREET</small>   In 1875, Mr. Joseph Whitham engaged Mr. Quiney as a Scripture reader or town-missionary, and put him to work in connection with a room

at Bradley Street, which had just been left by the Baptists. For fifteen months the cost was met by Mr. Whitham himself, but at the close of that period the supervision of the mission was transferred to the quarterly meeting. In March, 1883, when the scholars in the school had increased to one hundred, a body of trustees was appointed, and a plot of land was secured in Cooper Street, to which the mission was transferred. The foundation stone was laid on May 3rd, 1884, by Mrs. J. Whitham, of Woodlands. Purses were placed on the stone by seventeen Sunday school scholars; and the proceeds for the day amounted altogether to £182. The chapel was opened on October 5th of the same year. In 1897 an organ was obtained. The services will now shortly be transferred to the chapel in course of erection in Fleet Street.

BRADLEY HALL
The Bradley Hall mission in Leeds Road dates from 1894, though for some time previously services had been held in a private house in the neighbourhood. In that year the Hall was purchased for the circuit by Messrs. W. Tunstill, R. M. Prescott, and Wilkinson Hartley, and a preaching-room made by the removal of some of the inside walls. In 1897 the quarterly meeting directed the guarantors and committee to devise some plan of extension; and a school chapel is now in course of erection.

TEMPLE STREET
The Temple Street mission chapel was built last year. Messrs. S. Gott, R. M. Prescott, and John Hargreaves bought a piece of land upon which to build some houses. Of two at the end of the row the inside walls were left out, and the large room thus obtained was used for religious services. More recently a plot of land large enough for both a school and a chapel has been purchased, and upon this suitable buildings are likely to be erected before long.

RUPERT STREET
The little Rupert Street church meets in a room over the Co-operative Stores, from the proprietors of which the room is rented. A Sunday school also is carried on; and the mission promises to be a success.

## BARROWFORD.

The first Methodist chapel at Barrowford was built in 1801 (see page 51). In 1813 it was enlarged, the services being conducted during the building operations in a barn that afterwards came into the possession of Mr. T. Wiseman. In the following year the enlarged chapel was formally opened by the Rev. Richard Watson, who preached in the afternoon from Psalm cx. 3, and in the evening from Heb. xii. 22-24. At this time a new trust was formed, composed of the following:—John Watson, Henry Myers, Thomas Wilkinson, James Hartley, John Kaye, James Ayrton, Nathan Pickles, William Corlass, Thomas Corlass, Thomas Grimshaw, John Holt, James Clegg, C. Grimshaw, William Varley, Abraham Robinson, Robert Watson, and Jonas Lee. William Corlass had recently come to reside at Reedyford, and at once began to make himself useful. He commenced a class at Reedyford, and another at Barrowford, and for years sustained the office of local preacher.

About the same time there came to live in the village a man named William Law, who was a native of Heptonstall, and had been a sailor. Some property near Barrowford being left him, his release was purchased. Whilst at sea, he had contracted habits of intemperance, and when he settled at Barrowford he was a slave to drink. After a while he began to attend the chapel, saw the exceeding sinfulness of his sin, and was soon after converted. He earnestly sought the grace of God to keep him from falling, and knowing his weakness avoided temptation, on one occasion at least when on a journey turning into the fields and going a mile out of his way, in order that he might not have to pass the doors of a public-house. As might be expected from such resolution, he was preserved from falling, and became a holy, happy, useful man, leading two classes, and preaching with great earnestness; and great was the fruit of his labours. He died very suddenly in 1827. He had just time to utter the words "Come, Lord Jesus, and come quickly," when he was gone. His body was laid to rest in the burial-ground attached to Cross-stones church, near Todmorden. Some time afterwards a plot of ground was given by Mr. Ingham Walton for a burial-ground in connection with the chapel at Barrowford. In it there have been more than three hundred persons interred. It is now closed except to those who have a family vault.

In the year 1830 there were seven classes at Barrowford, and in addition to these and the services in the chapel, cottage prayer meetings were held regularly in the village and its vicinity. A plan for the conduct of these meetings in the above-named year is still extant: on this plan are named eleven places, eight of which were visited by the prayer-leaders once a fortnight, and three once a week. There were thirty-nine of these prayer-leaders, and in their anxiety to take in other places, they paid a visit to Newchurch-in-Pendle. The meetings were well attended, and there were great hopes of good being done, when to their surprise the prayer-leaders saw three persons from Higham in the meeting. At the close, the Barrowford leaders were told that they had no right to be there, that they were trespassing on ground belonging to the Burnley circuit. They asked the friends at Higham to undertake to hold meetings at Newchurch, but though no promise was given, the Barrowford leaders, not wishing to trespass, did not visit Newchurch any more.

The present school was built in 1834. In 1839 the Rev. Joseph Mortimer was appointed to the Colne circuit. A revival of religion broke out soon after in many places, and two or three hundred members were added to the societies; and a large love-feast was held at Barrowford in the summer of the following year. The weather was all that could be desired; and the people came singing from Colne, Nelson, and Barnoldswick, all arriving about the same time. The chapel was filled, and the love-feast was continued by adjournment in the evening.

The chapel was re-opened after alterations in August, 1860, when special services were conducted by the Rev. Peter Mackenzie of Burnley, and the Rev. T. Pearson of Sheffield. The collections amounted to £101 10s. On Saturday, April 6th, 1861, a new organ was opened, when two performances were given by Mr. W. R. Holt, of Bradford. The organ was built and presented by Mr. Grimshaw. The collections which were in aid of the debt amounted to £80 17s. 4d. New vestries were afterwards added, and the chapel enlarged. In June, 1875,

BARROWFORD OLD AND NEW CHAPELS.

a bazaar was held, by which £100 was raised towards the debt. In 1879 the chapel was again enlarged at a cost of £300, all expenses were met and the chapel freed from debt during the year, whilst in addition £171 was raised at the Sunday school anniversary and £120 at that of the chapel.

Barrowford took the lead in Nelson circuit financially in 1880, when there were as many as 250 scholars in the Sunday school. In 1881 Mr. Thomas Wiseman, of Bank House, presented an eligible site valued at £1,600, for a new chapel. A sale of work was held in April, 1884, towards raising money for the new chapel and for the conversion of the old chapel into a school. In 1886 the organ was re-built, and enlarged. The stone-laying of the new chapel took place on the 12th May, 1888, when the sum of £141 was raised. The top stone was placed in position April, 1889, by Miss Wiseman. The amount raised up to this time towards the new building was £2,800. The chapel was opened on Thursday, January 9th, 1890, by Miss Tunstill, who unlocked the door shortly before three o'clock. The Rev. C. H. Kelly was the preacher, and at the opening services altogether the total amount raised was £280. The total cost of the scheme was £4,200. Messrs. Tunstill Bros. contributed £500. A bazaar was opened on March 19th, 1891, by Miss Tunstill, towards clearing the debt of £900; and the sum of £239 16s. was raised. Another bazaar was opened in November, 1894, by Mr. Parkinson, of Burnley, for the same object.

It might be invidious to mention the names of those who by consistent lives have adorned the doctrine of Christ their Saviour at Barrowford; but some brief notice must be given of James Clegg, pronounced by James Nowell, who was a competent judge, "one of the best local preachers in this or any other circuit." He was born of pious parents, whose great desire was to see him "strong in the grace that is in Christ Jesus." After a little time at school, he was taught to weave on the hand-loom, but still went twice a day "to say a lesson" at school, his father selecting the books he read. They were Boston's "Four-fold Stake," and Edwards' "On the Human Will." It is needless to add that these works had little influence on the young lad, for the simple reason that he did not understand them. He was kept under wholesome restraint at home, regularly attended the services at Barrowford, and sometimes went with his father to Colne to hear Richard Reece, Robert Newton, and other famous preachers of those days. In the autumn of 1825 'Billy' Dawson preached at Colne on the occasion of the foreign missionary anniversary. There was a good deal of rain; and young Clegg, to avoid as much as possible getting wet, ran nearly all the way to Colne. He remembered part of Dawson's prayer:—" Lord, Thou knowest how many there are who intended being at this service: they go to the window or the door to see how the weather is, and it rains yet, yea, it rains yet. Lord, bless them yonder at their homes, and bless us here." His text was Acts xiii. 38, 39. Clegg often in after years expressed his astonishment that after hearing all these able men he should still remain unconverted. In December of the same year 'Sammy' Hick held services at Barrowford. He preached short sermons, and then held a prayer meeting. On the first Monday night at twenty minutes past nine, he said, " If no one comes out to be saved in ten minutes, I will conclude the meeting." At exactly half-past nine, as no one had come out, and while some man was engaged in prayer, 'Sammy' said, "We munnot tell lies," and pronounced the benediction; but, added Clegg, " Sammy little knew, he never did know, that during those ten minutes my companion and myself were awakened by the Spirit of God. He said to me, 'I cannot bear this any longer; if any other pray after this, I will be down on my knees.' I said, 'So will I.' But he dismissed the meeting. When we got outside we talked the matter over very seriously, and agreed that we would begin to serve God, and start from this night." The next Monday Sammy was once more at Barrowford, and in the meeting Clegg's companion found peace, but it was nearly six weeks before he himself experienced the sweetness of pardoning love. He at once joined a class which met on a week-night, but frequently went also to Mr. Law's, which met on Sunday morning. Law often used to put his hand on his head and say, " Lord, bless Jimmy, and make him a preacher." At that time Clegg gave a good deal of time to the visitation of the sick, and what he then saw and heard was often told in the pulpit when he became a preacher, and made a blessing to many. When Mr. Law died, he was appointed to succeed him as leader of the Sunday morning class.

James Clegg began to preach in 1832. Some few months afterwards he went for that purpose to Mount Pleasant. The Rev. John Barritt was in the congregation, and at the close of the service he met the young preacher as he came out of the pulpit, and taking him by the hand said, "I have rather liked thy sermon, but I don't like the colour of thy coat, and thy waist-coat is still worse." The garments referred to had been made for Clegg's wedding three years before, and were somewhat bright; he soon after procured a dress for the pulpit of more sombre hue.

Mr. Clegg also records that the zealous but eccentric Hodgson Casson preached twice at Barrowford, and in the evening had sixteen fits before he went to bed. He relates further that Dr. Warren 'stated his case' at Colne, but that no one was influenced. At Clitheroe, however, all the local preachers became 'Warrenites,' and the superintendent had to ask the help of the Colne local preachers. Eighteen readily rendered assistance, several of them going as far as Slaidburn.

'Billy' Dawson from the time of his first visit seldom, if ever, failed to preach once a year at Colne. His health at last apparently failing his sister urged him to take more rest. He replied, "Mary, I shall rest when I die." He reached Colne for the last time on Saturday, July 3rd, 1846, and died at two o'clock on the following morning.

## BRIERFIELD.

It appears that Mr. and Mrs. Henry Tunstill, the parents of Messrs. Robert and William Tunstill, removed in 1833 from Wheatley Lane to Brierfield. Brierfield House was not quite complete, so they resided for a time in the house now occupied by Mr. Jonathan Riley in Clitheroe Road. Mr. Tunstill had attended the Inghamite Chapel at Wheatley Lane, but Mrs. Tunstill had been connected with the Wesleyan chapel there. At the time of their removal to Brierfield there was no non-conformist place of worship, in fact it is said that there was no religious service held in the village.

In or about the year 1838 an attempt was made to introduce Methodism. Outdoor services were held, and afterwards a cellar was taken in Colne Road opposite to Lomas Row, entrance being effected by the descent of a flight of steps. Mr. Tunstill and his family were amongst the first to join the little church, and ever since the name of Tunstill has been honourably associated with Methodism. In 1840 the services were held in Mr. Tunstill's kitchen, and soon after a Sunday school was opened in a cottage in Colne Road. Afterwards a cottage in Burnley Road was hired. To make this room as serviceable as possible a portion of the bedroom floor was cut away, so that the preacher could be heard and by a little effort seen by those upstairs. The pulpit was in one corner, and the congregation of fifty or sixty persons were accommodated with seats, chiefly without backs. In 1843 the services were conducted by preachers from the Burnley circuit, and this continued until 1872 when Brierfield was transferred to Nelson circuit.

In 1844 Mr. Hartley Bracewell left Burnley and went to reside at Brierfield. It is stated that he obtained work at the mill on condition that he attended to the musical part of the service in connection with this preaching room. The cause prospered and very soon the rooms were inconveniently crowded; and an effort was made to get more suitable accommodation, but there was some difficulty in obtaining land. In 1848, a

Mr. William Tunstill, a mechanic, built two cottages on land belonging to Mr. Henry Tunstill in what is now called Halifax Road, and arrangements were made with him to take the building higher, and construct a room the length and width of the two houses. This room was fitted up as a chapel. There were seven or eight steps built about fifteen feet from the main building, and a wooden bridge led from these to the door. Just inside the door there was a high screen, which formed one side of the large square pew occupied by Mr. Tunstill's family, adjoining which was the pulpit. In the other corner was the singers' pew, the entrance to the pulpit being through this. In front loose forms were provided, and behind was a rising gallery of some six or eight pews. The room accommodated about 250 people, and was opened in 1849. The bills announcing the opening services had the unusual and interesting headline "Opening of a temporary Wesleyan Chapel."

In 1852 John Tattersall removed from Sabden, got work at the mill at Brierfield, and soon was so absorbed in the little Methodist cause that he was described as "minister, class leader, superintendent, and steward, all rolled into one." David and Jonathan Holt travelled from Burnley for years, both Sunday and week nights, to help in the work; Robert and George Johnson, Titus Wharton, Robert Geldard, William Ingham, Richard Calvert, William Lord, Richard Howarth, Richard Mann, Thomas Hargreaves, James Foulds, and others rendered faithful service for many years. Old James Clegg, of Barrowford, elsewhere referred to, once told the people in the present chapel, that on one occasion he walked from Barrowford to Brierfield up to the body in snow to conduct the service, and then walked back again, as there was no one to give him any refreshment. He added that he would have been thankful for just one piece of bread. Such an incident shows the hardships workers in early Methodism willingly underwent, and the changes for the better that have been effected.

In 1858 definite steps were taken towards erecting more central and convenient premises. A trust was formed during the time that the Rev. Levi Waterhouse was stationed at Burnley. There was difficulty in obtaining the land and also difficulty in raising the money. At first an outlay of £500 was contemplated, then £2,000, and afterwards Mr. William Tunstill, not being satisfied with the accommodation provided, offered, along with his brother Robert, to give £400, the estimated cost of making the chapel its present size. The foundation stone was laid on August 16th, 1860, by Mrs. Tunstill, who also gave the beautiful pulpit and communion furniture; and when the whole was finished the cost amounted to £3,400. The school, in which there are said to have been 500 scholars, under the chapel was opened on June 23rd, 1862, the Rev. John Clegg, so well known in this district, preaching on that occasion. The chapel was opened for service on Wednesday, October 8th, 1862, the Rev. Dr. Gregory preaching in the

BRIERFIELD CHAPEL.

afternoon, and the Rev. William Arthur at night. Subsequent services were conducted by the Revs. J. Clapham, J. H. Rigg, and Richard Roberts, the total collections at the opening services amounting to £420 13s. 7d. As this was at the time of the American War the collections may be considered phenomenal for so small a place and so young a cause. No doubt this handsome result was largely due to the gifts and efforts of Messrs. Robert and William Tunstill. The debt left on the chapel and school premises amounted to £1,800.

Such a debt was intolerable, and though the days were those of the terrible cotton famine, efforts to reduce it had to be made. The Rev. Joseph Rippon was appointed to the circuit in 1866, and thus describes the attempt he undertook as the pastor of the little Brierfield church. "I called on Mr. W. Tunstill," he writes, "and asked him how much he and his brother would give. 'Give?' he replied, 'we are losing £100 a week!' I said, 'Well, the debt has to come off, and I think you authorised the enlargement.' 'Oh, I admit our responsibility,' he replied, 'but a man must be good to give when he is losing money.' 'Well, you are good, so that is settled,' I said, 'and now, if I can raise £550, what will you give?' 'We will give another £550 to it.' 'And if I can raise £725?' 'We will give £725.' 'And if I can get £900?' 'We will give the other £900.' This was a very good beginning! I then went to 'the elect lady' Miss Barnes and stated the case, and she at once promised £300. Our members and congregation at Brierfield, who were almost exclusively colliers and factory workers, entered into the scheme with the greatest enthusiasm. We held a tea-meeting, and they promised to subscribe from 1d. to 2s. a week each for twelve months, so that with the help of £50 each from Messrs. John Butterworth and John Barnes, and sundry other subscriptions, we raised £1,450, and the Chapel Committee lent the other £350, to be paid back in ten years."

A new organ was introduced into the chapel in 1879, at a cost of £547. In 1881 there were 497 scholars and 56 officers in the Sunday school. On June 14th, 1884, the foundation stone of new school premises was laid on a site, given by the Messrs. Tunstill, behind the present chapel. The cost of the premises, exclusive of furniture but inclusive of land, was £3,400. Accommodation was provided for 900 Sunday scholars and 568 day scholars; and the day school was opened on August 3rd, 1885, with an attendance of one hundred children. The last report shows that the master and mistress, Mr. J. Gott and Miss Clegg, have raised the school to a very high position, and secured the largest obtainable grant for the year's work. Certain structural alterations were subsequently made at a cost of £400; and in 1897 the organ was enlarged and other alterations made at a cost of £300.

Another name connected with Methodism in Brierfield ought not to be forgotten. Mrs. Pattison was a member of society for seventy-five years. She was the daughter of Mr. Thomas West, an earnest Methodist, who filled almost every office open to laymen. On the death of her husband, Mr. John Pattison, who was a local preacher, she removed to her son's, the Rev. James Pattison, vicar of Brierfield. She was ardently attached to Methodism, and could relate many interesting incidents in connection with the body with which she was identified. When she died in July, 1885, at the age of ninety, she left all her class tickets from the year 1818. She was interred in Barkerhouse churchyard, Gt. Marsden.

## REEDYFORD.

The school at Reedyford, or Newbridge, as the district is occasionally called, was originally started by Miss Scott in a cottage about 1868. In 1873 premises were erected, which

REEDYFORD CHAPEL. (EXTERIOR).

were enlarged twenty years later, at a total cost of £2,200. The chapel was built in 1874 and enlarged in 1894, at a total cost of £3,600. Both of these premises formed a munificent gift to the Connexion on the part of Mr. William Tunstill. In 1895 a magnificent organ was put into the chapel through the liberality of Mr. Robert Tunstill, who has every reason to be proud of the choir he has so sedulously trained. Further reference to the relations of this active and generous family to Methodism will be found in the closing chapter.

REEDYFORD CHAPEL. (INTERIOR).

## SOUTHFIELD.

Methodism at Southfield appears to have been comparatively stationary for many years, and its history belongs chiefly to the past (see page 45). The barn which in Mr. William Sagar's time was transformed into a chapel has continued ever since to be used for that purpose. But its days are probably numbered. In 1895 a small committee was appointed by the quarterly meeting to select a suitable site in the Barkerhouse district, on which a chapel is to be built to supersede that at Southfield.

## ROUGHLEE.

Little is known of Methodism at Roughlee from the time of Wesley's last visit (see pages 12-19) until about the year 1807, when Abraham Haigh was the third preacher in the circuit, a young man who was exceedingly useful. Through his faithful ministry many young people began to seek the Lord, among whom were the brothers Towler—John, William, and Thomas. William was unwearied in his exertions to help forward the interests of Methodism at Roughlee, and for many years he went thither from Blacko through weather that would deter many a modern professor. In the year 1823 the chapel now standing was erected. It is entered by an ascent of many steps. Underneath it is a commodious school-room, formerly two dwelling-houses.

In connection with it there is a burial ground, probably the quiet resting place of some who listened to the voice of John Wesley.

In the year 1825 or 1826 "Sammy" Hick preached at Roughlee. Through his instrumentality much good was done. At a prayer meeting held after one of his services, whilst someone was engaged in prayer, he spoke to a man known as the "Barley Fiddler," and said "Thou hast a head as white as a plucking, how old art thou?" The man replied, "I am seventy-three." "Oh!" said Sammy, "there's a good chance for thee. The Lord converted my grandmother when she was eighty-two."

From the society at Roughlee have risen up three local preachers—James Dugdale, Robert Simpson, and John Hartley; but they all removed to other circuits, as have a number of members from time to time. Out of the many who have at Roughlee proved and shown the power of the Gospel in life and death may be mentioned two—Ann Fletcher of Greystones, who died in 1856, and Ann Holgate, who died two years later.

## BARLEY.

The continual disturbances to which the Methodists at Barley were subject (see page 45) led them to consider the possibility of building a chapel for themselves. With the exception of a few small farmers, they were all hand-loom weavers, their earnings were very small and money was very scarce; but they were full of zeal, and after meeting to consider the case resolved to do themselves whatever they could in the way of quarrying, carting, and building. In connection with the Hartleys of Bailey Green House was what was then called a "dandy shop," a building filled with looms, to which people went to weave as they go now to the "sheds." Some of the workers in this shop promised to get all the stone required for the building, if they could obtain the necessary leave. The leave was granted, Mr. Hartley closing his shop on Monday afternoons for the purpose and supplying the needful tools, and the stone was got; the farmers carted some of it to the site, and the rest was drawn by the weavers themselves, James Heyworth and John Crabtree yoking themselves in turn and the rest pushing behind.

The chapel was built on a piece of waste land, for which a title was obtained from the lord of the manor. When the walls were completed the trustees advertised for joiners to state a price for which they would put on the roof. Several attended and met the trustees: among them was William England, a local preacher. He said, "Well, friends, you see this is a very small job, and the people have struggled nobly, and are only poor; suppose we each go and work a day, we can do all the work required to put the roof on, and this shall be our share of the building." To this they all agreed, the chapel was roofed, and eventually opened for service in 1837, the trustees finding themselves £40 in debt.

A short time afterwards Mr. James Robinson, a churchman, met with James Howarth, and remarked that they had built a very nice chapel, but he understood they were £40 in debt. On being told that they did owe that amount, and did not know where to borrow it, Mr. Robinson offered to lend it to them for a short time. His offer was gladly accepted; but soon after efforts were made to repay the loan, and the Barley chapel was the first in the Colne circuit, to which it had been transferred, to be freed from debt. The trustees were Benjamin Frankland, superintendent minister, Ingham Walton, John Garnett, James Heyworth, Stephen Duckworth, William Heyworth, William Foster, Elijah Hartley, and John Hartley. In 1884 another chapel was erected on the same site, to accommodate 170 persons. It was opened the following year. The total cost was £850, but towards this sum on the day the foundation stones were laid as much as £132 7s. 10d. was contributed. The chapel was renovated in 1889; and £115 was raised by means of a sale of work in 1895.

At one time there was a strong feeling on the part of Methodists against the use of musical instruments in Divine services. So strong was this feeling at Barley, that when a double bass fiddle had been provided, one of the leading members of the society locked it up in his house and would not allow it to be used. At present the sentiment appears to have completely changed, and the popularity of the anniversary services is now said to be due chiefly to the attractive character of the music, Barley being one of the very few places in the neighbourhood where the charms of a string band are provided.

Among those at Barley who have been eminent for their devotedness to God and His cause, may be mentioned John Robinson, an old soldier who had lost one of his fingers; Mrs. Pickles, a woman of meek and quiet spirit, powerful in prayer and full of zeal for God; Ellen Starkie, an old Christian, who was a faithful leader of a female class; Ellen Grey, who was once heard to say in giving her experience in a love-feast, that she was so happy while weaving that she fancied her shuttle said, "Glory, Glory"; John Garnett and his wife Margaret, two faithful followers of the Lord (Mr. Garnett's barn was often used for "Charity" sermons and tea meetings); Robert Moorby, who had something to do with securing the land for the new chapel; Thomas Moorby, so true to the best interests of the Sunday school; and Ben Cliffe, who was an eccentric though zealous man. When going to a prayer meeting by the nearest, though not the public, way, he was accosted by the farmer through whose fields he was walking, "Where are you going that way?" "I am for Heaven," said Ben. "Then go the right way," said the farmer.

## CHAPTER VIII.

# BARNOLDSWICK.

THE Barnoldswick circuit was separated from Colne at the Conference of 1884, and is perhaps in geographical area one of the smallest circuits in Methodism. It includes only three preaching places, viz., Barnoldswick, Earby, and Mount Pleasant. The three may be said to lie at the three extreme points of a right-angled triangle, Earby and Mount Pleasant being situated at opposite ends of the hypothenuse.

The separation from Colne was effected mainly through the action of the Colne officials, and subsequent events have shown its wisdom. The steady progress of the circuit may be ascribed mainly to two causes, to the industrial prosperity of the district, whereby its population has greatly increased, and to the enterprise and activity of its ministers and people. At the present time (1899) the population of Barnoldswick may be estimated at seven thousand, and that of Earby at thirty-five hundred.

The third minister of the Colne circuit began to reside at Barnoldswick in 1862. The Rev. William C. Williams was the first, and his successors were the Revds. Joseph W Browne, Frederick Haines, Albert J. Popham, Andrew I. Wharton, John Clements, Matthew C. Pennington, Nelson C. Hesk, Josiah Goodacre, W. Boswell Lowther, William Brooks, Sampson Nicholls, Charles Bryant, and Vetranio Tyas.

The following is a complete list of the ministers stationed in the circuit since its separation from Colne, with the number of members reported in March of each year.

| | | |
|---|---|---|
| 1884,-85. | Vetranio Tyas | 153, 143 |
| 1886. | John Nelson | 134 |
| 1887-1889. | Edward Crump | 150, 133, 128 |
| 1890. | William Barber | 164 |
| 1891-1893. | William Millican | 180, 183, 188 |
| 1894,-95. | William Barnes | 208, 226 |
| 1896-1898. | Thomas P. Spencer | 218, 226, 256 |
| 1899. | James Hind | 262 |

The Rev. John Nelson is now a supernumerary living with his sons in New Zealand. During the Rev. E. Crump's ministry great depression fell upon the neighbourhood through the stoppage of Mr. Bracewell's large cotton factories, and many people left to seek the means of livelihood elsewhere. This was the time of the circuit's greatest poverty, and a grant in aid was made by the Connexion. The Rev. William Barber's stay was shortened through failure of health, which induced him to become a supernumerary. During the Rev. William Millican's ministry the cloud of depression began to lift, and several new weaving sheds were erected.

The following is a list of the circuit stewards from the formation of the circuit:—

1884. William Bracewell, James Brown.
1885-1887. James Brown, William Baldwin.
1888. William Baldwin, R. Kendall.
1889. R. Kendall.
1890-1894. R. Kendall, James Brown.
1895. William Baldwin.
1896,-97. William Baldwin, G. P. Hartley.
1898,-99. G. P. Hartley, I. Barritt.

Barnoldswick Methodism had its origin, as far as can be ascertained, in a cottage where preaching service was conducted weekly. About 1820 the first chapel was erected to accommodate 350 people. It served for a considerable time for both preaching services and Sunday school until two other rooms were added for the purposes of the latter.

In 1839 a schism occurred, in which at least one half of the society severed their connection with the Wesleyan cause, and started a place of worship of their own. They and their descendants now occupy the so-called Independent Methodist chapel, which was recently erected at a cost of about £5,000. In 1847 the membership of the Barnoldswick society was 57, and the contribution to the Colne quarterly meeting £3 15s. 2d. The membership to-day stands at 120, and the quarterly contribution averages £25.

A day school was commenced in the enlarged portion of the chapel in 1859 by Mr. W. M. Trever. Soon afterwards the present commodious premises were erected, and were opened in 1862. Mr. Trever continued as head-master until December, 1865, when he was succeeded by Mr. John Harding who left after two years' service. In 1867 Mr. John Taylor was appointed, and remained until December, 1873. On May 1st, 1872, the erection of a new west wing was begun, and completed in November of the same year. On January 9th, 1874, Mr. James Tipton took charge of the school, with Mr. W. C. Benton as second master. Mr. Tipton resigned in December of the same year, and was succeeded by Mr. L. W. Gill, who again was succeeded in 1885 by Mr. Isaac Barritt, the present headmaster. During the seventies, Mr. Bracewell built a new school to appease the unsectarian party, who disliked the idea of the Wesleyans having the monopoly in the education of the children. This school was leased to managers at a nominal rental, and carried on under Mr. Gaskell for some time under the name of the "Unity School." In May, 1878, the managers voluntarily discontinued the school, and the premises were used by the Methodists for their boys' department. These conditions obtained until June, 1885, when the boys were re-transferred to the Wesleyan premises, which were enlarged by the addition of a classroom. At present there is accommodation for 560 children, and the average attendance is 470. In the Sunday school are 400 scholars.

After the erection of such handsome school premises, the society began to feel that their chapel accommodation was not satisfactory, and the question of a new chapel was mooted. Mr. Bracewell, however, anticipated the people's desire by beginning the present substantial chapel, which was seven years

BARNOLDSWICK CHAPEL AND MANSE.

in building. The secret of his purpose was not disclosed till the chapel was nearing its completion. In 1877 it was finished, and opened on Good Friday, the Rev. Jno. Clements preaching the first sermon. In the evening of the same day the Rev. Peter

Mackenzie delivered his popular lecture on Queen Esther. The opening services were continued on the three following Sundays, and the total proceeds amounted to £517. With this money, together with the proceeds of the sale of the old chapel, which realised £500, the present manse was erected at a total cost of £1,800. The estimated cost of the chapel was £8,000, the organ alone costing £800; that of the schools £3,000. The chapel was given to the Connexion by Mr. Bracewell, who also bore the major part of the cost of the schools. The small fund of some £300, which had previously been raised with a view to a new chapel, was spent in putting an organ into the school, and in various improvements. The chapel accommodates 800 people comfortably, and at anniversary times 1,000. The premises are entirely free from debt, the cost of the manse having been raised by various efforts, including a bazaar in 1881 that was opened by Mr. T. H. Ingham. New class rooms were added in 1887; and in 1891 the premises were re-decorated.

The most prominent figure in Barnoldswick Methodism was Mr. William Bracewell, who was born at Green End, Earby, on April 5th, 1813. While a young man he joined the society at Earby, and became a member of the class led by Mr. Richard Holdsworth, of which class his mother was also a member. He became also a teacher in the Sunday school. He married in August, 1837, a Miss Metcalf, the only daughter of Mr. William Metcalf of Horton House, Horton-in-Craven. After his marriage he went to live at Horton, whence on Sunday mornings he came to meet with Mr. Joseph Marshall, who lived by the Old Coates Mill, and conducted a class in his own house. For a short time after this he lived at Burnley, where he carried on the business of a cotton

WILLIAM BRACEWELL.

manufacturer. In 1846 he began the erection of Butts Mill, at Barnoldswick, which he twice enlarged, and in 1854 and -55 he built Wellhouse Mill,—the two together containing about 160,000 spindles and 1,200 looms and giving employment to some 1,300 persons. To these factories he added a colliery, stone quarries, a corn mill, and farms, and thus became almost the sole employer of labour in the village. At the same time he was running two weaving sheds at Burnley. In 1879 his two sons now deceased were admitted into partnership, and the firm was styled "Wm. Bracewell & Sons." Up to this time Mr. Bracewell was said to have been the largest single-handed spinner and manufacturer on the Manchester Exchange.

While thus absorbed in large industrial undertakings, Mr. Bracewell always found time for religious work. He took a very active interest in the Sunday school and for nearly forty years was a superintendent. He supported at different times town missionaries who laboured amongst the poor with much acceptance. As a member of the Wesleyan church he filled at different periods almost every office open to a layman, and was a circuit steward at the time of his death.

On April 22nd, 1860, he was left a widower. A short time afterwards he married Miss Whitaker, of Colne, by whom he had two daughters, one of whom is still living at Barnoldswick as Mrs. Joseph Slater, of Newfield Edge. During the cotton famine of 1861-63 it is said that Mr. Bracewell kept his factories running, thus saving his employees from the terrible privations which visited the Lancashire towns at that time. It was largely owing to his activity and enterprise that the present branch line of railway was constructed from Earby, a private company in which he was the largest shareholder finding the capital for the line and the Midland Railway Company the rolling stock. He died March 13th, 1885, in the seventy-second year of his age. At his funeral the whole village put on signs of mourning, and he was followed to his grave at Bracewell Church by a procession nearly a mile in length. His name, his labours, his lavish generosity to the various religious bodies and especially to his own church will long be remembered by a grateful people.

Another prominent figure was Mr. William Baldwin, who came to Barnoldswick as a young man fifty-three years ago. He was born at Nelson in 1820. During his infancy, his parents removed to the small village of Blacko. He was converted when quite a young man, and in 1846 he married and settled at Barnoldswick. The church soon enlisted him in the active service of God. His name was on a local preachers' plan for fifty-five years, and for fifty-two he held the office of leader. Twice he was the circuit steward, and for many years continuously he acted as society steward. In the Sunday school he was teacher or superintendent for forty years. His geniality and generosity, and his loyalty to Methodism for so long will not soon be forgotten. He died in peace on July 1st, 1899, after a short illness, in the seventy-ninth year of his age.

Mention should also be made of Mrs. Thomas Hartley, a saintly old Methodist still living and in her eighty-third year, who (though somewhat feeble) can be seen in her pew almost every Sunday morning, delighting in the "courts of the Lord's house", though too deaf to hear the preacher. In 1834 Mrs. Hartley received her first ticket of membership. She still holds the office as leader to which she was appointed thirty-six years ago. Mr. James Nuttall, now resident at Thornton-in-Craven, and still a member of the Wesleyan church at Earby, was at one time a useful and prominent member and local preacher at Barnoldswick. He is remembered amongst other reasons for the remarkable career of his three sons, two of whom, Enos and Ezra, in their younger days were Wesleyan local preachers at Barnoldswick. Enos Nuttall entered the Methodist ministry, and was sent as a missionary to the West Indies, where he resigned and joined the Anglican communion. His preaching ability was soon recognised, and preferments were speedily offered him. He was made bishop of Jamaica, and eventually archbishop of the West Indies. A few years ago, while on furlough in England, he visited his old father at Thornton, and preached in the church of St. Mary-le-Gill to a crowded congregation. Ezra Nuttall is in the Methodist ministry at the present time in South Africa, where he was honoured a few years ago by being elected president of the South African Conference. Ebenezer Nuttall, now deceased, was a clergyman of the Church of England.

## EARBY.

When Methodism was first introduced into the village is not exactly known, but it was probably about the beginning of the present century. His Honour Judge Ingham, formerly resident for a long time at Marton, states that his grandfather was an intimate friend and companion of John Wesley, that Mr. Wesley preached for the first time in Yorkshire in the little Inghamite chapel at Salterforth, and that the pulpit from which he preached is still there. The late Mr. Edmund Lund's mother received her first ticket in 1815 from the Rev. Thomas Vasey when she was resident at Wycollar. The first Methodist services in Earby were held in a barn, whence the society migrated to a cottage. The early Methodists must have been very enthusiastic, for it is said that open-air services were held as early as six o'clock in the morning, and that anyone going up Aspen Lane late at night could hear praying in almost every house.

In 1821 the first chapel was opened. It consisted of a large room above two cottages, and access to it was gained by stone steps on the outside. About 1840 this building was altered; the cottages were converted into the lower portion of a chapel, with a gallery made out of part of the upper room at one end. This chapel continued in use until 1861, when the present place of worship was erected at a cost of £2,200. The foundation-stone was laid by Mrs. Bracewell, of Gargrave, who was the donor of the site, on July 10th, 1860. Since then £1,000 has been expended on repairs and decoration. The old chapel was used as a Sunday school until 1872, when the

EARBY CHAPEL.

present schools were erected at a cost of £2,000. The foundation-stone was laid by Mrs. Christopher Bracewell on July 10th, 1871. The old chapel was afterwards disposed of to the late Mr. William Crowther, who converted it into three alms-houses, which he generously endowed. The day-school was commenced in 1872 by Mr. S. Leach, who continued as headmaster until June, 1885, when Mr. Lindley, the present master, succeeded him. The school is adapted for two hundred scholars; in the Sunday school there are three hundred. The present chapel contains sitting accommodation for 410 people, and has recently been enlarged by the addition of a transept, in which seats are provided for about one hundred more. The cost of enlargement was £600, which is only part of a £2,000 scheme, projected for the future as occasion requires. Foundation stones were laid on April 15th, 1899 by Messrs. T. B. Hamilton, of Haslingden, Walter Bracewell, of Gargrave, Caleb Duckworth, of Colne, Mrs. Stables and Mrs. Charles Lowcock, of Skipton, and Mrs. Simpson, of Burnley. Three stones were laid by the following children:—Cissie Reid, Lilian Dodgson and John Douglas Green; and a public meeting was held in the evening. The enterprise began well, and is likely to prosper.

Amongst the prominent and useful members, who are now deceased, may be mentioned John Pickles, who for many years was the principal musician in the choir, a class leader, and a devoted superintendent of the Sunday school; Thos. Smith, a local preacher, and a man of kindly nature and much familiarity with Scripture; and John Taylor, another close student of the bible, who rendered good service in the church and school. Mention must also be made of Mr. James Brown, who is still going in and out amongst the people at the advanced age of seventy-one. He has been a church member for fifty-five years. Born at Bracewell, near Barnoldswick, he came to Earby at the age of twelve. In 1849 he became a local preacher, and had many experiences. He tells of walking to Barley and back to preach twice, taking his dinner with him for consumption on the way. On one such occasion he came to a stream which he had to cross as best he could. As he was walking along its banks for some distance to find a suitable place, his dinner fell into the stream and was carried along by the current. After several fruitless attempts to recover it, he at last succeeded, and sat down in the shade of a tree to eat it, and so well soaked was it with the immersion that (he adds) he ate it without requiring anything to drink with it. One of his frequent walks was to Barrowford where he would preach once, thence to Nelson or Colne where he would preach again, and afterwards back home to Earby. Rising at four o'clock in the morning, he would sometimes walk to Silsden, preach there three times, and then return home by taking the train from Silsden to Skipton and walking from Skipton to Earby. On one such occasion in the morning service, as soon as he had announced his text, three young men composed themselves comfortably in the corners of their pews for a sleep. Noticing this he successfully remonstrated with them, telling them of his early rising and long trudge, and pleading that if anyone should require a sleep it was the preacher. Mr. Brown is a self-made man, whose natural ability and wit have made him a stirring and effective preacher.

## MOUNT PLEASANT.

Mount Pleasant is a small but interesting cause on the hill side about half way between Barnoldswick and Colne. The chapel consists of two upper rooms of cottages made into one, access being gained by a staircase on the outside. It is furnished with pews and a rostrum, in front of which is a square

MOUNT PLEASANT CHAPEL.

space for the choir. The accommodation is sufficient for about eighty people. The chapel was built by John Barritt, but was purchased from the mortgagee and made Connexional property.

A notable character in connection with this neighbourhood was Mary Barritt, who afterwards married Zechariah Taft (see pages 69, 70). She was born near Mount Pleasant in 1772, was converted when a young woman, and possessing a strong personality and an inflexible will, with great evangelistic zeal, she made no small stir in the neighbourhood. She preached frequently in the local chapels, and also went on circuit, conducting evangelistic services at Whitehaven (where one hundred and eleven believers are said to have been added to the society), Redcar, Scarborough, York, Bridlington, Macclesfield, Buxton, Ilkeston, and Nottingham. In Nottingham five hundred additions are reported to have been made to the society in three months. The conversions of the Revs. Robert Newton, and Thomas Jackson, and of Mr. William Dawson, the famous Yorkshire local preacher, are ascribed to her preaching.

# CHAPTER IX.

## BIOGRAPHICAL NOTES AND SKETCHES.

OCCASIONAL reference has already been made to many of the honourable men and women who contributed in their degree to the founding or progress of Methodism in East Lancashire. Of these additional information has in several instances been obtained, and of others mention is yet to be made. For the Howorth family may be claimed a length of connection with the neighbourhood and a continuity of devoted service, that in few cases have been exceeded. According to the entries made in an old bible, one of the ancestors was a Simeon Lord, of Howroyd, near Todmorden, in whose time the male members of the family "left their homes and their business to join the army of Cromwell." A son of the next generation married a Susan Ingham, who lived at Hurstwood, and there in 1694 a nearer ancestor drank her first cup of tea. With this Puritan strain in their blood, to say nothing of the disposition to venture upon new beverages, it is no wonder that the family has not failed in its advocacy and exhibition of the rights of religious freedom.

The first to attach himself to Wesleyan Methodism was James Howorth, who was born at Hempsteads, Bacup, on May 27th, 1793, as a lad came over to attend the old Grammar School, and was afterwards apprenticed to Mr. Robert Munn, an enterprising grocer and draper. At that time he was a Baptist; but the associations into which he was thrown, and especially it appears the influence exerted by the Rev. L. Hargreave soon led him to throw in his lot with the Methodists. On June 10th, 1812, he first went to class, choosing as his leader Thomas Hudson, whom he accompanied the following Sunday to Burnley Moor (there is no other evidence known of the existence of a Methodist cause at this place), where Hudson preached from "Will ye also be His disciples?"

The next week Mr. Howorth went with C. Whittaker to a love-feast at Colne, and thenceforward there was little wavering in his attachment to the church he had chosen. Soon after his apprenticeship was over, he commenced business as a provision dealer in the shop lately occupied by Mr. T. Hoghton in St. James' Street, and in the course of time entered into partnership in the worsted trade with Mr. S. Howard. When the firm was dissolved, Mr. Howorth built the Mount Pleasant mill; and both there and in the mill at Cheapside he greatly prospered. In civil life he took no very prominent part, though for a time he served as a police commissioner. He was twice married—in 1818 to Miss Lord, who died four years afterwards, and in 1824 to Miss Martha Hartley. Both of these ladies were Methodists before their marriage, and both in all probability contributed to the strengthening of their husband's interest in the enterprise and activities of his church.

Of his connection with Keighley Green and Wesley chapels something has already been said (see especially pages 119, 120.) No good work appealed to him in vain for generous support or personal help. After an honourable and prosperous career he died on January 9th, 1858, counselling his sons to be "men of integrity and piety," and for his daughter condensing the secret of a wise life into a few compact words, "Study your bible, live near to God, acknowledge Him in all your ways, and He will bless you." A few weeks afterwards, on April 7th, his widow followed him; and by one who knew her she is described as possessing "a strong mind, a solid and dispassionate judgment, unwavering in decision where duty was clear," and as carrying on vigorously many kinds of religious and philanthropic work.

How well the sons, George and John, have followed the counsel of their father, most citizens of Burnley know. Integrity, and piety (or dutifulness, as the word originally meant,) have been now throughout long lives their most obvious characteristics. The one has continued to live in the town in which he was born, and few civil distinctions have been withheld from him; the other removed almost a quarter of a century ago to Bowdon, leaving behind him an influence that is not yet spent. Of both it will be possible to write more amply, when their work is fully done. Mr. George Howorth married a daughter of Mr. Thomas Smith, of Flaxmoss, near Haslingden. She was associated with him in every good work, and by her recent decease many hearts have been pierced with sorrow and the poor have lost a comforter.

The same restrictions do not hold in regard to their sister. She served the churches and the poor during her lifetime, and after for several years setting an example of the

JAMES HOWORTH.

MRS. JAS. HOWORTH.

GEORGE HOWORTH.

MRS. G. HOWORTH.

JOHN HOWORTH.

MISS HOWORTH.

utmost fortitude and patience was released from pain on May 4th, 1896. Her active connection with Methodism dates from the time when the girls were removed from the Sunday school at Keighley Green to the room under Wesley chapel, and continued until she was no longer able to meet her class in her own house. When her father removed to Park House, she began to cover the neighbourhood with a network of religious agencies, of which she was often herself both the inspiration and the servant. In 1863 she was persuaded to take charge of the young women's class in the Fulledge Schools, and there found her right sphere, exacting enough to sustain her interest, and gradually enlarged as fresh methods of doing good occurred to her fruitful mind. A society class was soon added; and as the years passed so many other things were added, that a bare list of the organisations she actively supported would include almost every variety of philanthropic effort. For a long time she was the secretary of the local branch of the Bible Society, and when her health failed she was elected to the less onerous post of its presidency. Her intelligent study of the Scriptures was in part the source of her missionary zeal. Of her private charities the ingenuity was as notable as the diversity. To be doing good in some way was her constant aim; and as soon as one avenue of gracious ministry was closed to her, her kindliness poured itself out through other channels, of which she was quick to discover the existence and diligent in testing the capabilities. To a stranger she would often seem reserved, strong of purpose but sparing in self-revelation. But beneath the apparent coldness beat a warm heart, and the slow speech was inspired by a mind that travel and reading had richly informed. She was a quiet woman, whose intellect restrained and disciplined her emotions, who evidently feared God and loved all His works. Her influence was steadily exerted to the help of any one within her reach who needed help, and to the sweetening of human society. And by her death the civil as well as the religious life of the town was impoverished.

A good portrait of Miss Howorth was placed several years ago in the young women's room at the Fulledge Schools, just as one of Mr. John Butterworth fitly adorns the young men's room. And in the chapel at the west end a memorial window of stained glass was unveiled in June, 1897. It consists of three panels, in which figures of Faith and Hope support a larger figure of Charity. Underneath the window runs a brass with the inscription, "To the glory of God and in memory of Miss Anne Howorth, who served God and this church and school with all her heart, and triumphed over pain on May 4th, 1896."

A contemporary of Mr. James Howorth was Mr. George Barnes, of whom a short memoir was published in the *Wesleyan*

*Methodist Magazine* for 1855, p. 1157. After stating that he was brought to Christ when about fourteen years of age and took a lively interest in every Methodist institution, it continues: "His character presented a combination of many Christian excellences—of unaffected humility and modesty, great sincerity, strict and invariable conscientiousness, gentleness united with firmness, prompt and punctual attention to duty, and uniform consistency. In his domestic relations he was considerate and affectionate; and in his commercial pursuits, a model of practical sagacity and unremitting application, controlled by Christian principles, and crowned with the divine blessing. He was a man of God, habitually cultivating the life of faith, and greatly enjoying both the private and public ordinances of religion. About four months before his death, he experienced an apoplectic seizure, from the effects of which he never fully recovered. . . A renewed attack, followed by convulsions and by a season of unconsciousness, at length ushered his spirit into the bliss of paradise." He died August 23rd, 1855, in his fifty-eighth year.

A nephew, who for nearly five years lived in his house more than fifty years ago, writes—"A thrill of affectionate admiration and veneration comes over me as I think of the uniform, unvarying consistency of the Christian life of Mr. George Barnes, as I daily witnessed it in his business relations, the privacy of the home life, and also in his connection with the Methodism of those times. Perhaps the feature that impressed me most was that I never once heard a hasty or uncharitable word escape his lips, and never witnessed the manifestation of a spirit or temper at variance with his religious profession. Family worship every morning and every night, the services of God's house, the Sabbath school, the weeknight service and his society class, were the habit and joy of his life during the round of the seven days every week; and I never knew him on any occasion willingly to forego any one of these engagements. One incident I remember well. It occurred on the day of changing their residence from Bank Parade to Grimshaw Street. After a busy, bustling day, when the last cart-load of all sorts of domestic articles had just been landed, and of course everything was in the utmost possible confusion and disorder, the good man asked us all to come into the dining-room for a few minutes, and then in simple but earnest prayer, amid the strange surroundings, sought God's blessing upon the new home."

Of Mrs. Barnes, who was the chief originator of the Dorcas Society, the same gentleman writes, "She was an intelligent and devoted class leader, trusted, beloved, and respected by ministers and people. The late Mrs. Peter Phillips and

GEORGE BARNES.

Mrs. John Butterworth were members of her class, and by them especially she was held in high esteem. Week by week, year after year, so long as health and circumstances permitted, her place in the house of God twice on the Sabbath, at the week evening service, and at her class meeting was very rarely vacant. The advancement of God's cause in connection with Methodism was a topic of daily conversation between Mr. and Mrs. Barnes; and next to the care of their own children, the interests of Burnley Methodism were to them both the dearest thing in the world."

Their daughter, Miss Barnes, lived for many years in Burnley. Her ill health made comparative seclusion indispensable, but the charm of her gentle character and the grace and promptitude of her bounty have rarely been exceeded. For some time she was a Sunday school teacher at Red Lion Street, and a collector for the missionary and other societies. Of her large benefactions, amongst which must be included a gift of £1,000 to the Victoria Hospital, several records will be found on the preceding pages. In the autumn of 1879, through the failure of her health, she removed to Southport, where for twenty years the influence of her Christian character and noble generosity has been widely and increasingly felt. Her interest in every philanthropic movement, and especially in the progress of Methodism in the Mornington Road circuit, has borne rich and valuable fruit. The handsome church at Leyland Road was in course of erection on her arrival, and Miss Barnes became one of its early members. In the building in 1890 of a new school and church-parlour she took a prominent part, not only laying one of the foundation stones but contributing largely towards the cost of the erection. Four years ago the church was greatly improved by the addition of choir stalls which Miss Barnes generously gave, the congregation defraying the debt remaining on the church. Mornington Road, Southbank Road, High Park Road, and Blowick have all been aided in their building schemes by this devoted Christian lady. Various institutions of the town, and the Manchester Mission have found in her a true friend. And in Southport, as in Burnley, she is as greatly honoured for her personal character as for her noble and generous gifts.

When Mr. Butterworth's portrait was unveiled in the Fulledge school on October 31st, 1885, an address of congratulation was presented to him, in which he was said to have been one of the superintendents when the schools were opened, and to have continued in that office until May, 1874, when he was seventy years of age. For use on the same occasion he appears to have committed to writing some reminiscences of his early life, and from these the following extracts are made. "I commenced to attend Sunday school in August, 1812, when I was a little over eight years of age, in a room over a blacksmith's shop belonging to the late Mr. John Wilkinson, and continued till the opening of the new school at Keighley Green in May, 1813. I was one of the scholars on the day it was opened. The scholars were some part of them taken into the vestry every Sunday, and were addressed by one of the superintendents or teachers, or by a visitor. I had more serious impressions produced upon my mind from those addresses than by any other means: they always followed me, I never could drown them.

"When I was thirteen years old, I left the town and went to reside at a place called Doffcocker, near Bolton; and during the time I was there I went to a Sunday school at Bolton, and to a good night-school. Though in a strange place yet I found friends, and such friends as I often think I should not have sought after, if I had not felt those serious impressions made upon me at Keighley Green school. From that time I was living in various parts of Lancashire till 1828, when I removed to Crawshawbooth. There I joined the society, and became settled. There was a good work begun in the Bacup circuit during the time that Mr. Fish was in it. He always claimed me as his spiritual child, and I felt quite as much pleasure in looking on him as my spiritual father. I was led to see myself as a sinner, and to feel something of the sinfulness of sin. I felt that I could not rest under the wrath of God, and I was determined not to rest till I could feel or hear the Holy Spirit of God whisper to me, 'Thy sins are pardoned, and thy name is written in the book of life.' Although I continued in this state for some months, I did not find rest till one evening I went with Mr. Fish to Goodshaw-Fold to a prayer meeting. As we were walking back, I unfolded the state of my mind to him; and when I had told him all I could think of, he turned round upon me, and asked me if I had given my heart to God, if I loved the Lord with all my heart, or if there were any sin that I could not give up. I told him I did not know of anything. He then told me that all I had to do was to believe and to believe then. I felt power to believe, and I went home rejoicing. Two years before I heard Mr. Brook, of Sheep Ridge, near Huddersfield, and there was a meeting after, to which I stayed and in which I wrestled to obtain liberty. I did not succeed, and was very miserable for more than a week, when I had a journey to a place near Rochdale. I had to walk over Blackstone Edge moor from Ripponden to Rochdale. I was alone, and several times I stopped and knelt down upon the moor in prayer. Once I felt such a power in wrestling as I never have experienced since, and I did shout with all my might on the open moor, 'Glory be to God, I will praise thee; though thou was angry with me, thine anger is turned away, and now thou hast comforted me.' I was at that time engaged in some business which kept me away from home for more than a week. It was business that was not very pleasant; and I think the blessing I received whilst crossing the moor strengthened and assisted me very much, so that I was very much better qualified for the work.

"It is now fifty-nine years since that time, but the blessings I received were the means of leading me to give my heart to the Lord, and of enabling me to decide upon anything that I had to meet which was not right. I believe if I had not joined the society I should have returned into the world again, and lost all that is good. But in giving my heart to the Lord and continuing in the society, I was better qualified to deny all that was sinful, my character was established, and I had always friends who were rendering me any assistance that I required, and never had any difficulty in finding employment. Providence seemed always to surround me, and to assist me in obtaining all that was necessary for any business I had in hand. My gratitude can never be sufficient to the Lord for all His spiritual and temporal blessings that He has conferred upon me all my life long."

The extracts read like quotations from a religious diary of the last century, but they represent admirably the kind of influence that made of Mr. Butterworth so strong a Christian man. He was born in the fourth year of the present century, and was of very humble parentage; but by industry and

MR. JOHN BUTTERWORTH.

MRS. BUTTERWORTH.

uprightness he gradually improved himself and his position, until he was able to retire from business in possession of an ample fortune and of universal respect. He was never very closely associated with the municipal life of the town, but served for a short period upon the School Board and for a longer one upon the magisterial bench. In the educational and philanthropic work of the town, on the other hand, few men took a more active part. He was one of the founders of the Victoria Hospital, and with it his benefactions will cause his name long to be associated. To the Wesleyan Town Mission, and to the establishment and effective working of schools he gave much attention. As a class-leader he was earnest, zealous, warmhearted, sound in judgment, and unremitting in his care for the religious prosperity of the members who met with him. Every other office open to a layman, except that of local preacher, appears to have been held by him, always conscientiously and often with conspicuous devotion. Several times he was a circuit steward, and when financial difficulty arose he would remark, "The Lord's cause must never be allowed to be in debt," and proceed either to clear the debt himself or to make a large donation with that in view. Prosperity never spoiled him : but always transparently simple, whilst yet grave and stately, those who knew him best recognised in him a type of Christian gentleman that must be graded not far below the highest.

In 1886 Mr. Butterworth committed the mistake, as he afterwards called it, of removing to Southport. Three years later on July 18th, he died. He was buried in Burnley cemetery, his body being followed to the grave by great crowds of friends, with representatives from the various public and religious bodies with which he had been associated. An impressive memorial service was held the following month in Fulledge chapel, when many gathered together from the town and neighbourhood to pay tribute to the Christian life and work of him they would see in the flesh no more.

Mrs. Butterworth was a quiet and kindly lady, born on March 1st, 1804. She was married first to Mr. Thomas Whitaker, and afterwards to Mr. John Butterworth, with whom she was associated in every good work. She died on December 13th, 1886; and the sole representative of the family in the line of direct descent is her granddaughter, Mrs. Pollard, of Park Avenue, Southport,—the heiress of many prayers and a loyal member of the church of her fathers.

Something has already been said (see especially pages 208-212) of the activity and munificence of Messrs. Robert and William Tunstill. They were born at Spencer Fold Farm in Pendle Forest, where their father appears to have farmed land under the Clayton family and to have employed a number of hand-loom weavers. The migration of the family to Brierfield and its relation to the Methodism of that place are described in the chapter devoted to the Nelson circuit. There one of the brothers continued to live until his death, and no increase of prosperity was able to shake his fidelity to his church or to mar the simplicity and genuineness of his spirit. Both brothers made few pretensions themselves, or were much affected by the pretensions of others. Their house at Brierfield was for many years the home of the preacher, clerical or lay: and a hearty welcome was given to the poorest and most illiterate, if his motives were thought to be pure. The message was to them more important than the messenger; and their seats in the chapel were occupied, whether the preacher was a dignitary of the church or the most uncultured layman on the plan.

Mr. William Tunstill married Mary, the daughter of Mr. Thomas Barraclough, a gracious and beloved lady. In business circles and civil life he quickly rose to a position of great influence. In 1869 he was appointed a County Justice, and when the Nelson Borough bench was created in 1893 a place on it was of course found for him. In 1882 he was elected to the directorate of the Manchester and County Bank, and two years later to that of the Lancashire and Yorkshire Railway; and of both institutions he has been deputy chairman for more than ten years.

In addition to service and honour of every kind within his own circuit, Mr. Tunstill has for many years been an influential member of the Connexional Chapel Committee, which

WILLIAM TUNSTILL.

is one of the most important of the administrative bodies in Methodism. Besides dispensing in grants the income of the Chapel Fund amounting to about £10,000 annually, the committee has the management of Loan Funds of £100,000 for new erections and the relief of debt. This, however, is only the smallest part of its duties, which include the consideration of all cases of new erection of chapels, schools, or minister's houses, the enlargement or sale of trust property, and the management of the trust estates in the country, nearly 8,000 in number. In the course of administration there arise month by month questions, legal, financial, and official, of the most delicate and complicated character. In dealing with these Mr. Tunstill's great commercial knowledge and practical sagacity in business details have proved of the utmost value. On the death of Mr. T. R. Healey in 1881, his ability and devotion received recognition by his appointment as one of the treasurers of the Chapel Fund, and three years later he became the senior holder of that office.

At that time circumstances transpired in connection with the chapel department, which rendered important changes possible. A work of re-construction commenced, which has been carried on during successive years with the result that this department of the Wesleyan Methodist church has been brought into harmony with modern requirements, both as to the spirit of its administration and as to its business arrangements. In these alterations Mr. Tunstill has taken a leading part ; and the popularity of the chapel office is in no slight degree due to his wise counsels and his sympathetic co-operation with his colleagues.

Not less distinguished has been the part he has taken in the reconstruction of the central premises at Oldham Street, Manchester, which have become the headquarters of one of the most remarkable mission developments in modern Methodism, and in the church of Christ at large. Mr. Tunstill's first speech in the Conference was in opposition to the proposed sale of the Oldham Street premises, and, in view of the opinion then prevailing, he displayed no little foresight and courage in associating himself with the comparatively few men who advocated the retention of the site and the erection of new premises thereon. The better counsels in the end prevailed, and Mr. Tunstill accepted the responsibility he had taken in the Conference, as one of the leaders of a forlorn hope, by a munificent donation to the building fund, and by consenting to become the treasurer of the new body of trustees, an office which he still holds. The difficulties in the way of carrying out the scheme proved to be of the most formidable kind, even more so than was anticipated, and, in dealing with these, Mr.

Tunstill's continuous advice and oversight contributed in great measure to the success of the undertaking. There can be no doubt that the rebuilding of these premises, and the wonderful mission work which has gathered around them, have proved to be the opening of a new chapter in the history of Methodism. Similar schemes have been started in many other large towns; and to a large extent the problem of how to reach the masses has been solved by these efforts. It must be a pleasant reflection to Mr. Tunstill that he has been able at a critical moment to render service that has proved so invaluable to the church of his life-long connection.

Recurring to earlier times, two of the most notable families in Burnley Methodism were the Hopwoods and the Fishwicks. The striking conversion of the first William Hopwood under the preaching of John Wesley himself has already been narrated (see page 57). The register of marriages at St. Peter's shows that his wife's name was Jenny Wood, and that the officiating minister was the Rev. William Halliwell; and it is a curious illustration of the state of education in those days that both bride and bridegroom shrank from the attempt to sign their names, and contented themselves with affixing their marks to the register. Mr. Hopwood was for many years a class-leader at Keighley Green, and there his Methodist work centred. He died on June 8th, 1838, and a tablet to his memory still stands on one of the walls of Wesley Chapel (see page 126). His wife survived until November 24th, 1840.

On a tombstone in St. Peter's churchyard are inscribed the names of several children who died

WILLIAM HOPWOOD (2nd).

in infancy. One son, William, married Ellen, a daughter of William Fishwick, and was for long an influential member of the congregations at Keighley Green and at Wesley. He resided at Oak Mount, and was alike generous in his contributions, and earnest and kindly in his spirit. His wife died on December 29th, 1848, and he himself twenty years afterwards on June 20th; and the bodies of both lie in St. Peter's churchyard. Of their children three sons, James, George, and William Fishwick, reached manhood; but only the last-named is still surviving.

But no name in the Methodism of the neighbourhood in the early decades of the present century was more prominent than that of William Fishwick, of Green Bank House. A brief memoir of him by the Rev. W. O. Booth was published in 1842. He was born on September 12th, 1791, a son of Webster and Mary Fishwick, ardent and somewhat bigoted church-goers, several of whose children afterwards became well known Methodists. Of the two daughters, Ellen married the second William Hopwood, and Sarah married the Rev. Thomas Stead. Richard died in early manhood, and George settled at Scorton, where he won the right to form the theme of a separate chapter in Taylor's "Apostles of Fylde Methodism." William was educated in the Burnley Grammar School, and afterwards associated in business with his father. In early life he was sprightly and the best of company. Referring in his old age to this period, he attempted to describe what he considered his hardened and reckless spirit by saying, "On one occasion I attended a ball with Alleine's 'Alarm to the Unconverted' in my pocket." It was probably the illness and death of his brother Richard, and the good reports of Methodism given by his brother George at Scorton, that caused the prejudices of the family at Burnley to give way. William noticed the change wrought in those he loved, and hearing of the enjoyment they found in religion determined to seek it for himself. He was deeply impressed under the preaching of the ministers, instructed and quickened by the reading of Dr. Bunting's great sermon on Justification by Faith, and in September, 1813, joined a class-meeting. For a time he was much tempted to rejoin his old associates and stay away from class; and on one occasion, "instead of yielding, he imitated Bunyan's pilgrim, and literally putting his fingers into his ears, and crying, 'Life, life, eternal life!' he ran all the way," until he was safely within the doors of the vestry. A few weeks afterwards he found the peace and strength he had so resolutely sought.

In 1814 he was appointed a class-leader, and in the duties of that office which he sustained until his death his best work was done. In the Sunday school his zeal as a teacher is said to have been untiring. He also took a deep interest in the establishment of day schools, and in the introduction of Methodism into outlying villages. When local missionary societies began to be organised, he undertook to canvass a district of the town for subscribers, and continued to the end exceptionally ardent in his support of foreign missions. Nor was there any other kind of philanthropic effort, that did not in its measure elicit his sympathy or with success appeal to him for aid.

He married in 1826 Elizabeth, the eldest daughter of Mr. Thomas Kay, of Longholme, but lost his wife five years later. In 1836 he removed to Longholme, but his interest in Burnley Methodism never abated. On December 26th, 1839, he died after a short but painful illness, and was interred in St. Peter's churchyard on the second of January following. A mural tablet was erected in Wesley chapel to his memory (see pages 126, 127); and the inscription on his tombstone reads, "He was distinguished by the possession of a powerful mind, sound judgment, general information, deep piety, extensive liberality, and unwearied zeal. The law of kindness was written on his heart, and fully exemplified in his conduct as a husband, father, friend, and master. Having fought a good fight, and kept the faith, he peacefully entered into the joy of his Lord, proving that to die is gain."

Thomas Kay resided in Burnley until 1820, when he removed to Thistle Mount, near Newchurch. Of his two daughters, Sarah and Elizabeth, the latter, as stated above, became the wife of William Fishwick. The son, John Robinson Kay, who afterwards removed to Summerseat, rose gradually to a position of the greatest influence in the industry of the county and in the Methodism of Great Britain. He was an intimate friend of Dr. Adam Clarke; and in the movement, that gathered force during his lifetime, to provide opportunities of secular education for the poorest children in the land, few men were wiser in their counsel or more lavish in their expenditure of themselves.

The first impression which Mr. Peter Phillips made was that of a charming, upright Christian gentleman. He was the son of the Rev. John Phillips, and was born in 1806 at Brechin in Scotland while his father was stationed there in the course of his itinerancy as a Wesleyan minister. The previous generation of the family had some connection with Warrington or its neighbourhood. Mr. Peter Phillips came to this town, to use one of his familiar expressions, when both as regards Burnley and Burnley Methodism it was "a day of small and feeble things." He commenced business as a chemist in the shop in Manchester Road afterwards occupied by Mr. Richard Thomas, an esteemed and devoted Methodist. About fifty years ago he set up as a stock and share broker, which business he carried on for a long time on his own account, then in partnership with his son, Mr. J. W. Phillips, who since 1870 has been in sole charge. Mr. Phillips married Miss Margaret Hitchon, whose father built and for a while lived at Ridge House. From

PETER PHILLIPS.  MRS. PHILLIPS.

the shock of her death on May 16th, 1875, when she was in her seventy-first year, he never entirely recovered. She was a woman in a thousand—kindly, gentle, and strong. In all religious work she took deep interest; but for many years she was the leader of a ladies' society class, in which she found her vocation and her joy. The testimony of her members to her helpfulness and their esteem was unanimous. The husband of one writes, "My late wife cherished an intense personal regard for her dear leader, for whose earnest Christian character she had a sincerely high estimation," to which she often gave expression. Another, still living, writes, "She took a deep and constant interest in the spiritual welfare of each of her members, and she was always the beloved and trusted friend of them all; and to those who survive, her memory is most precious."

Of Mr. Phillips it may be truly said that he had no enemies. His whole life and temper were such as to transform opposition, and to win affection and esteem. Constitutionally, he avoided contests of every kind; and wherever he moved, he made friends. He was naturally nervous; and though he repeatedly appeared in public, he never overcame this weakness. He was sociable and kindly, and his private charities were considerate and many. He was fond of books, familiar with their contents, and a capable critic in regard alike to matter and to style. In his early life he ventured even to increase their number by the publication in 1834 of a little volume under the title of "The Universal Restoration, and other Poems, Moral, Satirical, and Religious." The venture was afterwards referred to humorously by him as his "youthful folly," but the poems are such as no man need be ashamed of. They are full in phrase and ring of reminiscences of the poetry that was read in his youth; but a strong vein of quiet humour runs through them, the satire is playful and not bitter, and the rhymes and cadences show that the technique of the art had been fairly mastered. Genius is a rare gift; but the next best thing to the living fire is perhaps the skill of saying musically what will either profit or please.

Mr. Phillips was a trustee of almost every chapel in the circuit; he had held every important office in local Methodism; but it was in preaching that he delighted and excelled. He has been heard repeatedly to say that no office either in the church or out of it was to be compared with that of local preacher, and that he himself would give up every other office before that. In the pulpit he was intensely earnest without becoming either vehement or demonstrative. To persons of a certain temperament his preaching seemed sometimes too introspective and uniform, lacking in variety both of theme and of method. Texts, such as "Examine yourselves, whether ye be in the faith; prove your own selves," were great favourites with him. But there was a faithfulness, a loftiness of conception, a breadth of sympathy, a grappling with vital needs, about his preaching that lifted it altogether above the ordinary level. It is reported that another local preacher, who was the father of a family, was accustomed, when Mr. Phillips was planned, to tell his children to listen to him with the greatest attention, as they would be sure to hear a sermon worth printing in gold. To his less highly favoured brethren his kindness was thoughtful and ingenious. He often asked the writer in the winter season, when some elderly or poor local preacher was planned a long way from home, to send a cab for him so as to shelter him from the cold and rain, and save him from undue fatigue. Unostentatious generosity of this kind characterised Mr. Phillips in all relations of life and all departments of Christian work. He died in December, 1879; but his memory is still green, and his influence for good unspent.

At one time the Dugdales of Park Hill were well known in northern Methodism and outside its boundaries. Sketches of both husband and wife appeared more than a quarter of a century ago in the now defunct *City Road Magazine*, and from these a few particulars may be extracted. Thomas Dugdale was the son of William, one of the original proprietors of the Lowerhouse mills. He was born at Padiham on December

22nd, 1815, and according to his own statement received his first religious impressions from his mother. The family were in the habit of worshipping in the parish church of Padiham, and there whilst still a very young man Mr. Dugdale began to engage in religious work. He became a Sunday school teacher, and his abilities and diligence were so remarkable that, though only twenty-one years old, he was requested by the Rev. R. M. Master, vicar of Burnley, to take the superintendency of a Sunday school that had been recently established at Cheapside. He engaged in this work with great energy and success, insomuch that in the course of two years the scholars increased tenfold, from thirty to three hundred. At that time Cheapside was without any public religious services, and Mr. Dugdale proceeded to establish some. For about two years he preached every Sunday evening in the schoolroom, and every Tuesday evening he conducted a short service in a cottage. These efforts were very acceptable to the people, but were regarded by the then incumbent of Habergham-Eaves as a breach of the order of the Church of England. On that ground they, through his interference, were discontinued.

Excluded in this way from his former means of usefulness, and feeling the need of Christian fellowship, Mr. Dugdale was led to join the Methodists at Lowerhouse, and to take an active part in their services. He became strongly attached to the society class, was fully convinced of its Scriptural character, regularly attended the weekly meetings, was soon himself appointed a class-leader, collected successive classes, ever maintained the importance and utility of the institution, and deeply censured every attempt to misrepresent its nature or depreciate its value. While he resided at Lowerhouse he gathered together a company of aged females, and met them twice a week to teach them to read, and to explain to them the Scriptures. At this time also he was recognised by formal appointment as a local preacher.

THOMAS DUGDALE.

On February 2nd, 1843, he was united in marriage to Miss Sharples, of Holmfield, near Rawtenstall, a lady whose principles, spirit, and aims were thoroughly in harmony with his own, and with whom for nearly thirty years he enjoyed uninterrupted happiness. She died only a few weeks before her husband. In this year also Park Hill Wesleyan chapel was erected, and dedicated to the worship of Almighty God. Mr. Dugdale's connection with this building and his notable munificence have already been described (see pages 142, 143). He was now in the prime of life, full of zeal for the glory of God and free from the cares of business. Park Hill chapel was made the centre of earnest evangelistic operations, in which all the usual Methodistic agencies were employed. A large society was soon raised, three classes being met by Mr. Dugdale in a room in his own house. A Sunday school was established, of which for many years Mr. Dugdale was the superintendent. He liberally defrayed all the cost of its maintenance, and in other ways promoted its interests. Prayer meetings were instituted, religious tracts circulated, and the sick and poor visited. As a local preacher Mr. Dugdale was grave, natural, deeply earnest, free from the affectation of originality or oratory, with a sonorous voice, and occasionally he exhibited a solemn and tender vehemence under which congregations were overpoweringly affected. As long as his health permitted, he responded to every call, and in every place was cordially welcomed.

A few sentences will suffice to narrate the closing events of his life. His constitution was not robust, and his health had never been vigorous; hence in spite of the utmost care, he was compelled gradually to cease from his public labours, and to confine himself to his weekly class-meetings and the services of the chapel. These he attended with unabated interest nearly to the last. The long and severe illness of Mrs. Dugdale, and the sad calamity of her blindness, deeply affected him; and her death was a blow from which he never rallied. He passed away on August 5th, 1872, trusting in his Redeemer.

Mr. Adam Dugdale was a brother of the above-named, and in early life was connected with the church of England. His parents died when he was quite young, and possibly the influence of his brother may have had something to do with his joining the Methodist church. Though he resided at Rose Hill, Burnley, he attended Park Hill chapel for about twenty years. He was fond of music, and he gave a harmonium which he afterwards exchanged for an organ; and both of these instruments he played during the time of his attendance at Park Hill. He subsequently joined Wesley chapel in Burnley, and probably took the principal part in the great renovation of that chapel in 1877. This was part of a circuit extension scheme, towards which Mr. Dugdale promised £500; and the comfort of the pew-holders, particularly in the body of the chapel, and the fine rostrum which has hardly an equal in the country, were due largely to his enterprise. So devoted was he to Methodism that he made the duties of his church his business. He was a true gentleman, kind to the poor, and entirely free from

ADAM DUGDALE.

pride and pretension. His first wife was Alice, the second daughter of Mr. Thomas Whitehead, of Holly Mount, Rawtenstall. She was brought up a Methodist, and had been a member of society for some years at the time of their marriage. Probably through her influence he joined a class and finally associated himself with the innermost circle of Methodist influence.

Mr. Dugdale was not without family trials. He lost his wife, by whom he had five children, three daughters and two sons. The eldest son died through a horse accident near Park Hill. For his second wife he married Miss Annie Sutcliffe, only daughter of William Sutcliffe, of Bacup, one of the best known Wesleyans in the country. A week after his second marriage and when away from home the sad news was conveyed to him that his second son had passed away. His three daughters still survive, and, though no longer residing in Burnley, they maintain their connection with Methodism. Mr. Dugdale's last public act was to lay one of the memorial stones of the Colne Road chapel in May, 1879; but so unwell was he that he remained in his carriage during the whole of the service except the few minutes required for laying the stone. He was a member of the Town Council for three years, but contentious public life had no attraction for him. When the Borough Bench was established in 1871, he was one of the first magistrates appointed. He was born at Lowerhouse, near Burnley, November 8th, 1828, and died at Lytham on August 2nd, 1879. He was interred in the family vault at Longholme. Dr. Pope afterwards preached a funeral sermon in Wesley chapel, Burnley, in which he referred to Mr. Dugdale's thirty years' connection with Methodism, and to the unostentatious manner in which he had laboured to promote its welfare.

The name of William Lancaster has been connected with Burnley Methodism almost from its commencement. There was one of that name, who was one of the original trustees of the Keighley Green chapel; but whether he resided in Burnley, or in some other part of the Colne circuit, it is not easy to ascertain. It is not improbable that he was a descendant of the Richard Lancaster, who first provided a home for the Methodist preachers at Colne. There was another William Lancaster, who for several years was a leader, and whose two sons, Caleb and Joshua, still survive. A third William Lancaster came to Burnley from Gisburn, about the year 1798. At first he was employed in making the canal, and afterwards he took up the occupation of a hand-loom weaver. His name appears in the Keighley Green society stewards' book as leader of the Gannow class in June 1809, when he paid 5s. 3d. as its contribution to the circuit funds.

He first attended the leaders' meeting at Keighley Green on the 24th of August, 1810. At the end of 1818, he removed to Balladen, near Rawtenstall, but returned to Burnley in 1822. Three years later his name occurs again as that of a leader of a class at Keighley Green.

His son William was born on the 20th August, 1813. According to the usage of the times he was employed at seven years of age at a mill in Salford; and as showing the difference between the former times and these, it may be mentioned that he began work at half-past five in the morning, breakfast, which he had to deal with while he attended to his work, was taken to him at eight, at noon he had three-quarters of an hour allowed for dinner, after which work was resumed and carried on without intermission till half-past eight in the evening. There was no clock in the mill, but, as no building then intervened, he could see the clock in the steeple of the parish church. For the greater part of the year it was dark before the time for giving up work, and then he would anxiously watch for the appearance of a light in the clock tower, which indicated that the ringers were about to sound the curfew, when he knew that only half-an-hour's work remained. The only school he attended was the Sunday school at Keighley Green. Here he learned to read, and here he received his first lessons in writing, using the primitive contrivances of smooth sand and a pointed iron rod, to which reference has already been made.

In 1826 he became a decided Christian. His conversion was clear and unmistakable. In that year the celebrated "Billy" Dawson preached at Keighley Green from the text, "What shall it profit a man, if he shall gain the whole world, and lose his own soul?" Three boys were powerfully affected by the sermon, and at its close went forward as earnest seekers of salvation. But they did not receive any conscious blessing that night. After the service they stood and talked together on the grass-plot in front of the chapel. Said one of them, "We will not give it up: did not Jacob wrestle all night, and got the blessing? We will go somewhere where we can be quiet and alone." They at once set off for Royle Wood, about a mile from the chapel. Arrived at the wood they knelt down round an old tree root, and prayed in turn. But they could not stay all night, having early next morning to be at the mill. So after half-an-hour's prayer they returned to their homes—still unblessed. But on the way the eldest said, "Now we will never rest till we get salvation, we have been 'fearfully' near it to-day." Then turning to William Lancaster, he added, "We will go to thy father's class on Tuesday night." At noon on Tuesday two of them went to the mill, and calling William Lancaster to the door said, "We want thee to tell thy father to give out long hymns, so that the meeting will still be going on when we leave the factory: we are fairly 'set in' for salvation." As soon as the mill stopped in the evening, the three lads met and ran as fast as they could to the old chapel. As they entered they declared they could feel a gracious influence, for the members were singing

> See there my Lord upon the tree;
> I hear, I feel, He died for me.

In a few moments they knelt down and began to pray, and as the class continued, William Fishwick put his hand on young Lancaster's shoulder and said, "Thou art within touch of salvation; I feel thou art going to be saved." And "God blessed him there" that night; he and his companions, James Taylor and George Keighley, found peace.

About this time Mr. Thomas Farrer, the leading singer, noticed the lad's voice, and asked him to join the choir. Consent was readily given; but there was a difficulty in that he did not possess a hymn-book, and could not find a shilling with which to purchase one. There was, however, an arrangement at the school, by which a book could be had by the payment of a penny a month. In this way he became the possessor of his first hymn-book, which he took to the mill, and there he committed to memory the whole of the five hundred and twenty hymns it then contained. The chapel afterwards became the court house; and, when he was made a magistrate, and took his seat on the bench, he found himself in the very place in which he had formerly stood as a boy in the choir.

In 1834 Mr. George Fishwick, who had a mill at Scorton, came to Burnley, and told his brother William that he wanted someone to give out the work for the hand-loom weavers, and asked him if he could suggest anyone likely for the post. Mr. William suggested young Lancaster. He was sent for to the office, and after some conversation was engaged at twelve shillings a week, with instructions to go at once. As he had not enough money to pay the coach fare, it was decided that he should walk to Preston, and thence proceed by a packet that went to within a little distance of Scorton. He was to start at midnight, and when the time came for him to set out his father said, "Now, my lad, kneel down." They knelt down beside the old arm-chair, which Mr. Lancaster still treasures in his office, the very office in which he was engaged to go to Scorton, and the father prayed that he might be protected on the journey, and find favour with his masters. At Scorton he became a local preacher, and for twenty-four years travelled through the greater part of the Fylde, "holding forth the word of life." Often he would walk twelve to twenty miles, conduct

WILLIAM LANCASTER.

two or three services, and then walk home again. To these long walks in the fresh bracing air, and the change of thought and interest, he attributes his long life and good health.

After the death of Mr. George Fishwick he returned to Burnley on the first of April, 1857. On the first Tuesday evening after his arrival he went to his father's class, in which he had met for about eight years before his removal to Scorton. Only two of the members he had known remained. Before the meeting commenced his father said, "I am so weak I can neither stand, nor speak: here, William, you take the book." He took the book, and met the class; and before many weeks were passed the wearied leader at the age of seventy-eight had entered into rest. Hearing he was ill, a local preacher of the name of Charles Astin called to see him, and asked, "William, are you happy?" The dying man replied that 'happy' was not the right word to use, it was rapture and ecstasy. The son naturally succeeded to the leadership, which was thus in the hands of father or son for three quarters of a century.

For nearly forty years after his return to Burnley, Mr. Lancaster continued to serve Methodism as trustee of several chapels, circuit steward, and local preacher. In the last capacity his services used to be in considerable demand; and though he has now reached the age of eighty-six, he still occasionally appears in public. Every chapel and school in the circuit have been built within his lifetime. For sixty-five years he has been a local preacher. At one time for a short period he was a member of the Town Council. And now in extreme age he is waiting peacefully for the end, esteemed by all who know him.

Mr. John Thornton is happily still living, though increasing years prevent his taking the acive part in church work which he has done through a long life. He was born at Skipton-in-Craven, and was connected with Methodism there from his childhood. When a young man he was early entrusted with various church offices, such as the superintendency or secretaryship of the day and Sunday schools. He came to Burnley in 1853 as one of the officials in the Craven bank, and so has remained up to the present time. In Burnley he found a congenial sphere for his Methodist instincts, and identified himself with the activities of Wesley chapel. He was an earnest worker in the Sunday school as superintendent, a member of most of the committees and trusts, and for two periods of three years each has held the office of circuit steward. Since 1875 he has been the treasurer of Wesley chapel, for many years a class leader, and a Borough Justice since 1892.

Mr. Luke Collinge was born at Mereclough, on October 18th, 1810, and died suddenly at Blackpool on July 24th, 1883. Like many of the leading Methodists, and also the greater number of Burnley's prominent public men, he was a product of the village rather than the town. He was of humble parentage, and was never ashamed to allude to the struggles of his early life. At twenty years of age he removed to Burnley to take charge of the toll-bar, where the Wellington Hotel now stands in Brunshaw Road. There he commenced also the sale of books and periodicals. In 1839 he laid the foundation of what has developed into one of the largest furnishing businesses in Lancashire, and subsequently entered the cotton trade in partnership with Mr. John Stephenson, a Wesleyan local preacher, who afterwards removed to America. He was connected with the old Board of Commissioners, the Town Council, and the School Board, and for many years was the recognised leader of the temperance movement. He was a staunch teetotaller, but tolerant and charitable in regard to those who differed from him.

As a Methodist his deepest interest centred in the schools. This may have been partly due to the sense of his own disadvantages in early life, and also of the benefits he had received from the Sunday school. He was one of the first managers of the Red Lion Street day schools, and for about a quarter of a century one of the most popular superintendents of the Sunday school. He was a trustee of four or five chapels or schools. Conscientiousness, earnestness, and integrity, were always conspicuous traits in his character. Mr. J. S. Collinge, of Park House, is the only surviving son, his older brother William, who had served for one year with great ability as mayor of the borough, having died in October, 1897. During the mayoralty of the last-named an address was presented by the Mereclough Methodists, in which they stated, "You and your ancestors for over a hundred years have taken a deep interest in our work and welfare, having contributed largely to our building and extension funds; and our freedom from financial obligation and embarrassment is largely due to the generosity of your family and yourself. We also gratefully acknowledge our indebtedness to your father, who for fifty years was closely and officially connected with us, was a wise counsellor and guide, a sympathetic and generous leader, and a most devoted and faithful friend to our fathers and ourselves."

Mr. Richard Parkinson was born in 1817 near Colne. In his youth he had very few opportunities for education, as he had to go to work at a very early age; but he was gifted with indomitable energy, and when a young man he devoted all his spare time to self-education, and very soon became a well-informed man. He was in business in Trawden for a few years, and then removed to Nelson where he carried on some chemical works at Hollin Bank for a number of years. In

1871 he removed again, this time to Burnley, where his business as wholesale druggist soon became a large undertaking, and is still conducted under the name of Messrs. R. Parkinson & Sons. He took no very active part in politics, but was an earnest Methodist, and a warm advocate of everything belonging to that church. He was early converted, and became a Sunday school teacher and superintendent, a class leader, and a local preacher. For about thirty years he continued in the last named office. His sermons gave evidence of careful preparation. He had a clear enunciation; his style was deliberate, but not without fervour; and these qualities made him acceptable in all the pulpits where he preached. He was never happier than when engaged in a discussion on theology or the doctrines of Methodism. On one occasion when living in Trawden he had been having a heated discussion with another Wesleyan on these subjects until after midnight. His friend went away, but in about two hours he came back again, knocked at the door, and called Mr. Parkinson out of bed to commence the argument again, as an idea had occurred to his mind that, he said, would pulverise Mr. Parkinson's position. They set to again at three o'clock in the morning, and continued the discussion until breakfast time. A few years before he died his health failed, and he had to ease off business and to give up preaching; but his interest in Methodism never diminished to the day of his death, which occurred at Ilkley on February 20th, 1880. All his family are staunch Methodists and attend Wesley chapel, except one son who is the vicar of St. George's, Halifax.

James Smallpage was the eldest son of John Smallpage, of East Witton, Middleham, a local colliery proprietor and farmer. When his son James during a revival of religion in the Dales joined himself to the Methodists, he was subjected to much persecution. The change of heart and life, however, soon broke down opposing forces, and gradually led the whole family to throw in their lot with the Methodists. In the early part of this century James left home and came to Burnley, where the busier activities of commerce presented a fairer field for the energies of a young and industrious man; and his brothers subsequently followed him into the same district. James entered into partnership in the leather business first with James Hartley, late of Ightenhill, and afterwards with George and William Fishwick, of Keighley Green. He became a leader and a local preacher, and was closely allied with the devout Methodists of the time in strengthening the growing hold of Methodism upon the increasing population of the town and district. He married Elizabeth, a daughter of James Smith, of Lane Bridge, one of the early pioneers in the cotton trade of the neighbourhood.

Mr. Samuel Smallpage, a brother of James, lived at Brunshaw, and was a cotton spinner and manufacturer, but retired early from business. He was closely associated with every advancing movement, religious and educational, in the circuit, and contributed largely to the support and extension of all Methodist institutions. He was a superintendent of the Red Lion Street schools for twenty years, a class leader and a circuit steward. He retired to Ripon, and died there in 1875.

Of John Eagin, who died on March 20th, 1836, some characteristic stories have already been told. James Smallpage, his master, met in his class, and one week was absent. It was Eagin's practice to visit his absent members without delay. He had often been on errands to his master's house before, and had used the back door. This time he walked up the flagged pathway on a wet afternoon to the front door, and rang the bell. On the servant opening the door she asked him why he had not gone to the back. "Oh," said John, "I cannot go to the back door when I am on my Lord and Master's business." Another account of the story gives his reply as "My business to-day is not back door business: I have come to see thy master, and I have come to see him about his soul." Eagin was ushered in, and after a short conversation on spiritual matters master and servant, member and leader, knelt together in prayer.

James Crossley was a notable character who lived till he was over eighty. One boast of his was that he never had an overcoat on in his life, though as a local preacher and town missionary he had walked thousands of miles in all sorts of weather. He was pre-eminently suited for the work he had to do, visiting the poor, preaching to country people, and leading classes of earnest and simple-minded Christians. For some years he led a class at the house of Sallie Cawtherly; and if the members used favourite expressions of their own, they were of original minting. Sallie would often say, "I am thankful for the mercy I have received, and I am thankful because I am thankful." If anybody spoke about trouble she would reply, "I never trouble trouble till trouble troubles me." Her husband would say, "I am thankful that I am as I am; I might be better, but I might be worse; and I mean to double my diligence to make my calling and election sure," to which the leader would sometimes reply, "You might easily do that and be no for'arder."

For quiet, unostentatious work, especially in relation to the secretarial details of the church, few men deserve more honourable mention than Henry Marsden Ormerod. It is somewhat remarkable, that he was born in 1816 on the premises, where for forty-eight years he was afterwards a trustworthy, diligent and methodical servant in St. James' Row, near the Craven bank. At the age of thirteen he went as an office boy or writer to the place referred to, which was then occupied by Messrs. Alcock & Machonochie; and subsequently he became clerk to Messrs. Alcock & Dixon, Alcock & Holmes, Holmes & Son, and afterwards Holmes & Holmes. By his steady business habits and unblemished character, he rose to be general managing clerk, and was much esteemed by his employers. His long connection with all the details of the business made him a valuable servant, in whom great confidence was placed. In consequence of the alterations then about to be made by the corporation in St. James' Row, Messrs. Holmes & Holmes were obliged to remove to Grimshaw Street; and it was only natural that a person like Mr. Ormerod, who had been in one office so long, should deeply regret having to change. Strange to say he did not change, for upon the very day of the removal of the business Mr. Ormerod died. Before the erection of Fulledge chapel he attended Wesley. His secretarial books were models of neatness and accuracy. To the best of his ability he did all he could to help the good work in his native town, and held almost every office in the church. When Fulledge chapel was in course of erection, he and Mr. James Howorth were amongst the most frequent visitors to see how the work was progressing; and it might be said of them, "They counted the stones thereof."

Mr. H. D. Fielding was born at Middleton on August 25th, 1816, and died October 15th, 1890, in his seventy-fifth year. He came to Burnley about 1841, and commenced business as a cotton spinner and manufacturer. After carrying on operations at Bridge Street mill, he entered into partnership with his brother-in-law, the late Mr. John Barnes, at Bankfield mill, Curzon Street. Mr. Fielding was not long in showing interest in public life. He joined the Improvement Commissioners about 1843, and remained a member of that body until the town was incorporated in 1861. He was then returned as a councillor, but after his three years' term expired he left the borough to reside at Cheadle Hulme, where he remained until about 1869. He re-entered the council in 1877, and in November, 1881, he was elevated to the aldermanic bench. At the same meeting he had conferred upon him the honour of being unanimously chosen mayor in succession to Mr. John Howorth. He was re-elected for a second year of office. In his municipal work he was most prominently identified with the Improvement department. While on the Board of Commissioners he was chairman of the Streets and Buildings Committee for several years, and after the incorporation he presided over the same department, under the name of the Improvement Committee.

He resigned his position as alderman in November, 1889. In addition to his duties on the council Mr. Fielding was for three years a member of the Burnley Board of Guardians. He was placed on the Commission of the Peace for the Borough in May, 1881.

Mr. Fielding was a prominent member of the Wesleyan church. He served as day school treasurer for two long periods, the last extending from 1870 to 1885. During the time he held the office, Accrington Road and Whittlefield schools were built, and a large addition made to Fulledge schools. Mr. Fielding took a great interest in this work, and the fact that no better built schools at that time existed in Lancashire bears no small testimony to his care and oversight. He was also a circuit steward for three years. In matters of opinion he was at all times remarkably firm and explicit, and he never hesitated to state his own views. His dislikes were often strongly expressed, but at the same time his friendship was most valuable. He was a strong man, rather impatient of opposition, but unremitting in his attention to any good work he took in hand.

From the agitation, which followed the publication of what are known as 'the fly sheets' in 1848, the Colne circuit suffered severely. Disaffection was widespread, membership and congregations dwindled, and Methodism was at low water mark. It was while the circuit was in this condition in the year 1850, that Mr. Robert Wildman was appointed bank manager to the Craven bank. He was a man of fervent piety and exemplary character, and a fine musician with a rich powerful voice. He threw himself with energy into Methodist work and made his personality felt first in the Sunday school where he was very popular, and afterwards in the society. The singing gallery in the town chapel was empty, and he was requested to collect and take charge of a choir. He trained a number of the senior Sunday school scholars, wrote out music for them, and in this way filled the gallery. Under his superintendency the Sunday school prospered. There was a gracious revival, during which a considerable number of the scholars were converted and joined the church. Many of them regarded him as their spiritual father, and wished to meet in his society class. Thus he became the leader of four classes with a membership of one hundred. He then directed his energies to the reduction of the debt upon Albert Road chapel, and £900 was paid off. Mr. Wildman lived to see the old circuit made into three. The marble tablet erected to his memory in Albert Road chapel, mainly by the contributions of old Sunday school scholars, bears silent testimony to his excellence and usefulness.

## NOTABLE MEMBERS. 257

Time and space render it impossible even to enumerate all the earnest men who have served Methodism in East Lancashire during the century and a half of its existence there. Sixty years ago Dr. Thompson was an active and popular local preacher; and he was succeeded by Dr. Brown, another effective preacher, the brother-in-law of Mr. William Tunstill. Dr. Brown removed to London, where he died some years ago. Robert Brown, of Barrowford, and afterwards of Wheatley Lane, was one of the most intelligent preachers in East Lancashire. As he was fond of reading and scientific study, his thoughts turned in that direction, so that his preaching was characterised rather by its instructiveness, than by glow and fervour. Another most effective preacher was a man named Greenhalgh, a blacksmith. William Stowe, Charles Astin, James Dugdale, William Bradshaw and Robert Hudson, of Lowerhouse, rendered long and useful service in their day. David Platt was a popular preacher, rendered more so by certain eccentricities in the exhibition or illustration of the truths he was declaring.

In other departments Thomas Burrows, Joseph Lonsdale, T. Harker, Henry Nuttall, George Heys, of Lowerhouse, William Dixon, of Colne, John Wilson, of Thornton, William Waddington, who in the Sunday school and as class leader was much devoted; and William Nowell, who was not only circuit steward for one year, but also took a deep interest especially in mission and Sunday school work, have left behind them a record which enriches the heritage of the church. Richard Thomas, who is now spending the eventide of his life at Ealing, near London, was a quiet, unobtrusive worker and giver, and an honour to the church to which he belonged. He was connected with Wesley chapel for about thirty years. Mr. Roger Smith was a consistent and diligent member of the church and official of the society. He regularly attended to his appointments on the plan, and to his duties as a classleader. He visited his members periodically, and he was rarely absent from the leaders' meetings. He was a member of the society for fifty-two years, and a local preacher for forty-four. He died in November, 1879.

Of those still living mention must be made of James Nowell and Dr. Brumwell, who have retired from active work, but who for thirty years rendered service of more than ordinary value as local preachers. The present generation hardly knows what was involved in being a local preacher half a century ago. An instance of the self-denial and dangers the calling involved may be given. Fifty or sixty years ago a local preacher from Pendle Forest of small stature walked all the way to Mereclough, preached twice, and was returning home

R

by way of Towneley Park. In those days poaching was very rife, and suddenly the local preacher found himself on the ground entangled in a poacher's net. Of course he did not know what was the cause of his falling, but immediately a tall, powerful man came up and said, "What are you doing there?" The local preacher replied that he was simply walking home, and did'nt know what was the matter. The poacher was known as John O'Betty's, and was a muscular and violent man, who would allow nothing to obstruct his purpose. Happily he recognised the preacher, and said to his comrades, "Oh! you need'nt trouble, he will not harm anyone." Instead of molesting him he guided him past the net, and let him finish the remainder of his seven miles journey home undisturbed.

All these honourable men and women, and many more contributed each in his measure to the spread of Methodism and therefore of vital Christianity, and to each is due the gratitude of the community. They served their generation by the will of God; and their works yet follow them.

# List of Illustrations.

|  | Page. |
|---|---|
| John Wesley | Frontispiece. |
| William Grimshaw | 2 |
| Interior of Haworth Church in Grimshaw's Days | 5 |
| Colne Chapel, 1777 | 31 |
| Cottages on the Site of First Chapel, Padiham | 49 |
| Padiham Chapel, 1777 | 49 |
| Keighley Green Chapel of 1788, now the Court House | 59 |
| Peter Hargreaves | 92 |
| Wesley Chapel, Burnley (Exterior) | 124 |
| ,,      ,,      ,,      (Interior) | 125 |
| Lane Bridge Chapel | 131 |
| Stoneyholme Chapel | 133 |
| Piccadilly Road Chapel | 134 |
| Dorothy Lancaster's Cottage | 135 |
| Cottage in Cog Lane | 136 |
| Bartle Hills Chapel | 137 |
| Accrington Road Chapel | 139 |
| Park Hill Chapel (Exterior) | 141 |
| ,,      ,,      ,,      (Interior) | 142 |
| Fulledge Chapel | 145 |
| Brooklands Road Chapel | 149 |
| Colne Road Chapel | 151 |
| Mereclough Chapel | 154 |
| Worsthorne Chapel | 158 |
| Wheatley Lane Chapel | 161 |
| Colne, Albert Road Chapel | 168 |
| Trawden Chapel | 173 |
| Padiham, Wesley | 180 |
| Padiham, Cross Bank | 183 |
| Sabden Chapel | 184 |
| Higham Chapel | 187 |
| Lowerhouse | 190 |

| | |
|---|---:|
| Hapton | 191 |
| Rosegrove | 192 |
| Nelson, Old Railway Street Chapel | 195 |
| Nelson, Carr Road Chapel and School | 200 |
| Barrowford, Old and New Chapels | 205 |
| Brierfield Chapel | 210 |
| Reedyford Chapel (Exterior) | 212 |
|     ,,    ,,   (Interior) | 213 |
| Barnoldswick Chapel and Manse | 219 |
| William Bracewell | 220 |
| Earby Chapel | 223 |
| Barnoldswick, Mount Pleasant | 225 |
| The Howorth Family | 228 |
| George Barnes | 231 |
| John Butterworth | 234 |
| Mrs. Butterworth | 235 |
| William Tunstill | 237 |
| William Hopwood | 239 |
| Mr. and Mrs. Peter Phillips | 242 |
| Thomas Dugdale | 244 |
| Adam Dugdale | 246 |
| William Lancaster | 250 |

# Index.

Aberford, 76
Abergham Eaves, 61, 135
Accrington, 93
Ackroyd, John, 116
Ainsworth, George, 50
Altham, Moses, 191
Anderton, W., 159f
Armistead, W. H., 162
Arthur, Rev. William, 88, 210
Ashworth, John, 64
Aspden, Miles, 47
Aspden, Sarah, 167
Aspinwall, Sergeant, 47
Asquith, Mr., 169
Astin, Charles, 141, 257
Astin, Mr., 155
Astin, Joseph, 167
Astin, "Susy," 105
Atmore, Charles, Diary of, 37f, 60f, 68, 109
Austin, Rev. G. B., 83

Bailey, John, 121
Baldwin, Starkie, 143
Baldwin, Thomas, 170
Baldwin, William, 221
Ball, Hannah, 113
Balmford, "Saley." 64
Banning, William, 66, 153
Bannister, John, 19
Bannister, Richard, 15
Barber, Rev. John, 106
Barber, Rev. William, 218
Bardsley, Samuel, 58, 69
Barley, 44f, 214ff; trustees of chapel, 215
Barnes, George, 98, 100, 127, 229ff
Barnes, George, junr., 98
Barnes, John, 146, 160, 211
Barnes, Mrs., 230ff
Barnes, Miss, 99, 102ff, 133, 138, 148, 211, 232
Barnoldswick Circuit, 217ff; ministers in, 217f; origin of Methodism, 218; day school, 218; circuit stewards, 218; Mount Pleasant, 225

Barritt, Isaac, 219
Barritt, Rev. John, 62, 69f, 207
Barritt, Mary, 63, 70f, 225
Barrowclough, Rev. Jonathan, 198
Barrowclough, Thomas, 13, 236
Barrowford, 1779, 50ff; trustees of chapel, 51, 204; formation of "Barrowford and Nelson" circuit, 197, 203ff
Baxter, Benjamin, **195**
Beaumont, Dr., **120**
Beech, Rev. J. H., 147
Bell, Benjamin, 151
Bennett, John, 1
Bentley Wood Green, 54, 135
Berry, Rev. James R., 90
Berry, John, 188
Best, W. T., 147
Birtwistle, George, 165
Birtwistle, Richard, 60
Blacko, 51
Blake, Rev. Malachi, letter from Mr Williams, 4
Blezard, John, **192**
Blocksedge, Mr., **199**
Boint, John, **62**
Bolton Hall, 73
Bond, Rev. William, letter from, 87, 89
Booth's, Rev. W. O., Memoir of W. Fishwick, 240
Boothman, Sarah, 138
Bottomley, George, 169
Bowers, Rev. John, 85, **120**
Bracewell, Mrs. Christopher, 223
Bracewell, Hartley, 208
Bracewell, John, 62
Bracewell, Thomas, 161f
Bracewell, William, **219**ff
Brackenbury, Rev. T., **202**
Bradburn, Rev. Samuel, 50, 113
Bradford circuit book, Extract from, 27
Bradshaw, William, 257
Brailsford, Rev. Wilson, 95
Bramwell, Rev. William, 38, 69f
Bridge, Mrs. Abel, 57f

## INDEX

Brierfield, transfer to Nelson circuit, 95; introduction of Methodism, 208ff; debt, 211; Sunday and Day Schools, 211
Brimicroft, 56
Brooks and Pickup, 148
Broughton, Thomas, 144
Brown, Dr., 144, 257
Brown, James, 224
Brown, Richard, 45
Brown, Robert, 257
Broxup, Richard, 44
Brumwell, Dr., 257
Bunting, Jabez, letter from John Gaulter, 71, 115, 194, 240
Burnley, 53ff; Wesley's visits to, 55ff; members in 1763, 56; accounts in 1789, 61; leaders in 1790, 61; leaders in 1802, 65; Burnley circuit, 1810-1899, 74ff; income in 1810, 74f; plan of 1811, 78f; preaching places in 1830, 78; lay preachers in 1830, 78; plan of 1837, 80; Local Preachers' minute book, 1818, 80f; ministers in 1810-1899, 81ff; supernumeraries in, 83; supplies in, 83; circuit stewards, 1815-1899, 95ff; value of trust estates, 100; Chairmen of District, 101; division of circuit, 103f; Keighley Green chapel, 104ff; Leaders of, 104; choir, 109; society stewards, 1789-1847, 109f; trustees, 110, 113; Sunday school, 113ff; day school, 118; Sick Society, 118; prayer-meetings, 119; Wesley chapel, 119ff; erection of, 120; trustees of, 121f, 126; treasurers of, 122; chapel-keepers, 122; jubilee, 125f; mural tablets in, 126f; Red Lion Street schools, 127ff; Band of Hope, 129; mission school, 129f; trustees, 130; Lane Bridge, 130ff; Stoneyholme, 132f; Piccadilly Road, 133f; Rose Hill, 134f; Accrington Road, 135ff; Bartle Hills Sunday School, 138; Whittlefield, 140; Wood Top, 140f; Park Hill, 141ff; tablet of Thomas and Mrs Dugdale, 143; Ighten Hill, 143f; Fulledge, 144ff; trustees of, 146; Sunday school, 147; Hull Street Mission 148; Brooklands Road, 148ff; stone-laying, 150; contributors to, 150; Colne Road, 151ff; Mereclough, 62, 153ff; trustees of, 153; Sunday and day schools, 154; Worsthorne, 155ff; Articles of Agreement, 155ff; stone-laying, 159; Wheatley Lane, 159ff; trustees, 160f; stone-laying of school, 160f; trustees of school, 160f; places given up, 162f; Sunday School Union, 163f; establishment of schools, 164; week-day bible classes, 164; day schools, 164ff; Town Mission, 166f; district meetings, 167
Burrows, Thomas, 257
Butterworth, John, 94, 99, 103, 115, 130, 138, 140, 147, 150, 232ff
Butterworth, Miss, 150
Butterworth, Mrs., 232, 236

Calderbank, Joseph, 187
Calvert, Richard, 209
Casson, Hodgson, 207f
Castle Clough, 136
Catlow, Mrs. J., 172
Chadwick, Rev. Samuel, 91, 149
Chatburn, 53
Clapham, Rev. James, 146, 210
Clapham, Rev. J. E, 134
Clark, Dr. Adam, 70f
Clark, William, 159
Clayton, Colonel, 168
Clayton, George, 129, 167
Clegg, James, 52, 206ff
Clegg, Rev. John, 210
Clegg, Miss, 211
Clegg, Thomas, 196
Clegg, William, 193
Clements, Rev. John, 219
Cliffe, Ben, 215f
Clitheroe, 53
Cliviger Coal Co., 154
Clough, Wesley's visits to, 50f
Colbeck, Thomas, 13, 19
Collinge, Lawrence, 153
Collinge, Luke, 154, 251f
Collins, Rev. William, 38
Colne Circuit, 1776-1810, 28ff; Wesley's visits to, 29f, 35; Ministers in 1776-1810, 67f; plans, 1786, 71f; Colne Circuit, 1810-1899; 168ff; debt on chapels, 169; Sunday School, 169f; ministers in, 1810-1899, 170f; supernumeraries, 171; circuit stewards, 1865-1899, 171f; Collingwood Street, 172; Langroyd Road, 172f; Trawden, 173f; Foulridge, 174; Laneshaw Bridge, 174f; Black Lane Ends, 175; Cotton

# INDEX.

Tree, 175; extension of, 67, 195
Condy, Rich., 46
Cork, S., 172
Corlass, William, 204
Countess of Huntingdon, Life and Times of, 4
Cowgill, B., 135
Cowgill, Mr. and Mrs. Geo., 103, 134
Cowpe A., 139f
Crabtree, John, 172, 214
Crane, Roger, letter to Mr. Sagar, 32f; letter from J. Wesley, 33
Crawshaw, John, 53
Croasdale, William, 200
Crompton, Samuel, 85
Cronshaw, R., 182
Crossley, James, 154f, 254
Crowther, William, 223
Crump, Rev. E., 218
Cuerdale, James, 155
Cutler, Ann, 58, 69

Darney, William, 1, 3ff; as Wesley's helper, 8; collection of hymns, 8; appointments, 10; character and preaching, 10; death, 10
Davies, John, 118
Dawson, "Billy," 118f, 206f, 248
Dawson, John, 130, 175
Dawson, Robert, 191
Dawson, William, 120, 225
Dean, Richard, 159
Derby, Lord, 169
Dewhirst, John, 50, 178
Dickenson, Rev. George, 130, 174
Dineley, 162
Dixon, Thomas, 56, 62
Dixon, William, 257
Dodgeon, Miss, 165
Dodgson, John, 47
Douthwaite, A., 167
Driver, Thomas, 61, 109
Dugdale, Adam, 123ff, 245ff
Dugdale, Mrs. Adam, 103, 132
Dugdale, Colonel, 190
Dugdale, James, 100, 214, 257
Dugdale, Misses, 103, 140
Dugdale, Robert, 81
Dugdale, Sarah, 143
Dugdale, Thomas, 142f, 243ff
Dunnockshaw, 54
Dutton, John, 170

Eagin, John, 66, 77, 254
Eagin, Thomas, 121
Earby, introduction of Methodism, 222ff; Sunday and day schools, 223; stone-laying, 224

Easton, John, 62
Eastwood, Benjamin, 137
Edgar, Mr., 164f
Edmondson, Rev. Jonathan, 68
Edwards, Miss, 165
Elliott, Henry, 196
Elliott, John, 196
Elliott, Reginald, and Sons, 200
Eltoft, Mr. 67
Emmett, Miss, 58
Emmott, Barnard, 161
England, Mr. and Mrs. William, 52, 214f
Entwisle, Joseph, 39, 60, 68
Everett, Rev. James, 85

Farrar, Rev. John, 89
Farrer, Thomas, 105f, 111, 249
Fielding, Benjamin, 105
Fielding, G. E., 122
Fielding, H. D., 255f
Fishwick, George, 121, 240, 249
Fishwick, William, 100, 107, 109, 116, 120, 126f, 239f, 249
Fletcher, Ann, 214
Fletcher, John, 113
Fletcher, Miss, 165
Fletcher, Mrs., 137
Floyd, David, 81
Foster & Andrew, 147, 202
Foster, John, 44f
Foulds, James, 62, 209
Fowler, Thomas, 100
Frankland, Rev. Benjamin, 183

Garnett, John and Margaret, 215
Garrett, Rev. Charles, 147
Garrett, Rev. Philip, 86, 101, 115, 128
Gaskell, Mr., 219
Gaulter, John, Letter to Rev. Dr. Jabez Bunting, 71
Gawksholme, 5
Geldard, Robert, 209
Gill, L. W., 219
Gillies, Dr., letter from Grimshaw, 2f
Gloyne, Rev. C., 39
Goom, Henry, 105, 112
Gott, James, 202, 211
Gott, S., 203
Gray & Davison, 122
Great Harding, 13
Greenhalgh, James, 81, 257
Greenwood, Henry, 196
Greenwood, John, 140, 167, 202
Greevs, Rev. J. W., 146
Gregory, Dr., 210
Grey, Ellen, 215

# INDEX

Grimshaw, William, account of, 1ff; letters to Dr. Gillies, 2f; letters to John Wesley, 6ff; "Answer" to Rev. G. White's sermon, 18; visit to Padiham, 20; death, 23
Grimshaw, Mr., 205

Haigh, Rev. Abraham, 51, 213
Hall, Rev. S. Romilly, 130
Halliwell, Rev. William, 239
Halstead, Robert, 193
Halstead, William, 64ff, 153, 193
Halstead, Rev. William, 87
Hamilton, James, 115
**Hannah, Dr.,** 142
Hapton, 191f
Hardacre, Richard, letter to William Sagar, 42
Hardcastle, **Rev. Philip,** 128
Harding, John, 218
Hargreave, Rev. Lawrence, 83f
Hargreaves, Abraham, 51
Hargreaves, Colonel, 159
Hargreaves, Crawshaw, 91
Hargreaves, George and Hannah, 155, 185f.
**Hargreaves,** James, 159
Hargreaves, John, 112, 203
Hargreaves, Peter, 56
Hargreaves, Rev. Peter, 87, 90ff
Hargreaves, Robert, 185
Hargreaves, Thomas, 209
Hargreaves, Rev. Thomas, 90f
Harker, T. 257
Harrison, John, 183
Harrison & Harrison, 152
Harrison, Towneley, 62
Hartley, Christopher, 61, 109, 112
Hartley, Grace, 46
Hartley, James, 81, 144, 160
Hartley, John, 214
Hartley, Mrs. Thomas, 222
Hartley, Wilkinson, 202f
**Hartley, William,** 44, 174f
Hartley, William, 201
Harvard, Rev. G. C., 146f
Haslindgen, 93
Hastling, Rev. Henry, 101, 148
Haworth, 2f; visits of Charles and John Wesley, 6
Haworth Round, 1748-1776, 12ff; ministers, 25f
Haworth, Dion, 54
Haworth, James, 170
Healey, T. R., 238
Heap Barn, 6
Heap, J. Swain, 90f
Helm, Nicholas, 182

Helm, Paul, 192
Hey, James, 200
Heys, George, 191, 257
Hick, "Sammy," 107f, **207, 214**
Higgin, Lawrence, 196
Higgins, H., 167
Higgins, John, 155
Higham, introduction of Methodism, 52f; members in 1763, 52; 1812, 184ff; trustees of first chapel, 185; first baptism, 185; Friendly Society, 189
Highfield, Rev. Mr., 42
High Wycombe, 113
Higson, Mr., 172
Hindle, Robert, 182
Hoghton, 73
Holbrey, Rev. George, 126
Holden, Gilbert, 81
Holden, Thomas, 140f
Holdsworth, Richard, **220**
Holgate, Ann, 214
Holland, Thomas, 21
Holmes, Mr, solicitor, 99
Holroyd, Mr., 123
Holt, David and Jonathan, 209
Holt, James, 129f
Holt, Thomas, 162
Holt, W. R., 205
Hopkinson, James, 196
Hopper, Christopher, 36, 69
Hopwood, George, 163
Hopwood, William, senr., 57, 107, 112, 120, 126, 157f, 239
Hopwood, William, junr., 78, 98, 240
Horn, Mr. and Mrs. J. S., 164f
Horne, William, 50
Houlding, E., 135
Howarth, Richard, 209
Howorth, George, 125, 134, 144, 147, 227
Howorth, James, 98, 112, 116, 119f, 127, 144, 226
Howorth, John, 78, 147f, 227f
Howorth, Miss, 123, 148, 227ff
Howorth, William, 178
Hudson, Mr., 180
Hudson, John, 50
Hudson, Thomas, 226
**Hunter, James, 20, 23**
Hurstwood, 67

Ickornshaw, 196
Ingham, Rev. Benjamin, 1, 4; extract from account book, 76
Ingham, Judge, 222
Ingham, T. H., **220**
Ingham, **Susan,** 226

Ingham, William, 209
Illingworth, Charles, 162
Illingworth, W., 83, 86
Isherwood, Mrs. Dolly, 51

Jackson, John, 152
Jackson, Rev. Thomas, 120, 225
James, Dr., 152
Jeffries, Rev. John, 126
Jobson, Rev. F.J., D.D., 138
Johnson, Miss, 118
Johnson, George and Robert, 209
Jones, Mr. and Mrs. Edward, 134, 148, 165

Kay, Henry, 98, 121
Kay, J. Robinson, 128, 241
Kay, Thomas, 109, 185, 241
Kay-Shuttleworth, Sir James, 130
Kay-Shuttleworth, Sir Ughtred, Bart., M.P., 129, 144
Keeling, Isaac, 84f, 162
Kelly, Rev. C. H., 166, 206
Kelly, James, 130ff, 167, 179
Kennerley, Mr., 129
Kershaw, Richard, 45f

Lambert, William, 191
Lancaster, Caleb, 129, 247
Lancaster, Joshua, 247
Lancaster, Miss, 140
Lancaster, Mrs. J., 134
Lancaster, Mr., plumber, 120, 128
Lancaster, Richard, 28, 247
Lancaster, T. E., 134
Lancaster, William, 71, 99, 107, 126, 144, 149, 163, 202 247ff
Lane, John, 28f
Langstaffe, Reuben, 81
Latham, Rev. G., 87
Laugher, Miss, 135
Law, William, 194
Law, Robert, 135
Laycock & Sons, 174
Laycock, Simpson, 196, 199
Leach, S., 223
Leach, William, 157
Lee, Jonas, 46, 163
Levell, Rev. William, 195
Lewis, Miss, 118
Lindley, Mr., 223
Livesey, John, 188
Livesey, William, 56
Lomas, Rev. T. H., 130
Longridge, M., letter to Mr. Sagar, 40
Lonsdale, Joseph, 257
Lonsdale, Mr., 122

Lord, John, 50, 186f
Lord, Joshua, 78
Lord and Whitworth, Messrs., 121
Lord, William, 209
Lowcock, Thomas, 52
Lowerhouse, 189ff
Lun, James, 63
Lund, Edmund, 222
Lupton, Mr. W., 129, 134
Lyth, Dr., "Early Glimpses of Methodism in York," 76

Macdonald, Rev. F. W., 126
Macdonald, Rev. G. B., 118, 120, 146
Macdonald, Rev. J. A., 148
Mackenzie, Rev. Peter, 88f, 130, 146, 153, 205, 219
Mann, Richard, 209
Marsden, Leonard, 193, 196, 200
Marsden, Thomas, 194f
Marshall, Jos., 220
Maskew, Rev. Jonathan, 25
Mather, Rev. Alexander, 34f, 47f, 68, 75
Matterson, Rev. Robert, 91
Matthews, Mr., 164
McKenny, Rev. John, 146
McKitrick, Rev. W., 80
McLean, Rev. John, 120
McNeal, Rev. Geo. H., 91
McOwan, Rev. Peter, 194
Melson, Dr. J. B., 70
Mercer, Robinson, 143
Metcalfe, Mr., 44
Midgeley, Rev. William, 106
Midgley, Mr., 165
Miller Barn, 6
Millican, Rev. W., 218
Milner, Rev. Mr., 6
Milnes, E., 175
Montgomery, James, 85
Moon, William, 81
Moor, William, 66
Moorby, Robert, 215
Moorby, Thomas, 215
Moore, Benj., 125, 177
Moore, Rev. John, 146f
Moore, Joseph, 81, 188
Moore, Lilian, 188
Moorhouse, Joseph, 179
Moorhouse, Thomas, 192
Mortimer, Rev. Joseph, 195, 205
Morton, Rev. Robert, 148
Moss, Rev. R. Waddy, 148
Mundella, Right Hon. A. J., 165
Murray, Mr., 164
Myles, Chronological History of Methodists, 8

# INDEX

Narrowgate Mill, 45
Nelson circuit, 1810-1899, 193ff; trustees of chapel, 195, 197; formation of Barrowford and Nelson circuit, 197; ministers in, 1865-1899, 197f; growth of Methodism in, 198f; leaders, 199; circuit stewards, 1865-1899, 199; day schools, 199; township, 201; District Synods, 201; Railway Street, 202; trustees of, 202; Cooper Street, 202f; Bradley Hall, 203; Temple Street, 203; Rupert Street, 203
Nelson, Rev. John, 1f, 4, 25, 75, 218
Newbridge, 212
Newchurch-in-Pendle, 185
New Laund, 61f
Newton, Dr., 115, 118, 142, 225
Newton, Miss, 165
Nowell, James, 100, 206, 257
Nowell, John, 86
Nowell, Thomas, 100
Nowell, William, 257
Nuttall, Ebenezer, 222
Nuttall, Enos, 187, 222
Nuttall, Ezra, 222
Nuttall, Henry, 193, 257
Nuttall, James, 222
Nuttall, W. H., 129

Oakenshaw, 93
Ormerod, H. M., 147, 254f
Osborn, Dr., 142, 184
Osmotherly, entry in Society Book, 9
Owen, Thomas, 118

Padiham, visit of Darney to, 19; members of "Darney's Society," 20; Wesley's visits, 20f, 48; first trustees, 21; 1777, 46ff; first Sunday School, 50; 1810-1899, 176ff; ministers in, 1847-1899, 176f; circuit stewards, 177; leaders, 178; Hall Hill chapel, 179; trustees, 179; history of Wesley organ, 179ff; Giles Street School, 181f; Hall Hill Mission, 182; Cross Bank, 182
Parker, Robert, 193
Parkinson, Richard, 252f
Parkinson, William, 133, 206
Pattison, Mrs, 212
Pawson, John, letter re Grimshaw, 24; letter from Mr. Sagar, 40f
Pearse, Rev. Mark Guy, 134
Pearson, Rev. T., 205
Pemberton, Rev. W., 121

Pendle Bottom, amounts contributed by Society in 1796, 62, 163
Pendle Forest, 1, 161
Phillips, Rev. John, 85f, 241
Phillips, John W., 86, 123, 130
Phillips, Peter, 14, 86, 123, 241ff
Phillips, Mrs., 230f
Pickles, John, 224
Pickles, H., 169
Pickles, Michael, 62
Pickles, Mrs., 215
Pilkington, T., 144
Platt, David, 81, 257
Platt, Mr., 166
Pollard, Edward, Miss and Miss Sarah, 98
Pollard, George and Henry, 144
Pollard, James, 121
Pollard, William, 112, 149
Pope, Dr. W. B., 152
Posnett, Rev. J. L., 142
Potter, W. B., 129f
Prescott, R. M., 203
Priestley, Rev. J., 132
Procter, John, 162
Procter, Robert, 159f
Procter, Mr., 100

Quiney, Mr., 202

Radcliffe, Rev. W. T., 172, 184
Raikes, Robert, 113
Randles, Dr. M., 150, 179
Rattenbury, Rev. John, 142, 169
Read, W., 159
Redman, Lawrence, 155
Reece, Rev. Richard, 117
Reedyford, 212f
Richardson, John, letter to Mr. Sagar, 36
Ridall, Mr., 37f
Ridehalgh, James, 50f
Riding, Abel, 152
Riding, John, 54f
Riding, Robert, 62
Riding, Thomas, 117
Rigg, Rev. Dr., 159, 210
Riley, Jonathan, 208
Riley, William, 192
Rimington, 53
Rippon, Rev. Joseph, 95, 211
Roberts family, the, 188
Roberts, Rev. Joseph, 153
Roberts, Rev. Richard, 210
Robinson, F., 139f
Robinson, H. J., 83
Robinson, James, 215
Robinson, John, 215

# INDEX. 267

Robinson, John, leader, 53
Robinson, Miss, 165
Robinson, Thomas, 198
Robinson, William, 44
Rosegrove, 192
Rossendale, 1
Roughlee, Wesley's visits to, 13ff; leaders in 1748, 15 ; 213f
Rowell, James, 75
Rylands, Peter, M.P., 123

Sabden, 183f; Sabden Bridge, 97 ; Sunday school, 184 ; Sabden Hall, 185, 189
Sagar, Captain, 175, 193
Sagar, Howarth, 202
Sagar, John, 196, 200
Sagar, Miss, 45, 196f
Sagar, Mr. (leader) 142
Sagar, Richard, 168f
Sagar, William, 31ff, diary of, 32 ; letter from Roger Crane, 32f ; death, 33 ; letters from J. Wesley, 35ff ; letter from Mr. Richardson, 36 ; letter from John Pawson, 40f ; letter from R. Hardacre, 42
Saunders, Mr. and Mrs. Henry, 142
Scarlett, General, 130
Scarr, Thomas, 81
Schofield, James, 149
Scott, "Kitty," 65f
Scott, Miss, 212
Scott, Rev. S. O., 126, 132
Scott, Sir Walter, Journal of, 106
Scurrah, Dr., 178f
Seagrave, Rev. Robt., M.A., 2
Sharp, Abraham, 20
Sharpe, Miss, 165
Shaw, Richard, 130
Shent, William, 25, 75
Simpson, James, 128
Simpson, John, 155
Simpson, Robert, 214
Simpson, Rev. W. O., 182
Simpson, William, 81
Simpson, W. M., 172
Slack, Rev. Benj., 157, 161
Smallpage, Jas., 78, 121, 144, 253
Smallpage, Joseph, 130, 163
Smallpage, Samuel, 94, 123, 144, 254
Smith, Rev. G. Harvey, 177
Smith, John, 179ff
Smith, James, 144
Smith, Richard, 51, 179
Smith, Roger, 257
Smith, Thomas, 224
Smith, T. H., 130

Southern & Ormerod, Messrs., 99
Southfield, 45f, 213
Spencer, Jeremiah, 60
Spencer & Moore, Messrs., 98, 123
Stamp, John, 93, 101
Stanley, Rev. Jacob, 10f
Stanley, Rev. Thomas, 93, 101
Starkie, Ellen, 215
Starkie, Edward, 186, 188
Starkie, John, 188
Starkie, Robert, 177
Starkie, Rev. Starkie, 177
Stead, J. Fishwick, 85
Stead, Thomas, 85
Stephenson, James, 179f, 192
Stephenson, John, 179
Steward, William, 178f
Stott, Henry, 122
Stott, John, "Methodism in Haslingden," 54 ; 122
Stowe, William, 257
Strachan, Rev. Alex., 86f
Sutcliffe, Mr., 176, 195

Taft, Zechariah and Mrs., 63
Tattersall, John, 51, 188
Tattersall, John, 209
Tattersall, Richard, 188
Tattersall, William, 87
Taylor, George, 144
Taylor, Rev. G. C., 89
Taylor, John, 138
Taylor, John, 224
Taylor, Rev. Thomas, 21, 24, 29, 34
Taylor, William, 50
Thomas, Richard, 123, 241, 257
Thompson, Dr., 257
Thompson, Henry, 50
Thompson, James, 165
Thompson, Martha, 56
Thornber, William, 190
Thornton, John, 123f, 163, 251
Thursby, Rev. William, 130
Tickle, John, 50
Todd, William, 189
Todmorden Society Book, entry in, 9, 22
Towler, Hagar, 51
Towler, John, 213
Towler, Thomas, 167, 213
Towler, John, William, James, and Thomas, 167, 213
Towneley, Mr. P. E., 108, 116
Tueart, Mr., 166
Tunnicliffe, Charles, 186
Tunnycliffe, Charles, 50, 68f
Tunstill, Mr. and Mrs. Henry, 208
Tunstill, Miss, 206

Tunstill, Robert, 208, 212, 236
Tunstill, William and Mrs., 196ff, 208f, 236ff
Tunstill, William, 209
Tyerman, Rev. Luke, 146

Varley, James, 196
Varley, John, 173
Varley, Mrs., 188
Vasey, Rev. Thomas, 68, 106, 174f
Vercoe, Rev. W., 147

Waddington, Charles, 179
Waddington, William, 124, 147, 179, 257
Waddington, Miss, 140
Walker, Miss, 165
Walmsley, Thomas, 100, 179
Walton, Ingham, 204
Walton, James, 51
Walton, L., 165
Walton, R. T. Wroe, 193
Walton Robert, 175
Wamsley, John M., 90
Wamsley, Philip B., 90, 100
Ward, William, 157
Watkinson, Rev. W. L., 141, 182
Watson, Joseph, 196
Waterhouse, Rev. Levi, 209
Watson, Rev. Richard, 203
Webster, Rev. Joseph, 154
Wesley, Charles, 6
Wesley, John, 6; visits to Roughlee, 13f; letter to Rev. G. White, 14f; visits to Padiham, 20ff, 48; visits to Colne, 29, 35; letters to William Sagar, 35ff; death, 38; notice of Sunday schools, 113ff
Whalley, James, 50

Wharton, Titus, 209
Whitaker, Dr., History of the Parish of Whalley, 18f
Whitaker, James, 178f
Whitaker, Miss, 148
Whitaker, Mrs., 149
Whitaker, Thomas, 62
Whitaker, William, 45
White, Rev. George, 16ff; Sermon against Methodists, 17
Whitehead & Holland, Messrs., 196
Whitehead, Jesse, 200
Whitehead, Rev. S., 148
Whitehead, Thomas, 141
Whitham, Mr. and Mrs. J., 202f
Whitham, W., 117
Widdop, 14
Wilding, W. P., 160, 162
Wildman, Robert, 256
Wilkinson, Henry, 191
Wilkinson, H. H., 53, 184f
Wilkinson, John, 2, 51
Wilkinson, Jos., 196
Wilkinson, Thomas, 62
Wilkinson, William, 172f
Wilkinson, W. J., 87, 90
Williams, Mr., 3f
Wilmore, Jos., 188
Wilson, John, 257
Winterbottom, James, 121
Wiseman, T., 203, 206
Wiseman, Miss, 206
Wood, John, 19f, 42f, 50, 64
Wood, Jonathan, 54
Wood, Thomas, 178
Wray, Rev. J. Jackson, 147

Yorkshire and Haworth Circuit, 24
Young, Dr., 134

www.ingramcontent.com/pod-product-compliance
Lightning Source LLC
Chambersburg PA
CBHW031932230426
43672CB00010B/1900